THE BILLIONAIRE BACKPACKER

A book that could quite possibly change your life

MARTIN COLE

Publisher - Shifting Consciousness

Copyright

Copyright © 2017 by Martin Cole
All Rights Reserved. No part of this publication may be reproduced, stored in a
retrieval system, or transmitted, in any form or by any means, electronic, mechanical,
photocopying, recording, or otherwise, without the prior written permission of MJC
Training Trust Ltd except for the use of brief quotations in a book review.
This is a work of fiction interlaced with real events. Any resemblance to real persons is
coincidental.

Dedication

To my wonderful wife Denise who spurs me on to ever more adventures in life.
Thank you for booking my flight to Peru before I could change my mind.

To my sons Steven & James
You have taught me that the youth of today also hold wisdom if we take the
time to listen.

Foreword

Imagine starting your life over again but with all the life experience of today. It would be a dizzying journey of success and achievement that would leave those around you standing in awe. They would have no clue where your wisdom, foresight and abilities came from. A sought-after person you would be for sure.

The Billionaire and the backpacker story is inspired by true events. The messages woven through the story will reveal to you the potential for a restart - a reboot of your life. It's a book that could quite possibly change your life!

The billionaire and the backpack takes you on a captivating journey from the sidewalks of New York to the Peruvian jungle where an ancient ceremony revealed that nothing is without meaning, consequence and maybe even destiny.

Take this book home tonight and expose yourself to the very real possibility of a life changing story.

Part One

Chapter One

Rows of desks chairs and computer screens are separated from several palatial offices by clear glass walls that can be made private with the flick of a switch. In one of these offices sits a man whose mind is connected to a bank of computer screens with as much purpose as an umbilical cord to an unborn child.

The foot soldiers start to file in and fill the rows of chairs. Some look like they have been up for hours; others still removing sleep dust from the corners of their eyes. Jackets are hung on the backs of the purpose built chairs. Telephones poised on speed dial as the digital ticker tape prices start to peel across the full length of the room. A bell sounds, and the room begins to boil.

Ben used to occupy one of those seats, but now he had a box (or cages as the wannabe traders called them) all of his own, cages they would do anything to take up residence within. The truth is that most of them would be lucky to see the inside of the ensuite bathrooms, never mind sit at the leather inlaid desks.

Ben started young; he was just nineteen when he walked onto the floor for the first day. There were seven others that day and observing them would have clearly indicated that some were not going to last. In fact, Ben and only one other, Jake, remained at the firm.

Ben now forty-three, cut a very sharp attractive figure that still intrigued younger women, even when he wasn't wearing one of his five thousand dollar suits.

Jake had not yet made it to a cage of his own, and the truth was he knew he probably never would. Sure he was good but not a master; not a mover and shaker as they like to think of the cage masters.

Jake gave a quick tap on the door and walked into Ben's office. Ben didn't move a muscle or break his gaze from the screen.

"Ben."

Nothing for a few seconds, which seemed like an eternity in this business. Ben looked up.

"Morning Jake, Start accumulating all the short selling you can when it hits 1142."

"1142? That's, what… 75 points lower than the current price!"

Ben just held a slightly defocused gaze on Jake.

"Right.. I'll tell the boys and girls. Where are we looking to come ashore?"

Ben looked back at his screen

"1232."

Jake's head twitched, but he knew better than to display any doubt.

The first day on the floor was a baptism of fire, with everyone taking great delight in causing as much stress as possible by treating the trading virgins like rag dolls being pulled back and forth like children fighting over a single toy.

Ben bypassed that, as he came from cage stock. Ben's late father had spent years in one of the cages and had a reputation of the master of the universe. He had taught Ben from an early age that nothing you see on a market screen is the truth. The truth lies behind the facade of the charts and resides in the minds of men.

'Learn to read the minds of men, learn to read the beliefs they hold about the future, and you will know all you need to know,' was the mantra that he drilled into Ben from the age of twelve.

Ben had entered his glass cage at an unprecedented age of twenty-two. Twenty-one years in the cage had given him everything the world believes they want. The country mansion, the chic apartment walking distance from Wall St, a car and motor cycle collection with enough money to float a battle ship but this was a mere drop in the ocean he had made for the firm. Behind boardroom doors, he was referenced as 'asset one.'

Mary, Ben's assistant, knocked. Her natural blonde curls were the first unforgettable feature of this beautiful power house of efficiency.

Ben motioned his head to come in.

Mary had joined the firm a little after Ben; she had grown to be of high value not only for her efficiency but also her tactile ability to handle some of the prima donna traders.

In their early years at the firm, Ben had tried several times to get more from her than her efficiency but this fizzled out as he placed her on a pedestal as a friend and confidant, to share part of his life that he could share with no other.

Jake continued to spend at least an hour a day fantasizing about her, but she had long since found her soul mate.

Ben's relationship with Mary was now one of respect for what he called her wisdom. She had an uncanny ability of reading people the same way that he read the minds of the masses that fuel financial markets. He had grown accustomed to the notion that Mary's ability was of far more value than the mere production of money. He had continually raised her salary to the point where Ben had one day been questioned about her value. It was a short conversation, and no-one ever went there again.

"Lunching in or out today?" said Mary.

"Early finish, I'm going to the roost for the weekend."

The roost was Ben's name for his country estate, about 45 minutes out of the city.

Around lunch time, Ben made his way across the floor. Some days a trader would meet his gaze, not knowing what the correct reaction would be, so usually took the safe road of breaking the contact as soon as possible. Ben could be like his father at times, aloof and somewhat condescending although in his favor, he was for the most part unaware of this trait.

The elevator doors opened. He pressed G. The garage is two levels below street level.

"Afternoon sir," said the attendant as the doors opened. Being instantly recognized, the attendant had already stood a little more erect.

Chapter Two

Two floors up on the sidewalk, a girl in her twenties is laden under a heavy backpack. Her hiking boots are a stark contrast to the polished city leather that is outpacing her.

There is a ruggedness about her, which is softened by cascading curls of auburn hair. She turns the heads of the passing suits but remains oblivious to her natural beauty.

Christine is a loner; she has traveled to India, Pakistan, China, Columbia, and Peru. Why she was on Wall Street looking at fast walking leather shoes she could not fully understand, but then neither was she trying.

A Mercedes approaches street level from an underground car park. The driver feels a stinging pain on his cheek. He slapped his cheek and knocked a wasp to the floor, but it was still alive. As he slammed his foot down to try and end its life, the edge of his shoe came into contact with the accelerator and the car lunged forward.

On the security monitor, the garage attendant saw a backpack bounce from the windshield of the Mercedes. The attendant dialled 911.

Being Wall Street, in moments an ambulance and cop were on the scene.

Christina was writhing in agony.

The cop leaned over and told Christina the ambulance was on its way.

Ben, standing behind the cop, blurted out

"I'm sorry."

A hand was placed on Ben's shoulder; it was security from the building.

"Sir, you don't want to get involved in this."

Ben stood up and backed away to where the car was.

Christina kept eye contact with him until it was broken by surrounding security.

The ambulance arrived, and the cop came over to Ben. One of the security guards stepped forward and intercepted him.

"She was Jaywalking, and we have it on camera."

Ben slid his hand up to his cheek that was by now swollen and red.

A lawyer appeared from the building and took control of everything. The cop felt overwhelmed and succumbed to the pressure of the suits.

The ambulance driver asks Christina if she had insurance.

"No."

As she's lifted onto a stretcher, she wanted to scream, but stubbornness would not allow it. Her eyes caught one last glimpse of Ben as she was placed in the ambulance.

The ambulance took off, and the security team disbursed. The garage attendant appeared at the same time as Mary.

"I'll call the limo up, sir."

Mary walked up to Ben and turned his cheek. "Nasty, I have something in the office for that."

"Just call down when you're ready sir, and I'll have the limo ready," the attendant called out as Ben and Mary walked back down into the garage.

Chapter Three

B ack in the office, Mary applied some antihistamine cream to Ben's cheek. The glass cage became a viewing box for the floor until Mary pressed a button that provided privacy.

"What happened?"

"This girl stepped out, and I hit her. She was not looking where she was going."

"So the sting on the cheek didn't play a part?"

Ben put his hand up to his cheek.

"Can you call Anna at the roost and tell her that I will not be home until later and she can take the rest of the day off?"

As Mary left the room, she flicked the switch to make the office visible again. Ben pressed the button to light up his trading screens. The price was getting close to 1142. He looked out across the floor.

1142 flashed on the screen and traders started to pick up telephones. Over the next hour, the price rose steadily to 1172 against the heavy selling that Ben had instructed Jake to carry out.

Jake knocked and entered the cage.

"Err... it looks like it's all being absorbed Ben; we are 26 million short at an average of 1136."

The slight tremor in Jake's voice was ignored.

Ben looks up from the screen at Jake.

"Oh, ye of little faith."

Jake cracks a half smile. In the next three minutes, the price falls.

1169

1160

1140

1125

"Christ Ben, it's on! I'll get to it."

Three hours later, there was a roar that rippled down the lines of desks as the price hit 1048.

Jake burst into the cage. "This has to be the gilded cage Ben.. 96 Million. 96 million fucking dollars. Upstairs are gonna be smiling on you again today."

Ben receives 5% of the profit with 2% shared amongst his team, who were still punching the air fuelled by adrenaline. Ben remained emotionless.

"Scaggys tonight?" asked Jake.

Ben looked out of the window across the Cityscape

"Yeah, maybe..."

Two hours later, Ben walked across the now near empty floor and pressed G on the elevator.

"Hello sir, nasty business with that young girl today, sir. Jose is just bringing up the limo for you."

The limo pulled up, and Ben stepped in.

"Where to sir? Scaggys?"

"Yes sure, why not? It's been a hell of a day."

Before Ben reached the bar the yelling and champagne popping reached fever pitch. Jake dragged Ben off to one side towards a booth seat, where a couple of attentive ladies had been well placed.

"Jake, not tonight mate. I'll stay for a drink and then I want to get away for the weekend."

Four hours later, Ben stumbled a little as Jose opened the door of the limo. It was raining, and the lights from other vehicles caused all manner of colors to reflect in the raindrops streaming down the side windows. Suddenly, the colors pulsated in red and blue as traffic crawled at a snail's pace, past an ambulance attending a road accident.

"Jose."

"Sir?"

"Where is the nearest hospital from the office?"

"That will be Seven Oaks, sir. Are you not feeling well?

"No, I'm fine. Just swing by the hospital."

Jose turns off at the next exit.

Fifteen minutes later, they were approaching what looks like a cross between a private English estate and a Las Vegas casino entrance. A doorman appeared flanked by a doctor and nurse. Ben stepped from the car.

"Would you like a chair sir?"

"No, I'm just here to visit."

Ben approached reception.

"Good evening Sir, how can I help you?"

"I am looking for a girl that would have come in today. She was involved in a car accident. I think she had a problem with her leg."

"Name, sir?"

"Sorry, I don't know her name."

The receptionist looked back at the screen.

"Well sir, I can tell you that we have had no admissions for any leg issues for the last 48 hours, so she has not been admitted to Seven Oaks."

Ben thanked the receptionist and returned to the limo.

"All sorted sir?"

"No, she wasn't there."

"Who, sir?"

"The girl today who had the accident."

"Oh yes, I heard about the Jaywalker. Sir, that girl wouldn't be at this hospital, not here."

"Where would she be then?"

"Likely at Swagman Memorial downtown."

"Take me there."

"You sure sir? That's not the nicest area to be driving a limo."

"Let's go."

"Yes, sir."

Twenty minutes later, eyes were staring from street corners. Jose flicked a switch to lock the doors.

"Aint a fresh looking place, is it sir? Hospital is up on the right here."

Jose parked the limo right up to the entrance and Ben stepped out into what felt like an imminent battle zone of unarmed drunks.

The receptionist was not used to seeing a five thousand dollar suit on her shift and instantly gave it attention.

"Miss, I'm looking for a girl that had a leg injury today."

"Name sir?"

"Ben, Ben Hammond."

"No sir, the girl's name."

"Sorry, I don't know."

"Sir, we have probably fifteen girls that I could match to your description right now and anyway unless you are her kin, I am not allowed to tell you anything."

Ben reached into his pocket and pulled out a hundred dollar bill from his wallet and tore it in half. He passed one-half to the receptionist and put the other back in his pocket.

"When you find me this girl, you'll get the other half of the bill."

The receptionist picked up the phone and made a call, then another and then another.

"Sorry sir, no-one knows anything."

Ben turns to walk away.

"Sir, I tried. Can I have the other half? Please?"

Ben handed over the other half, and as he did, he saw a rucksack behind the receptionist.

"That's it, that's her bag."

The receptionist picked up the phone again and spoke in Spanish, she smiled.

"Sir, down the hall, third left about half way along."

As Ben walked away, the receptionist pulled off some sticky tape to repair the torn bill.

Halfway along the corridor, Ben started looking in each room he passed. The place was chaotic; people were yelling at each other, nurses were trying to keep the peace and work at the same time.

A trolley was heading towards Ben, and he recognized some long curly hair; it was Christina.

"Stop." He called out to the nurse.

"Can't stop sir, theatre waiting."

Christina was barely able to open her eyes but immediately made a connection to Ben and tried to grab at him. She caught his coat and pulled him towards her.

"You... You... Bastard!" She slipped back into semi-unconsciousness.

"Sir we have to go, they are waiting. She will be back in about two hours."

The nurse pushed Ben to the side, moments later he found his way back to reception.

"Find who you're looking for, Sir?"

"Yes thank you. What time is visiting?"

"You can come anytime sir, anytime time you want," as she placed the hundred dollar bill in her top pocket.

"Her bag."

"Yes, sir?"

"I will take that for safe keeping."

"No sir, can't let you take that. You told me you're not family."

Ben stepped away from reception and made a call to Mary.

"Mary, sorry to trouble you at this time of night but I have a problem and don't know how to handle it." Twenty minutes later, a seven oaks ambulance pulled up. Out stepped the driver and partner, along with a security guard. Ben greeted them. "Come with me."

Ben walked back up to reception.

"These two gentlemen here are going to wait until the young lady comes out of theatre she will then be discharged to the care of Seven Oaks Hospital. This other gentleman is in charge of patient security and will be responsible for all of the girl's belongings. Is that clear?"

"Err... Yes, sir."

Ben turned to the three men. "Are we all clear on this?"

"Yes, sir."

Jose was waiting with the door open as Ben approached the limo.

"Where to sir?"

"Home, Jose, home to the roost."

———

The Seven Oaks Hospital doorman greets Ben with a "Morning sir, shall I park for you?"

Ben nodded and went straight to reception.

There were three reception nurse staff, who immediately acknowledged Ben as he approached. Before he had quite reached the counter, one of them greeted him with an automated response "Good morning sir. How may I help you?"

"There was a girl transferred from Swagman Memorial last night. She would have arrived via ambulance along with a security guard."

The receptionist glanced down, ran her finger down a single sheet of paper. "Yes sir, we established her name is Christina, her passport was located in her belongings. She is just down the hallway to your left, in room six."

Ben started to walk away.

"Sir, I will just need your name for visitors records."

"Ben, Ben Holloway."

"Holloway. Thank you, sir."

Ben arrived at room six. The door was open, and he could see a nurse brushing out the girl's hair.

The nurse had already been alerted to the visitor. She scanned Ben up and down and smiled as he entered the room. She then turned back to Christina.

"You have a visitor, Christina." There was no response.

The nurse turned back to Ben.

"Don't worry; she will be fully awake in a few moments. The anesthetic is wearing off now. I am just making her hair pretty for when she wakes up."

"But she was operated on last night in Swagman Memorial before she arrived here. Why is she still sleeping?"

The nurse checked the chart hanging at the foot of the bed.

"Yes sir, that is correct, but I see here that she had an X-ray on arrival and the doctors decided to remove the cast and reset her ankle."

Christina started to stir.

"There sir, here she is with us now, she will be wide awake soon."

Ben stepped outside the room to take a call.

It was Mary checking that everything was taken care of last night.

By the time Ben came back into the room, Christina was sitting up slightly, her eyes trying to take in the surroundings but unable to move as fast as the internal questions were firing.

"Where am I?"

"You are at Seven Oaks Hospital Miss. I'll leave you alone now with your visitor".

Ben tentatively approached the bedside.

"I'm"

"I know who you are. You're the one who hit me."

"You can sue, and I will not contest it. You will get a large payout, and then you will have plenty of money to do what you want. Probably enough to travel first class and not be backpacking."

Christina's eyes cut to Ben's core.

"You must be some asshole. Why the hell do I want to sue you? I want my leg working back, not money."

"Sorry, I... Er… I thought…"

"No, you didn't think, and that is likely your problem. You assume everything in life, and you naturally assume you are right as well."

"Whoa… Hold on. That is what normally happens. Everyone will sue for anything they can."

"Well, clearly not everyone. Don't you find that everyone is an overused term?"

Ben stepped back from the bed.

"Do you want anything?"

"Yes"

"Ok. I can organize that. What is it..?"

"I want out of here and to be on my way."

"I'll find out how long you have to be here. By the way, you don't have to worry about hospital costs, I have taken care of all that."

"Please just find out when I can leave."

Ben went back to reception, who called up a doctor to speak to Ben. As Ben arrived back in the room, Christina was struggling to sit up.

"Here, let me help." Ben reached for one of the pillows.

"I can manage, thank you."

Ben ignored the remark and adjusted her pillows as the Doctor arrived.

"Good morning everyone," said the doctor.

"Everything is looking good with your leg. Well, it's more your ankle. That's why we reset it last night. It's quite a tricky fracture."

"When can I leave?"

"You can leave tomorrow Miss, but you cannot walk on that ankle for at least six weeks."

"Six weeks! What am I going to do for six weeks?"

"You can stay here," Ben says.

"Get out. Both of you, get out."

Ben attempted to respond.

"Look, I have asked you to leave. Now go."

Both The doctor and Ben left the room closing the door behind them.

The doctor turned to Ben.

"Don't worry; the anesthetic makes some people irritable when they come round."

Ben decided to leave and made his way back to reception.

On the way home, Ben mentally replayed the last couple of hours and concluded that the girl was an ungrateful bitch. He had taken care of everything for her, offered her money, put her in a $5,000 a day hospital. Yes, she was an ungrateful bitch, and he will have nothing more to do with her. The lawyers can sort it out.

Ben, feeling free again, drove home and spent the weekend relaxing around the roost.

Chapter Four

I t was 7 am. The automatic curtains opened to a crisp, bright morning. Coffee was wafting up from the kitchen.

Anna called from the bottom of the sweeping staircase.

"Mr. Ben, breakfast is ready."

Anna had been in service 'as she likes to put it' for Ben as a cook and general housekeeper, for some fifteen years now. She was the sort of person that you know you could just hug, and you'd get a big smothering one right back.

There was no reply to her call, but as she heard the familiar sound of the door closing, she knew that Ben was taking a shower.

Ten minutes later, Ben was in the kitchen with scrambled egg and bacon, which had just the right amount of curl to offer a soft crispness.

Anna cleared away the plate and served the second coffee.

"Mr. Ben, what's troubling you? I know this look, and something is wrong."

"Anna, you are like a fussing hen.." Ben rubbed her shoulder smiling.

"I was just thinking about a small accident yesterday. It's nothing, Anna."

"Mr. Ben, if you say this is nothing, then I must be wrong, but I still think."

"Anna!" "Everything is OK… Oh..before I forget, I'm going to visit someone this morning so no need to bother with lunch. In fact, you can take the rest of the weekend off."

Ben drank the last of his coffee and headed for the garage that housed a Mercedes, a Jaguar and a two berth campervan. The Jaguar burst into life.

It was 5 am on Monday and still dark as the curtains remotely open. Every muscle in Ben's body was automatically programmed to carry out the rituals of rising early, taking a shower, spending 15 minutes on the running machine, take a second shower and shave, and be in the glass cage at 7.30am.

It was 9 am when Ben exited the lift and walked across the floor. It was like everyone's routine had been shattered with Ben coming in late. Jake appeared from Mary's office.

"Hey Buddy, everything alright? We missed you, what's up?"

Ben was late because he drove to Seven Oaks Hospital and sat outside in his car for an hour, trying to make his legs carry him in, to see the girl again. Eventually, he got angry again and continued onto the office.

He couldn't understand why he could not get Christina out of his mind. He was always in control of his life. In fact, he was always in control of his next thought and action. This feeling was an alien experience and not something he wanted to continue.

He decided to throw himself into the day.

Seated in front of the screens, he asked Jake if anything was showing signs of movement and what news was out today.

Jake quickly reeled off:

"The yen is looking weak against the GBP and the US Dollar. The Swiss franc is steady and has been for three days."

Ben opened a EURO chart and took a quick look.

"Ok, Jake. Here is what I want you to focus your attention on today. Keep a close eye on the Euro for signs of any up move against the Yen. If this occurs, start accumulating Swiss Franc positions up to six million. I'll leave it in your capable hands."

Jake left to give instructions to the team.

Mary knocked and entered the office.

"Good weekend?"

"Yes thanks, very relaxing apart from the hospital fiasco."

"All sorted now?" Mary replied.

"Sort of, she hates being in the hospital."

"She being?"

"Her name is Christina, and she's an aggressive little bitch."

"Aggressive towards you, or the situation?"

Mary was one of the few people that could get Ben off his often linear one track thought pattern.

"Probably she's angry at the situation in general. Have you asked her?"

"There is no asking her."

"Have you tried listening?"

21

"I have things to do. I can't be molly coddling people."

Ben spent the rest of the day monitoring trading positions and planning for market movements that might develop over the next few days.

Things were quiet on the floor; it was 4:00 pm when Ben called Mary in. "I'm getting off early today. Am I all clear for the rest of the day?"

The truth was that nobody would question any action that Ben took at work and anything that was scheduled would be reworked around him. But that never stopped him showing the respect he held for Mary by asking her.

"I am going to take your advice and drop in on the girl one more time to see if I can help."

Mary lifted one eyebrow without moving her head a millimeter.

"Yes, I will listen…" He cracked a half smile at Mary as he emphasizes 'listen.'

Seven Oaks gave an immediate sense of peace to visitors; maybe it was the manicured gardens, the magnificent portal entrance and the demeanor of the highly trained staff. But today it was not working.

Ben found himself feeling uneasy again, as he got closer to room six.

He knocked on the half-open door. Christina was motionless, gazing out of the window.

"Hi, how's it going?"

A no reply immediately sent a ripple through Ben's stomach.

"Look, I thought I would just pop in to see if I could do anything. Can I contact your parents? — Get you anything?"

Christina slowly turned her head.

"I think you've done enough already, don't you?"

"I've told you I'm sorry."

"No, you never said you were sorry. You didn't say it when you hit me, and you haven't said it since then."

The earlier ripple in Ben's stomach turned to a full knot.

"You know what? You're right. I would like to make a full apology right now. Is that OK?"

"I suppose so."

"OK. I am sorry for running into you, but I got stung by an insect, and that distracted me. How's that?"

"Half of it was OK. Everything up until you used the word 'but'. Do you know why people use the word 'but'?" "It's because it negates whatever comes after it."

Ben wanted to throw his hands up in the air but bit his lip instead.

"I'm sorry."

Christina responded by running her fingers through her hair and exhaling loudly, and then returned to gazing out of the window.

"It's going to kill me being in here for six weeks. I have places to go, things to do. I want my life back."

Ben's face started to contort into a harried expression.

"Look… I've done what I can do. Bar taking you home; there is not much else I can do."

"Ok, that's a deal. Take me home."

Ben felt himself swallowing deeply as an obligation to his words took over.

Christina looked dead into Ben's eyes, and he experienced something he had not felt in a very long time - vulnerability. It was most uncomfortable.

"I'll be back in a moment."

Ben went into the hallway to make a call. "Mary, this girl wants to come home with me."

"I hardly think I am the person you should be consulting about your relationships."

"No… no. I mean Christina, the girl in the hospital."

"Look. I don't think that is a good idea, but you will have to make that call."

Ben started rubbing his chin with his thumb and forefinger, something he always did before placing large trading orders. It was a little thing he did that he believed triggered clear decision making. He dialed again.

"Anna, we have a guest coming to stay. Can you make up a downstairs room, overlooking the garden?"

"Si, Mr. Ben. A lady, Mr. Ben?"

"Does that matter?"

"Yes, Mr. Ben. Flowers are nice for a lady."

Ben wanted to explain that this guest was not a lady and flowers were not needed but sensed it was not worth the effort to explain. "Yes, OK. Whatever you think is best."

Ben went back into the room, and Christina gave him a look filled with expectation, followed by her first smile.

The smile contained more power than he was prepared for, and it caught him off guard.

"Er..OK, I will get an ambulance to take you home."

"No need. I can go with you."

Ben suddenly felt he had been manipulated and wanted to escape the whole deal.

"Are you sure this is a good idea?"

"Yes. We don't need an ambulance."

"No, I mean… staying with me at home?"

Christina's smile changed to a frown.

"You offered, I agreed, and it was a done deal. Now you have changed your mind. What the hell is going on?"

Ben knew he was heading into trouble and wished he'd just kept his mouth shut.

"No nothing is wrong. It's just that I have to go into town... into town for a meeting." Ben was shifting body weight from one foot to the other. "Let's just organize the ambulance and keep it simple."

Christina's smile returned, which sent butterflies into Ben's stomach for the second time today. This time, however, it was different. This time he became aware that the smile was from coming from a much younger female than he would ordinarily be attracted to.

Chapter Five

Anna had just finished preparing the room when she caught sight of an ambulance arriving. By the time she reached the outside of the front door, she was already calling out "Marcelo ... Marcelo."

The gardener, who was close by, dropped his tools and sprinted to the ambulance.

The driver opened the door to Anna's rotund frame, who was now paying the price for the short dash with heavy panting.

"Mr. Ben... Mr. Ben... What is the matter with...?" "Ma'am, nothing to worry about; we have brought Miss Christina Wilkins."

"Miss Christina..?"

The driver's mate opened the rear door and started lowering the wheelchair to the ground.

"Miss Christina, what a lovely name. My name is Anna. I take care of Mr. Ben. Marcelo. Where are your manners? Miss Christina has some luggage."

As Marcelo pulled the rucksack from the ambulance, he caught the zipper which opened to reveal a white plastic bag with what looked like a tree root protruding from it. He grabbed hold of it and tried to push it back into the rucksack but then paused to examine it. He turned to Christina and gave a soft smile.

"Marcelo, go ahead and put Miss Christina's luggage by the front door. Mind the floor; you are all dirty."

Marcelo followed orders without saying a word. He dropped the bag at the door and turned to Christina, as Anna was pushing her into the house. Their eyes meet again, and the same smile appeared on his face.

"Miss, would you like me to put the roots somewhere cool and damp?"

Christina didn't blink an eye. "Yes, please."

Anna wheeled Christina into the reception area. She felt uncomfortable with the ostentatious wealth of the place.

"This is such a big house."

"Yes, Miss and only Mr. Ben here but now you will stay with us, and this is good."

"Let me show you around. Your room is on the left of the staircase. It's normally Mr. Ben's reading room, but he said to make up a ground bedroom, so I chose this one which has a lovely view to the garden. Across here on the right side is the big lounge room."

Anna wheeled Christina into the lounge. It was huge, with three soft seating areas and the largest TV she had ever seen. There was a reading area that contained at least 500 books and to the side of that, what looked like an audio area where one could sit semi-secluded.

Anna then spun the chair around and went back towards a centralized sitting area, in front of the fireplace.

"And here is Mr. Ben's favorite chair, where he likes to sit and watch the fire."

The open fire hearth was big enough to walk into. You could easily sit beside a small fire. On each side of the fireplace were large French doors that opened onto a patio area, extending out into the garden. Hanging above the fireplace, was a large picture of a couple in their twenties. You could tell it was one of those crazy pictures that get taken when a little too much alcohol brings out the sillies. Christina could make out that the male was a much younger Ben. The girl was holding up a paper eye mask with cat-like eyelashes painted on it.

"Is that Ben's wife?" Christina asked.

Anna chuckled.

"Mr. Ben is no married. Mr. Ben should have a lovely wife. I tell him all the time."

"It's a lovely picture, Miss Christina. No?"

"Yes, beautiful."

"Let me show you your room now."

Anna wheeled Christina in an almost straight line across from the lounge entrance towards her room. As she reaches the far side of the staircase, she points to the right to a single door.

"That's Mr. Ben's office and here is your room."

Anna wheeled Christina into a room, which approached the size of a small apartment.

There was a king size bed, a sofa and a coffee table which were placed so as to look out of the French doors onto the garden.

"The bathroom, Miss Christina, is right over here behind the sliding door."

Christina took control of the wheelchair and spun it around to face Anna with a beaming smile.

"Anna, please. You don't have to keep calling me Miss Christina. Christina is just fine. You can call me Charlie if you like" she said with a chuckle.

"Charlie…. You're too pretty for a Charlie."

Anna walked away chuckling Charlie.

"If you need anything Mis...er... Charlie, there is a bell on the table beside the front door. Just ring that and I will hear you."

"Thank you. Anna" Christina called out as she left the room.

Christina wheeled herself over to the French doors and opened them. It was a glorious day, and the smell from the garden instantly filled the room. She could see Marcelo working some way away, who looked up as the French doors opened. Christina raised her head, to acknowledge that they had seen each other. Marcelo waved back and continued with his work.

The front door closed with a bang, as the breeze from the open french doors pushed a gust through the house.

Ben had arrived home. He rang the bell and Anna appeared.

"Hola, Mr. Ben."

"Anna, has our guest arrived yet?"

"Si. Miss Christina is in the blue room. She is a lovely girl, Mr. Ben. Lovely girl."

Christina appeared in the doorway of her room.

"Do you realize we have never introduced ourselves?" She said.

Anna left them both facing each other.

"Mmm... I think you're right. Things did not get off to a good start with us."

"Well. if you hadn't—"

She broke off that sentence just as quickly as her brain triggered her to start it.

Ben quickly jumped in "How about we do that properly this evening at dinner?"

"OK."

Ben didn't feel he wanted to turn this into a chatty time right now. In fact, he was troubled by having even considered letting Christina stay here. He had the same feeling he experienced when he very occasionally made a mistake with financial market analysis. That same stomach churning roll was just lurking beneath the surface which was his trading indicator telling him that he may have been misled into taking the trading position he had committed to.

With trading, he could always change his position quite quickly, but this was different.

What he had instigated with Christina was a commitment that was going to have to run its course, and this did not resemble a warm fuzzy feeling.

"I have some work to do, so shall we just say... later?"

"Fine, no problem."

Christina turned and wheeled back into her room. Just as Ben was about to turn the door handle to his office, Christina called out.

"Do you have internet access that I can use?"

Ben turned around to see Christina with a laptop resting on her knees.

"Yes we do, but I can't grant you access to that until your computer is checked."

"Why do you want to check my computer?"

"It's not a check of your computer regarding what you have on it; it's more for security."

"What do you think I am? Some hacker? All I want to do is check my emails."

"Look... I'll call someone in on Monday to make sure you have Internet access OK?"

Ben closed the door behind him, and Christina went back into her room. He heard the clunk of her door closing, which immediately injected the thought that he might be able to leave his office without more conversation taking place.

"Fuck that insect..." he murmured as he stroked the offending area, where any mark of the sting had long since vanished.

Chapter Six

C hristina had managed to lower herself into the bath. It was the one time she wished it had been a lot smaller, to keep her back propped up against one end and prevent the plaster cast from sliding down into the water.

She imagined how good it would probably feel with the water finding its way under the plaster. She hadn't felt this relaxed for a very long time and was suddenly jarred back to the present as she slightly slipped backwards in the bath.

She draped a towel over the wheelchair and managed to edge over the side of the bath back into the chair. With the overhang from the towel, she managed to pat herself dry and then cover herself with another towel.

She wheeled herself back to the side of the bed and then realized that the French doors were still wide open. The now cooling breeze felt quite sensuous against her damp skin.

She located the draw cord on the curtains and pulled them closed, leaving the doors open behind them.

Back at the bedside, she eased onto the bed and slid under the top cover as she watched the curtains gently swaying.

"What is the meaning of all this?" she mouthed.

"Christina… Christina…" A hand touched the bedside and Christina jarred awake. It was cool in the room.

Anna's hand rested on her shoulder, which was exposed above the covers.

"Let's close the doors, Miss. I mean Christina."

Anna opened the curtains, closed the French doors and as re-closed the curtains, it revealed that it was now early evening.

"Dinner is in one hour, Christina. Can you manage? Do you need some help to get dressed?"

"No, thank you. I can manage."

"I came in to see if you had any laundry, but you were so sound asleep, making funny little noises like a cat sleeping, that I did not want to disturb you. I have done your laundry for you and is folded on the chair."

"Thank you, Anna, there was no need for you to do that for me, but thank you."

"You're very welcome… M…I mean Charlie." Anna chuckled with Christina.

The dining room was just as ostentatious as the lounge. Ben was already seated at a table that could have easily seated twenty-five people. There was another place setting immediately to the left.

"This is going to be awkward," Ben said.

"What's to be awkward about? I thought we were just having dinner?"

"I was referring to your chair being low and getting to the table."

Christina squirmed a little as she knew there was antagonism in her voice and that Ben had experienced a significant amount of that each time they met. She told herself that she would not be such a bitch.

"Sorry about that, I had a long sleep today and did not wake up too well."

Ben got up to help her from the wheelchair to a chair at the table. She pushed up and stood with all her weight on one leg, keeping balance by holding onto the table. Ben pulled the wheelchair back and then took her hand to steady her down onto the chair.

Ben had held many women's hands. Why this hand was noticeably different, he had no idea.

"There… that was not a bad team effort" he said.

For the first time, Christina felt comfortable in Ben's presence.

Christina, while not a strict vegetarian, had decided about a year ago not to eat meat and had probably only been forced to on five or six occasions.

Anna appeared pushing a serving trolley. She circled to Ben's side.

"Good evening," she said.

Christina replied, "Good evening to you, Anna."

Ben smiled in acknowledgment.

"Lamb with lots of vegetables," Anna said, lifting two covers that revealed all the food.

"I made lots of vegetables as my niece is always telling me that young people like vegetables. She only eats vegetables which I no understand."

"Thank you, Anna, that is lovely," said Ben.

"We will serve ourselves this evening."

"OK, Mr. Ben. I'll leave everything here for you and go and prepare your favorite dessert."

Ben's mouth watered at the thought of sticky date pudding with hot custard and a ball of ice-cream just starting to melt together. All thoughts of main course vanishing for a moment, Anna disappeared back towards the kitchen.

Christina pulled the food cart a little closer and took her plate to the food.

"Mohamed to the mountain," she said.

"Mohamed to the mountain. Are you religious?"

Christina chuckled at someone thinking Mohamed to the mountain indicated a religious stance.

"None in particular; it was just something my mother used to say when transferring food to a plate. It was just to get me to take the plate to the food so as not to drop anything."

"Your mother sounds like a very smart lady. Does she live locally?"

"I think I will have vegetables tonight, although the lamb does look lovely."

Christina finished serving herself and watched Ben take a large helping of lamb with just a few vegetables, which was in stark contrast to her plate.

"Your mother and father, you were saying?"

"I didn't mention them, you did."

Christina instantly sensed the part of her she did not like had just re-surfaced again, just as quickly as Ben did.

"Sorry, I did not mean to pry" he replied.

"No… no. It was me just making things awkward again."

She smiled at Ben to soften the situation, which it immediately did.

"My father is probably dead."

"Probably… I don't understand."

"Well, I have never met him. He left my mother when she got pregnant, and she never saw him again."

"I am sorry I brought that up, sounds like an awful thing to do to anyone."

"I like to think of him as being a bit of a shit."

Ben picked up a bottle of wine.

"Well, we could drink to that if you like?"

"No, thank you. I never touch alcohol."

"Your mother?"

Ben was digging, trying to find out if someone was nearby where Christina could go and stay.

"Are you trying to get rid of me?"

Ben sensed his thoughts had been read and shifted uncomfortably.

"No, no, don't be silly. You can stay as long as you want... need to."

Christina met his gaze full on.

"What about your mother, father, wife?"

"My mother died when I was six, so I never really got to know her. From then on, I was taken care of by my father, and then, later on, I was off to boarding school. Finished boarding school and followed my father into trading financial markets.

That's my potted history, pretty uneventful."

"And you get all this?"

She made a large arc gesture with her arms indicating Ben's home and lifestyle.

"Er... yes."

"You must be very content in your work."

"You didn't mention your father."

Ben knew the tables had turned and now he had become the interrogated. A discussion of his father was not going to be allowed.

They both turned their attention to their plates and made small talk about the food, and the lovely day it had been.

Anna appeared with a smaller food cart, and Ben's face lit up. She cleared the plates back onto the larger cart and then placed the desert on the table.

The ice cream was just starting to melt into the custard, and the sticky date pudding was standing like an iceberg.

"And one for you, Miss Christina."

"No, not for me."

Ben jumped in.

"Aw. Come on; you have not lived until you have tried this."

"I just don't eat sugar."

"You're a diabetic?"

"No, I'm not diabetic. I just choose not to poison my body with sugar."

"Poison with sugar… never heard anything so ridiculous."

Anna took the dish away.

"No, Anna. Let Mr. Ben have two helpings so that it can be doubly good for him."

"Yes, Anna Ana… Leave it here; I will try to poison myself twice. We can manage now, thank you."

Anna took the larger trolley back to the kitchen, leaving Christina's dessert on the table.

"Are you really going to eat all that?"

"Last time I checked, I didn't need someone telling me what is good or bad for me."

"Go ahead, pig out on it. You seem to have everything else in excess."

Anna came back into the room and deliberately breaks the tit for tat conversation.

"Mr. Ben, Christina, maybe you are feeling tired. I have made a nice fire, and I will bring you some coffee in there soon."

"Thank you, Anna."

Anna sensing she had defused the situation, left again.

"You do drink coffee, I assume?" Ben asked.

"Yes, and I'm sorry for my pig out remark but."

Ben cut her off. "You told me something once about the word BUT. Let us leave it at that, eh?"

Christina felt an inner smile at having to take some of her own medicine.

Their eyes met in a way that acknowledged a peaceful solution had been reached.

Chapter Seven

T he lounge was sumptuous, and Christina sank low in the softness of the sofa.

The coffee drifted her off to Columbia and a roadside hut, where she had enjoyed what she thought was the best coffee ever tasted. The truth was it had been a long time since that time, which likely gave it some added likability.

"Where are you?" Ben laughed.

"Am I that dull to the fairer sex?"

Christina gave her first full on beaming smile at Ben, which flushed his face.

"Sorry, I was off in some distant place, remembering a particular coffee."

"Time travel. What a wonderful dream, eh?" said Ben

"Or maybe a reality when you think about it," she came right back.

Ben, sensing they had found some common ground, started to enjoy the light heartedness of the present moment.

"So you'd do it, would you?" he asked.

"Do what?"

"Time travel?"

"Yes, in an instant."

"Where would you go?"

"Oh I don't know, think of the possibilities. The things we could experience again."

"Mmm... It would certainly make my job a lot easier and more profitable."

"Do all men think straight to the profit potential?"

"I don't know; it seems like a natural thing to think of to me."

"But don't you have enough?"

"Seems to me like we just have different perspectives. I like to accumulate wealth and possessions. You must have things that you like to accumulate for yourself? Surely that amounts to more than what you have in your backpack?"

Christina's eyes dipped into the coffee cup and exhaled deliberately.

Ben felt the back of his neck tense up.

"Sorry, what I meant by that was-"

Christina cut him off.

"What you meant is not that important. What you believe is. You have some beliefs about what a backpack is. What if I had more wealth than you?"

"Oh, I doubt that."

Ben's neck now went into spasm at the thought, fuck... you have done it again. Shut up and let her talk.

"How about we get back to time travel?" Even as those words came out of his mouth, he knew that was not going to happen until she wanted to.

"Oh no, please let us continue with the profit potential. What does your wealth provide you with?"

"Nice things. I can do things I want to do when I want to do them."

"OK take a year off and let's buy a random plane ticket and see where it takes us."

"That's a lovely thought, but right now, given my life and my work, that would be a ridiculous thing to do."

"What, you couldn't afford it?"

"Of course I could afford it, and I do intend to travel and see the world when -"

Christina cut his sentence short by raising her hand to signal him to let her speak.

"Let me tell you a story that my mother used to tell me. It's about a man behind bars."

"An old man stood behind bars expressionless. He had spent a lifetime here. He had seen each of his children take up their place behind these same bars and he was helpless to stop them.

One day, a visitor, a young man, arrived and stopped in front of the old man's cell.

'You look like you have been here a very long time.'

The old man took a step forward and came close up to the bars.

'I can't remember when I came in, but I do know I have been here for a lifetime. I suggest you leave this place before you meet your jailer.'

'I only came here to visit.'

'We all come to visit,' said the old man 'but very few ever leave.'

'When do you get out?' asked the young man

'Ah... when...' Replied the old man.

'When is what happened on my visit so many years ago. Once I was like you, I was young and full of ambition and wanted to achieve great things. Then one day, I found myself trapped here. I suggest you leave before the same thing happens to you.'

The young man laughed nervously.

'I've done nothing wrong, old man. I'll not end up behind bars.'

'I am warning you to leave now, while you can.'

The young man grew frustrated with the old man.

'I will leave here when I am good and ready!'

The old man repeated:

'Ah, your jailer approaches,' which frustrated the young man even more.

'You are a fool, old man. There is no jailer here.'

'Young man, the jailer here cannot be seen, cannot be touched. In fact, many things here are not as they seem.'

The old man reached out and grabbed the collar of the young man and slowly pulled him through the bars until they were standing side by side.

'You see… even the bars you cannot touch,' said the old man.

The young man was shaken and made a lunge forward and passed back through the bars to where he had been standing a few moments ago.

'You're mad old man, mad. You stay behind bars that are shadows.'

The old man reached out and again dragged the young man back to stand beside him.

'Let go of me,' the young man cried out. The old man tightened his grip and then reached for a tin cup, which he rattled on the prison bars.

Shadows are they.

The young man, now terrified at being trapped in prison, struggled free and pushed through the bars once again, leaving the old man on the other side.

He turned back towards the old man. 'How is this possible, how can the bars be steel for you and yet I can pass through them?'

The young man was now excited at the thought of being able to pass through metal bars that others could not. He started to imagine himself as a great magician' showing off his wonderful powers to others.

'What are you thinking?' asked the old man

'I think when I leave here, I am going to be a great magician.'

'Ah… your jailer approaches.'

'You are a fool old man. I don't know why you cannot pass easily through the bars as I can.'

The old man smiled and said 'Maybe I have given you special powers.'

'Yes, I think you have, and I am grateful. When I get out of here, I will return to help you.'

'Ah… your jailer approaches' repeated the old man.

'I've have had enough of this,' said the young man.

'When I get out of here, I am going to be a great magician. When I am a great magician, I will make lots of money; when I make lots of money, I will live wherever in the world I want. When I have achieved these things, I will be the happiest man in the world.'

'Your jailer has arrived,' said the old man.

The young man now furious, turned to leave and as he did, prison bars blocked his way. He laughed and waved to the old man.

The young man lunged forward to pass through the bars but they were solid, and he could not leave.

He turned to the old man and asked.

'What is going on, why can't I leave?'

The old man ignored the young man, which angered him even more.

'Old Man!' he yells. 'What is your name?'

The old man looked across into the young man's prison cell.

'My name is when.. and I am your jailer.'

"My mother used to then finish up by saying…

'My dearest Christina, all of your life, beware the prison bars of when. This small word has the power to imprison you and steal from you all that could have or might have been. The word WHEN pushes everything forward. The word when takes things that are within your grasp and pushes them just out of reach. Most people will go through their entire life using the word when as part of the sentence they use to tell you what they want to experience in their life. Do not let when eat away at your lifetime. Time is the only true resource you have at your command, do not use it when, but use it now.'

She would then kiss me and tell me how much she loved me."

Ben and Christina's eyes met, as the number of blinks for both of them increased to try to hide watery eyes.

"Time for bed for me. Can you help me into the wheelchair?"

Ben leaped up.

"Of course."

Ben felt a strong urge to hold Christina but felt just as strongly against it. He helped her into her chair and gently rubbing her shoulder, he said.

"Thank you for sharing that story with me tonight."

Christina knew that she had to escape this emotion now if she was to stop the floodgates from opening.

"Ben… could I ask you to see if it's possible for me to use crutches within a few days instead of the wheelchair?"

"Yes, of course, I'll see what I can do."

"Thank you, good night."

Christina wheeled herself into her room and closed the door as quickly as she could before the floodgates opened.

Chapter Eight

The next morning, Anna tapped on Christina's door.

"Breakfast, Charlie?"

Christina was already awake and dressed. Hearing Charlie made her smile. When Christina and her mother were fooling around, they would call each other by different names. Charlie just came out one day and stuck.

"OK coming, can you open the door please?"

Anna did as was asked.

"Good morning Anna, how are you today?"

"Fine Miss Christina... fine. It's a beautiful morning. Breakfast is on the table in the dining room. Mr. Ben is already there."

Christina moved quicker in the chair now, as she was getting used to it and in a few seconds was by the table side.

"Morning," said Ben.

"Good morning to you too."

"You're the chirpy one today. Are you a morning person?"

"Only when I'm hungry." She laughed.

Ben helped her onto a chair.

"Mmm. Oatmeal with honey, nothing better."

"I thought you didn't eat sugar?"

"I don't. Honey is not the same as refined sugar. It's refined sugar that does all the harm. It's the most addictive substance on the planet," Christina added as she stirred a large spoon of honey into the oatmeal.

"I love it when it becomes thinner and mingles with the oatmeal. There is something quite pretty about it."

"The most addictive substance on the planet... don't you think that's a bit of a strong statement to make? What about say — "Heroin, that's what you were about to say' right?"

"Er... yes."

"Heroin is always the one that everyone brings up. It's interesting, isn't it, that ninety percent of people instantly think of heroin being the most addictive substance."

"I wouldn't say it's interesting; I just believe it to be so."

"Why do you believe it? Media convinced you and millions of others, so it becomes truth."

"Well, I'll just stick with my sugar for now if that's ok with you" Ben came back.

"Anyway, let's not disagree so early in the day."

Christina wanted to explain about the demon sugar but sensed that was better avoided.

"I have a campervan in the garage that hasn't been out for a while. How do you feel about spending a day up at the lake?"

"Almost like a date, you mean? People will talk and point at such a big age gap...."

Ben had an emotion flush but managed to stop his face at the pink stage, where you hope no-one noticed.

"I'm sorry, I didn't mean to say that. It was a stupid remark... Yes, I would love to go to sit by a lake."

They finished their breakfasts, and after a bit of a struggle getting into the high level of the camper, they were on their way. There was little conversation apart from the scenery and it being a nice day. Ben pulled off the main highway and onto a rough stony track.

"It's about a mile up here, a bit bumpy now and then but that's not a bad thing as it keeps people out."

"That is just the thing that would make me want to explore the track," she said.

"Really, why?"

"Sometimes overcoming obstacles reveals the greatest finds in life."

"Now that I have to agree with. Take this place for example. I was on the main highway back there one day, when a gust of wind rolled a bush across the road. I swerved and ended up sliding onto the start of this track. At the same time, there was a pick up truck coming towards me, and he saw what happened. I reversed back to let him pass, but he started waving his arms at me. It turns out there was some wire that had wrapped itself onto the tire, and it was doing more damage as I reversed."

"So you found some wire?"

"No, I found this." Ben pointed to the right side of the road. They were now driving alongside a large lake. They rounded a bend, and there was an old ramshackle house. A man sitting on the porch pitched forward in his chair, then leaned back and waved.

Ben waved back.

"That was the guy in the pick up that day with the wire incident."

"He said he had some wire cutters back at the house and invited me to hop in the truck with him to fetch them."

"Sounds like a whodunit story to me," Christina replied.

"Actually there was a whole other side to it. I don't think the old man had spoken to anyone much in years and boy could he talk. I had his life story while he was searching for the elusive wire cutters.

He had lived here for 50 years with his wife. She died some years ago, and he lost the will to go on. Even though he had a small mortgage, he could no longer service it. The bank was about to take the property and evict him because he refused to sell the place. He would have had plenty of money left over after the sale, but he just did not want to leave the place."

"I can see why. The lake and setting has a magical feel to it," Christina replied

"Magical… not sure about that one but it recharges me whenever I come up here."

"So how come the old guy is still here?"

"I bought the place. Everything, lock stock and barrel, as they say."

"I thought you said he refused to sell."

"That's right, but I bought the place on the understanding that I could have access to the lake and stay up here in the camper whenever I want, and he could live here for the rest of his days.

"I try to get up here at weekends. If I am on my own, then we sit and talk most of the night. He is a wise old fella sometimes.

If I have company with me, then I never see him. His name is Jeff."

"Company being of the female type, you mean?"

Ben felt another pink flush coming on, but once more, he managed to control it.

"I have brought one or two people up here if the situation was right."

"What's the right situation sorry, I'm being nosy."

Ben turned and smiled "Yes, you can be a little that way, can't you? Here is my favorite spot."

Ben swung the camper around in a small clearing. He stopped the engine and pressed a button that automatically leveled the camper. Another button sent out a shade from the side, creating a comfortable place to sit outside.

"I'll grab a couple of seats and then help you out."

Ben went round to the back of the camper and opened up a storage area holding a folding table, two chairs, two sunbeds and the wheelchair. He placed the two chairs and the table under the awning and then opened Christina's door.

"Do you want to sit in the wheelchair or a chair?"

"I'll take the chair."

Ben moved closer to Christina's side. He grabbed hold of her left arm and placed it over his head and onto his shoulder. He slid his right hand around her waist and started to turn her left out of the camper.

"Just let your weight rest on my shoulders, and you can hop along to get to the chair."

The method worked rather well until the third hop when the soft damp grass provided a perfect slide for Christine's heel and down she went pulling Ben down with her.

They both fell and ended up side by side, laughing. Ben stood up and helped Christina to her feet, then did the hop thing again to reach the seat.

"There you go. Teamwork was not too bad, eh?"

Ben went inside the van and came back with two glasses of Anna's homemade lemonade.

"You'll like this; Anna makes it. It's pretty good." Ben said as he handed her a glass. She took the glass and hesitated.

"Sorry… it's the sugar. I don't consume sugar."

"Just taste it and tell me what you think."

"No!"

"I tell you what, put your top lip in the glass to wet it and then taste what is on your lip. Is that too much to ask?"

Christina wanted to say yes, it was too much to ask but did not want to spoil what had been so far a lovely day.

She tasted her wet top lip.

"Honey, it's made with honey."

"Yes, I asked Anna to make it up this morning and got her to use honey instead of sugar. I quite like it myself when you get used to the difference."

"That's sweet."

"Sweet of me or sweet of the honey?"

Christina gave him one of those smiles of hers that almost opened a small window revealing some acceptance on Ben's part. He liked that smile a lot.

"So tell me about your travels, where have you been?"

Christina turned to look directly at Ben and paused just long enough for Ben to say

"What… What is it? What have I said wrong?"

"Oh nothing, but umm I have something else on my mind."

Ben leaned back in his chair. "Hey, it's a beautiful day, I think we're enjoying being with each other. It's your call on the conversation."

"Well, actually, I wanted to ask your opinion about something that happened to me."

"Ok… shoot, as long as it's not bad stuff. Everyone tells me that I am not a very good agony aunt."

"I was in the jungle —."

Ben cut her off. "The jungle, Christ. What were you doing there? Snakes, spiders and all that stuff. Holy crap, no way would I be going there anytime soon."

"Like I was saying before you interrupted."

Ben sat back in his chair again.

"Sorry, didn't mean to interrupt."

"Well, it was about six or seven months ago. I had taken a river boat trip from Parinadi to Iquitos. Just before we arrived in Iquitos, I met someone on the boat who was on a return trip back to visit a shaman. You know what a shaman is, right?"

"Like a witch doctor, you mean?"

"Well, not exactly but that will do for now."

"He was going back to see the shaman for some health issues. He didn't want to talk about his health but said that he had approached me to tell me about this shaman because he had a feeling that I needed to know."

"Sounds like an excellent chat up line to me."

"Well, he was pretty handsome, but as he was traveling with a girl and she was standing beside him, I didn't think it was that."

"So, you're on a boat heading to a place called Iquitos that you know nothing about. You meet a stranger who says he felt compelled to talk to you about a shaman. Have I got it right so far?"

"Yes."

"Sorry, I'm just struggling to understand why you would want to be doing this sort of thing."

"Do you always have to have a reason for everything in life?

Ben bit his lip.

"Ok, so this guy tells me that the shaman's name is Almedio and he is part of the Bora tribe. I asked him how I would get to see this Almedio and he said he had no idea. He just felt compelled to give me his name. In fact, he said, "I have no idea if you will ever meet him or if you are supposed to meet him."

"Can I just interject there for a moment please?" asked Ben

"Yes, ok."

"If this young man was going to see this Shaman, he must have known where he was and how to get there. Why did you just not agree to go with him and see if it was meant to be?"

"Good question and I did suggest that to him, but he said that was not how it works."

"All seems a bit strange to me," said Ben.

"Yes, it seemed that way to me, and I grew suspicious, which must have shown on my face. The girl traveling with him must have sensed my uneasiness and jumped in to say that the same thing happened to John. John was the name of the young man.

They had been tramping around Peru when a series of strange events led them to Almedio. She said that since neither of them could tell for certain that they were even doing the right thing, that it was not even worth thinking about. If it were meant to be then, it would happen and to just let it go at that. Seemed like a good idea and we said our goodbyes as the boat docked."

"As soon as I arrived in Iquitos, I didn't feel safe, but then I had been to other places where I felt the same and nothing happened, so I put this down to what I think of as new nerves and brushed it off."

"Sounds to me like something I would not be very comfortable doing."

"I think that's an ok feeling to have about situations like this, but if you don't ever find yourself in a situation like that in life, then maybe it's a pretty good measure of how stuck you are in your comfort zone."

Ben smiled and said. "I like comfort; I like the known, there is something quite safe and reassuring about it."

"You're right."

Ben could not believe it; he was right about something in Christina's eyes. However, the inflation of his chest was soon punctured.

"Reassuring is good up to a point, and I suppose if you had found your purpose in life and you are engaged in that purpose on a daily basis, then that would be reassuring. However, the truth is that only a tiny percentage of people ever find their real purpose in life."

"How do you know that? I mean that seems like a sweeping statement to make" Ben came back.

"Ok point in question then... your life."

Ben crossed his arms and exhaled deeply.

"My life. Is that a good example?"

"Why not your life?"

"Well, I have achieved a lot... Now I don't want this to come across the wrong way, but I have a life of luxury. I have earned that."

"But is the luxury the real act of living? Do you remember the prison bars of when?"

"Yes, I wanted to talk to you about that sometime."

"Well let's talk about it now."

"You mentioned that you trade money, I believe?"

"Yes, I trade currencies and make money by exploiting differences in the value of one currency against another."

"So is that who you are or what you do?"

"I suppose it's what I do."

"So who are you and what is your purpose?"

"Whoa that's heavy stuff; a big question."

"Well, on the last day of your life, do you want to be sitting in your office trading currencies?"

"Of course not, I want to be out enjoying myself."

"What is enjoying yourself? What is it that makes you feel complete?"

Ben shifted in his chair, his folded arms now pushed right up so his hands were under his armpits and incoherent thoughts raced around and collided with each other.

"That's a tough line of questioning, young lady."

"It is, isn't it? and it's only us that can figure it out for ourselves."

Ben's arms dropped down to his lap.

"The story, the prison bars of when is telling us how we use the physical here and now to try and catch the imagined future. It's like the story of the carrot and the donkey. The donkey spends its whole life believing its walking towards the carrot, but it never attains it. Worse still, the donkey spends its entire life walking in a circle, drawing water for others without every getting to live the life of carrot eating."

"My girl, you have thoughts beyond your years. How on earth did you get into all this mind stuff?"

"My mother was my first teacher… but let's just continue with the prison bars."

"Most people get up in the morning, go to jobs they do not enjoy to earn money, to pay to a banker for the roof over their heads and money to a supermarket to keep food in their bellies. They do this for five or six days a week. Normally on the sixth day, they buy a lottery ticket and in doing so, engage in the purposely given dream that money - that thing they are exchanging their life TIME for, will give them more life."

Ben's head rolled forward until his chin rested on his chest. Christina looked out across the lake and watched a duck execute a water ski landing.

"You know what?" Ben said

"What?"

"I'm getting it, well I think I am.

Out in front of my office is a floor with maybe a hundred

traders. They look at my office as a destination, their future. They have this thought that if they can make it into that office, they will have arrived. But it's just an office. I know they have these thoughts because I had the same when I was on the outside."

"Most people do not live their lives, they exist," Christina replied. Ben came quickly back.

"But then I have made it. I am living the dream."

"Whose dream? Is doing what you do your dream? Does doing what you do provide you with more life? Because that is I think what we are talking about - more life, more living, more aliveness."

Ben rubbed the back of his neck. "This is all getting a bit heavy… Hey, we came here to enjoy the lake."

"You know, you're right, but didn't you want you to hear about Almedio and some wire on your wheel that you needed wire cutters for?"

Ben's eyebrows squeezed together.

"How about for now we have lunch instead?"

Ben went inside the camper.

"I like to keep it simple when I come up here. Cheese and crackers ok?"

"Sounds great."

Christina saw a duck out on the lake and noticed how the one had now become many. Ben returned from the camper with crackers, cheese and two large mugs of coffee. They sat and watched the ducks a while until Ben commented on how they always seem to move in unison.

"They are like those formation swimmers you see, but not quite so tightly organized. Don't you think?"

"Yes, I was just thinking how they are a good example of humans."

"Do you ever stop?" laughed Ben

"I never used to think like that until I met Almedio."

Ben pressed his lips tightly together to stop any chance of a smile breaking out.

"I was wondering when he was going to show up."

"Show up is exactly the way it happened, funnily enough. I'll tell you how I met him later but first, do you have anything to draw on as I want to show you how this was explained to me."

"Sure."

Ben returned from the camper a few moments later with a new A3 size drawing pad and a selection of pencils.

"I will admit here and now that I am not a hundred percent sure how all this works, but it gets more and more interesting as you get further into it."

"Do you have a boat by any chance or is that a silly question?"

Ben squeezed his lips tightly together again to try and stop a smile, but it escaped.

"Yes, I do."

"Does it have a screen with a sweeping arm that beeps when it picks things up?" Ben's forehead wrinkled slightly. "Let me try and draw it as it was explained to me."

Christina drew a large circle and divided it into four, eight and then twelve. She numbered each section 1 thru 12 Next, she drew in five small circles and labeled them A thru to E.

"Ah, I know what you mean. It's called a radar. The captain tried to explain it to me one day, but I didn't fully understand it."

Christina's eyes popped "You have a boat with a captain?"

"Well, he's not full time, but if I don't want to drive it myself, then I hire a captain for the trip."

Christina's mouth dropped open slightly.

"Well, here is how Almedio described it to me."

"Whoa, hold on… a guy living in the jungle explained to you how a ship's radar works?"

"Well that's another story, but for now let's stick with what he said… ok?"

"Fair enough, but I can't wait to hear that one."

"So basically this is what he said using this drawing.

'When looking at a radar screen, your vessel is at the center point of the screen. Imagine that this center point is your current life and circumstances.

The course of your vessel and your direction will be the vertical line straight up from the center. This is the direction you are moving in.

The letters you see on the screen (A to E) will be other vessels – obstacles; in fact, anything that is in the range of the circle to your current position. Think of these as just dots.'

"Imagine now," Christina continues, "that you are out at sea with no land in sight. Looking at your radar screen, you can see there are five dots within your radar range. Dot (B) is quite close and will need keeping an eye on.

Looking at (C), you might think that you are now past this vessel and clear of any collision risk. However, this may or may not be the case, and you will only know this if you continue to monitor your radar, as it updates with each sweep of your range.

(C) Could well be maintaining the course of the line (5) meaning that if you were stationary, you could collide.

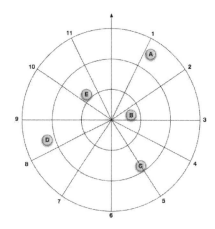

There is also the speed differences of the vessels compared to your own to consider. Have a play with the radar image and imagine different movements of the dots (A-E) to gain an understanding of the fluidity of the dots about your position and direction. Also, consider the effect of changing direction."

"So basically it's like we are floating around waiting for stuff to bump into us?" Ben said.

"That is what I thought, but it turns out that it goes a little deeper than that."

He went on to say.

'A radar gives you an overall perspective of everything that is around you. By learning to read this instrument, it's possible to safely navigate the ocean in complete darkness, with an awareness of all that is around you and more importantly, what is around you that you should give increased attention to.'

"He said how important it was to live a connected life. Not a connected life to what is presented to us as life but a connection to our purpose."

"Purpose being?" Ben said.

"The purpose of our lives; why we are here and what our purpose is while we are here in this life."

"So he was saying that we all have a purpose in life and we should follow that purpose?"

"Yes."

"So what is your purpose?" Ben said.

"I don't know."

"This seems to me to be a bit wobbly in logic. Everyone has a purpose; everyone should follow that purpose. Didn't that make you a little bit skeptical of this guy?"

"Well, yes it did until he started talking about connecting the dots. He went on to explain that looking back in life; we can easily connect them and relate them to what happened in our lives."

"Ok, I can go along with that. I have done that many times. In fact, I do that in my…" Ben paused, and an unconscious smile appeared.

"In your what? Were you going to say your work?"

"He told me that a person who was at the highest level of performance in their chosen field had almost certainly developed the skill of connecting the dots with a degree of forwarding connectivity. He also said that only in rare cases would that person be acutely aware of what they were doing."

"Bizarre."

"What's bizarre?"

"Well, there was a guy that started work on the same day as I did. His name is Jake, and I have tried many times to show him what I do, to show him how to predict the most likely outcome for the future movement of a particular currency. As hard and as often as I try, he just cannot see it. I said to him one day "You have to connect the dots." He replied, "Yes, I understand that, but how the hell do you connect them for what has not happened yet?"

I have to admit that I don't know how I do that. I don't know how I can look at a computer screen and read what is likely to happen with a high degree of accuracy."

"That is pretty cool when you think about it," Christina replied.

"Yes, I suppose it is."

"He told me that the secret to living a connected and meaningful life was to learn how to decipher the dots that are coming at us all the time.

We have to learn to understand which ones are about us at that moment, and which ones are leading us towards living out our purpose.

He said that there are two types of purposes. For example, you might be engaged in a thing that is your current purpose, let's say to get a particular job done, but that particular job might not be fully linked to your core purpose."

Ben rubbed the back of his neck and then his chin as he sat back in the chair, only realizing then that he been leaning uncomfortably forward, listening to everything Christina had been saying.

"As I was listening to Almedio telling me all this, I really wanted to understand it, as I felt it could help me in my search."

"Your search… what are you searching for?"

"That's not important right now."

Ben leaned forward again.

"Maybe it is important. Maybe that is why we are having this conversation. Maybe…" Christina cut him off mid sentence.

"Maybe it is, but maybe I don't want to discuss that with you."

Ben gently bit the inside of his mouth.

"As I said, I really wanted to know how this worked so I asked him if he would show me. To which he said no, you couldn't be shown how to connect live dots."

"Live dots?"

"Yes, live, he said. Historical dots, dots that you could connect by looking back were easy for understanding and were able to give you some future direction. However, it was very common to get distracted and take off in a different direction in life that may not be aligned with your core purpose."

"Ok, so we have historical dots and live dots?"

"Exactly and to understand and interpret live dots, we need to engage in some training. Training that involves taking the concept of the radar and applying it to our day-to-day lives. From the moment we wake up, we need to be in automatic radar mode –" Ben interrupted.

"That sounds like quite a hard thing to do when you think about it."

"That's what he said; he said that this was most people's reaction but went on to explain that this radar like mode of consciousness is natural for us and yet less than five percent of the population is aware of what it is they are doing.

We might know this five percent as innovators, that seem to change the world in ways that race around the planet into millions or even billions of hands.

These people have almost certainly taken control of their mental radar and use it to guide them towards success in anything of their choosing.

'Almost certainly, he said, the people that change the world are the people that are aware of the radar and are at the same time in alignment with their core purpose.'"

"This is fascinating and scary," Ben said.

"That is exactly how I felt and to be honest; I still am scared by all this. In fact, you are the only person I have shared this with, and I have no idea why."

"Hey, maybe breaking your ankle was a dot?"

"No, that was because some idiot ran into me with a car."

Ben opened his mouth to say something but caught Christina's eyes and thinking better of it, decided to get back to the dots.

"So there are now dots, live dots, and historical dots. How on earth do we understand and read the live dots? This seems to be the whole crux of this thing."

"Almedio said that dots are anything and everything from the spoken word, an overheard comment, the smile on the next person you meet, the car you catch out of the corner of your eye, the shape of a raindrop on your windscreen, the jet flying overhead."

"Wow, that makes it a bit of a crap shoot then?"

"Exactly what I thought but then he put it this way. He said you could think of dots as ethereal bytes of communication that may or may not be relative to you."

"Ethereal bytes of information," Ben repeated.

"Yes, ethereal bytes of information but, relative to you. So yes, while a lot is going on, we are only interested in the bytes that are relative to us."

Ben's eyebrows squeezed in a little as he said "That narrows it down a bit but not much. The funny thing is, when you think about it, you can often have a conversation with another person, and you can sort of understand what they should be doing because of what they are telling you about their lives. It's like you can spot these dots in others' lives, where they can't see them."

"Yes, and it's the same for us. Someone can sometimes look at us, and they are better able to see what would make us happy and give more direction to our lives. What we need to do is to develop the ability to use it in our own lives."

Ben leaned back in the chair again. "How on earth do you make a start on something like this?"

"He told me that first, you must convince yourself of the truth of this. Without acceptance of ethereal bytes of information as a valid and genuine connection to something that is circling the planet as intelligence, we will never truly embrace the fact that we can live lives that give us a deep connection with whom we really are and our life's purpose."

Neither Ben nor Christina realized how long they had been sitting at the lakeside until they felt the first pangs of hunger.

Ben stood up and looked directly into Christina's eyes. As much as he wanted to hold her right now, there was another side of him that felt different.

"It's been an enjoyable day. I can't say I understand everything you've talked about or if I believe it to be true, but somehow I feel that it has been mind expanding."

Ben looked at his watch. "Wow, later than I thought. Let's head home. We'll call Anna on the way and tell her we will be late for dinner.

Ben pulled the camper right up as close as he could to the front entrance. Marcelo was just packing away the last of his tools and came over to them.

"You want me to park the camper, sir?"

"Yes please Marcelo, but first grab the wheelchair, it's just inside the side door."

Ben walked around to the passenger's side and opened Christina's door as Marcelo brought the wheelchair.

"Same as before, left arm over shoulder. I'll hold your waist and spin you out to the side here. Marcelo, chair ready?"

"Yes, sir."

"Ok, here we go."

It went the same this time as at the lakeside, except that Christina's right arm now came around and held onto Ben's right shoulder, so she faced him directly for the first part of the lift. This did not go unnoticed by both of them.

Marcelo closed the passenger door, and Ben pushed Christina towards the front door as Anna opened it.

"You are late, Mr. Ben, Christina. No worry, I have dinner ready for you as soon as you have washed up."

As soon as they were inside, Christina took over wheeling the chair and went straight to her room. Ben headed upstairs and on the way, asked Anna to have dinner ready in say forty-five minutes.

"Forty-five minutes. Yes, Mr. Ben."

Ben dropped his clothes to the floor and stepped into the shower while his mind went straight to Christina and how she would manage in the shower with the plaster cast.

Ben liked to air dry after a shower whenever he had time. A

quick half dry with a towel and then just lay on the bed and let the air dry the rest of his body.

Christina was air drying at the same time.

Anna knocked on both their doors, in turn, saying dinner in ten minutes. Both occupants stirred from a cross between daydreaming and light sleep.

Christina wheeled out from her room as Ben reached the first step of the staircase.

Christina had on a white blouse with a loose skirt, replacing the T-shirt and jeans which had the seam torn open to make it easier to pull them over the plaster cast. Ben thought the tomboy part of Christina had been replaced by a bright, beautiful young woman. He was in no doubt as to which one he preferred.

"Famished, how about you?" he said.

"Yes, starving."

As both sat at the table, Anna arrived with the serving trolley.

"Your favorite Mr. Ben, a Sunday beef roast. For Miss Christina, I cook something different. For Miss Christina, I cook a roast vegetable dish topped with parmesan cheese."

Ben opened his hands, palms up.

"Anna, what would we do without you?"

Anna laughed "Probably go hungry Mr. Ben, probably go hungry."

Christina beamed a smile at Anna.

"Thank you Anna, it looks lovely and smells delicious."

Ben caught Christina's eye and winked. "Actually it looks fantastic. We could swap if you like."

"I don't think so."

They both finished up the dinner without saying much. Anna appeared as if she had a timer that told her when the plates were to be cleared. As always, there was the second smaller trolley for dessert.

As she approached the table, she said" Christina, I have made something for you. I made dessert but no sugar and only a little honey. Mr. Ben, you can try it as well… no?

"I'm sure it's fantastic Anna," Ben replied.

The both enjoyed the dessert and complimented Anna on her return.

"Coffee in the lounge, Mr. Ben?"

"Yes, please."

"I have lit a fire, Mr. Ben as it's a little cooler tonight."

Ben moved to help Christina into her chair, but she stopped him.

"It's ok; I have to learn to do this myself at some point."

Ben hovered, hoping she would require help but she made it look easy.

"I will check on the crutches tomorrow for you."

"Great, it will be good to be back at full height."

Christina followed Ben into the lounge, where he sat on one end of a large sofa facing the fire. Christina positioned her chair and then sank down at the other end.

"It's been a good day, hasn't it?" she said.

"It has, and we've managed to get through it without bickering at each other so a double good day, I would say."

Christina pinched her lips together as a large smile appeared.

"Listen, I have been thinking about your story of the 'prison bars of when.' It got to me a bit but then I thought that you need money right, you need the means to do the when things?"

"When things?"

"Yes, I came up with the idea of 'when things' so that I was aware of what it was that I was saying when about. Sort of like a mental list if you like."

"That's a pretty neat idea," Ben replied. "I can imagine asking someone: 'What are your when things?' It really does prompt you to think about the concept."

As they finished up their coffee, Ben turned to Christina and said: "I have a real early start in the morning. There is some big financial news coming out that I need to prepare for. So if you are all good, I am going to have an early night."

Christina tried to get up, but the sofa was too low. Ben, seeing her struggle, reached out for her hand.

"No... I have to manage myself."

"Ok, but it's only a hand."

Christina reached back to Ben and took his hand so he could help her up. They were now very close to each other, and there was a pause as they looked at each other, just long enough to feel awkwardness.

Anna arrived to clear away the coffee cups, and Christina turned and sat in the wheelchair.

"Anna, you can take the rest of the evening off. We are both having an early night."

"Si Mr. Ben, thank you."

Chapter Nine

Christina woke to Anna's now familiar knock.

"Miss Christina, breakfast will be ready in the kitchen in 10 minutes."

"Ok, I'll be ready."

Christina had a quick wash, wheeled herself over to the curtains and pulled the cord to open them.

Marcello was only 3 feet away from the French doors, attending a small tree planted in a half wine barrel. They both startled each other.

They waved, and Marcello continued to tend to the small tree.

Christina, after a slight wrong turn into Ben's office, located the kitchen's two-way door and used the chair to push it open. The spring on the door was quite strong, and Anna quickly pulled the door wide open.

The kitchen was huge, like every other room in the house. There was a large center island that was at least twenty-five feet long. Stainless steel everywhere. It looked like a small army of chefs would have no trouble avoiding each other preparing a banquet for a hundred guests.

Anna had made toast, poached eggs and bacon. Christina stood up hobbled on one leg and then lifted herself onto a tall stool at the center island.

"Toast and eggs for you, Miss Christina?"

"Yes, great. Is Ben coming for breakfast?"

Anna passed a plate to Christina and slid the eggs and toast closer. "Mr. Ben left early for work."

Anna walked towards the far end of the kitchen and opened the back door, which let in a rush of crisp morning air.

"Marcelo…"

Marcelo appeared as if he had been waiting only feet away from the door.

"Take off your boots and wash your hands."

Anna instructed him like a mother hen, wanting to keep everything ship shape and in order.

"Yes, Anna. Thank you, Anna."

Marcello was surprised to see Christina in the kitchen and nervously straightened his jacket and swept his hand through his hair.

"M-morning, Miss," he said as he started to blink rapidly.

"What's the matter Marcello, have you not seen a pretty girl before? Come and eat breakfast."

Marcello grinned from ear to hear and took the plate that Anna slid into position opposite Christina.

"The bacon is for Marcello."

As Christina pushed the eggs and bacon closer to him, they exchanged smiles before he dropped his head towards his plate, as he took two eggs and two rashers of bacon.

"Not so hungry this morning Marcello? You normally have four rashers of bacon."

Marcello looked at Christina, blinking even faster now.

"I only want two."

"You can have the other two; I don't eat meat."

Marcello instantly took the other two rashers and more toast.

"I have to go on an errand, so you two young ones can talk without me here."

The kitchen door swung back and forwards a few times as Anna departed.

Now it was Christina who fidgeted on her seat which matched Marcello's rapid blinking.

The silence became a little uncomfortable before Christina started things off.

"Do you like gardening?"

"The root you gave me is in good condition. I know what it is, I have seen it before. How did you get it past border control?"

"How do you know what it is?"

"I was born in Peru, and that should tell you that I know what it is. Have you ever taken it?" Marcello asked.

"Yes."

"And?"

"You're very curious, do you always question like this?"

"Sorry, I want to know what it's like. My parents told me what they thought, but they had never taken a ceremony with it, so I always thought they were not able to know what it was like. My mother made me promise that as long as she was alive, I would never enter a ceremony. Three years ago she died, and I am released from that obligation, but here in the USA I did not have any possibility of taking part in a ceremony."

"Well, it's hard to explain a ceremony because it depends on how the ceremony finds you."

"How can the ceremony find you?"

"What I mean is that if you just decide that you are going to do a ceremony out of curiosity, then probably all you will get from it is more curiosity."

Anna came back into the kitchen.

"I see you two are getting on fine. I thought you might," she chuckled.

She then cleared the breakfast plates, and as she removed Marcello's plate, she said: "Now don't you have some gardens to tend to?"

"Yes I do, thank you for breakfast."

"You're welcome but don't you forget it's only a little treat now and then and I'm not to be treated like I was your mama."

Marcello smiled and nodded to Christina as he left for work.

"Miss Christina, he is a good boy. I think he is around your age, do you think?"

"Er yes, I think so."

"Good, that is good. Same people the same age that is good. I was wondering if I should invite Marcello for breakfast again tomorrow. What do you think?"

Christina's head started to tilt from side to side as she realized what Anna was up to.

"Errr I don't know. Sorry, I was thinking of something else."

Anna's eyes were fixed expectantly on Christina in a silence that seemed to last a long time.

"Yes, ok, breakfast is probably a nice thing to do."

Anna returned a mission accomplished smile.

"I have to go to town today on some errands, would you like to come?"

"Not today, thank you. I am going to rest my leg, and I have some reading I need to catch up on."

"Ok, well I won't be here for lunch, so I will leave something out for you."

"Thank you."

Christina turned on the stool and dropped into the wheelchair.

She called out to Anna as she wheeled away. "Have a nice day in town."

Anna was already busy preparing her some lunch to leave out.

Christina went back to her room, managed to open up the French doors and sat on the terrace, just looking out at the gardens.

Everything was so neat and tidy; straight lines manicured lawns. Her mind drifted back to Peru and what the jungle had been like in stark contrast.

Anna's taxi ended that thought, as it pulled up in front of the house. Anna appeared right on cue and climbed in. As the taxi pulled away, Anna caught sight of Christina, and they exchanged waves.

The taxi disappeared, and just as quickly, a DHL van appeared. The van was moving quite quickly and almost skidded to a halt on the gravel driveway. The driver jumped out, slid open the side door and started moving parcels around. He then played air guitar for about three seconds before pulling out some crutches wrapped in clear plastic. He slid the side door shut and turned to go to the front entrance of the house when he caught sight of Christina.

He pulled out his ear buds and walked towards her at the same high speed that all delivery drivers seem to walk at.

"Morning Miss. Delivery for Mr. Ben Williamson. Can you sign for it?"

"Yes, I can."

The driver passed the tablet to Christina for her signature.

"Thank you… Shall I leave the package here?"

The driver passed the crutches over and headed back to the van at the same rapid pace while replacing his ear buds.

Christina laid the crutches across her knees and turned the chair around to go inside. Trying to separate the crutches, she realized she needed something to cut the strong plastic tie that was holding the two crutches together. She knew exactly where to find that something. She wheeled over to her rucksack, opened up a small side zipper and pulled out a multi-tool. This little tool had been so useful on her travels. Holding it always caused a smile to appear on her lips, as it made her flash back to unexpected funny things she had used it for. The pliers had to be the most useful tool, with its ability to grip and cut even the strongest of wires. They cut through the plastic tie with ease. She replaced the multi tool, spun the chair around, locked the wheel and stood up on the crutches. She liked the higher perspective and started practicing around the room.

Chapter Ten

Ben had been busy most of the morning. Instructions for the day had been given to Jake to pass to the team. Mary knocked and walked in with two coffees.

"Good weekend?"

"Interesting."

"Wouldn't have anything to do with a young lady, would it?"

Mary could always speak her mind to Ben. She had long since earned his respect on matters of relationships. She had saved many a situation from blowing up on the floor by engaging others in what she called 'no regret negotiation.'

She handed Ben a coffee and Ben motioned for her to take a seat.

"Yes, actually it was down to her. We went up to the lake — "

Mary's coffee stopped half way to her mouth.

"Is this going to be something I probably don't want to know about? She's very young, Ben."

"It's not like that. I mean I don't -"

"You don't what?"

"Look, we just had a great weekend. It was interesting because I have never met anyone like her before. Where she has been in the world is quite amazing, when you think that she was a girl traveling on her own."

"So what's happening with her? When can she leave?"

"I don't know; I suppose when her leg has healed. Did you send the crutches to the house?"

"Delivered this morning at about 11:00 am. Maybe she has left already."

Ben's head tilted forward, and faint lines of a frown appeared.

"Not something you'd like to happen then?"

Ben looked up as his eyebrows squeezed together.

"What do you mean?"

"Oh, nothing, just an observation. Just ignore me, you know what I'm like."

Jake appeared at the door. Ben flicked his head back, and Jake stepped in.

"Sorry, Mary... Just to let you know Ben, it looks like it's all on. Things are starting to move our way."

"Ok, I'll leave it up to you now" Ben replied, as he held Jake's gaze which meant 'You can go now.'

"Catch you guys later," Jake said as he spun around and left.

"You were saying?"

"Well, it's just that she has an interesting perspective on a few things in life."

"Want to give me an example?"

"Well, one thing that made me think was a prison story she told me."

"She's been to prison?"

"No, no. It was a story about putting things off, you know, like how we say (When) I get this, when I get that, when the weekend comes, I'm going to do whatever.'

It was about how we use the word when to push things off into the future and so we never actually do the when things at all. In fact, we spend a lifetime in when moment avoidance".

Mary leaned forward and chewed gently on her bottom lip. There was no instant come back from Mary; they just looked at each other across the desk until Ben raised his shoulders and turned his palms outwards.

"See. It even made you think," he said.

Mary was still processing when avoidance. Then suddenly said, "I'd like to take the afternoon off, if I may, Ben."

"Yes, of course. You know you don't have to ask."

Mary got up, leaving the empty cups and a few moments later, Ben saw her walking across the floor towards the elevator. He watched Jake raise his hand to attract her attention, which she ignored completely.

Jake looked back at Ben's office, and as their eyes met, Jake threw his arms up to question at a distance. Ben returned a shrug of the shoulders then beckoned for Jake to come over.

"What was that about? She looked like a woman on a mission."

"Probably some errands she had to do. Look, I have some things to do as well. I take it you are hundred percent to see today through?"

"It will go like you said, eh?" Jake replied.

"Pretty sure it will, but you know what to do if not."

Jake's breathing became shallow as his hands started to sweat.

"Yes, I'll sort it, no worries."

Chapter Eleven

Ben arrived home just after 4:00 pm, which was unusual but his mind had been overly occupied with the events of the last few days.

He kept scanning back and forwards, running through the days from beginning to end, trying to see if the crazy dot theory Christina had told him about had any substance. He just kept hitting walls of confusion that instantly manifested into frustration.

Nothing was sticking. His mind ordinarily controlled, logical and calculating, kept breaking from any train of thought and jumped from one thought to another and then another. His stomach rolled as he thought about trying to do his work under these conditions, which would be impossible for him. He started to feel something he had never experienced before – vulnerability.

Christina heard the front door close and hobbled over to see who it was. "Thanks for these."

Every troubling thought vanished from Ben's mind.

"Well, it didn't take you long to get onto them, did it?"

"Great to be standing up again."

"I spoke to the Doctor, and he said that you are fine to get around on them but to elevate your leg if the cast starts to feel tight. I have some work to finish up so we can catch up later at dinner if you like?"

"Ok."

Ben closed the office door behind him. This was a small room by comparison to the rest of the house, but still, it was an office space with a small lounge-like sitting area.

There was a slight hum from the computer which was always left on, as waiting for computers to boot up frustrated him. He pressed the monitor on button and typed.

'Almedio, Peru' as a search.

Nothing came up on page one, so he started digging into much lower page results. A topic in a forum came up. It read 'Is it better to go to a retreat or try to go bush, so to speak?'

The word retreat peaked Ben's interest, enough for him to click on the link.

It was a free and open forum. Ben spent several minutes looking at different posts and Almedio was nowhere to be found. However, he did notice that one word was cropping up in several of the posts by various people. The word was Ayahuasca.

Ben typed this into the search bar. The first result said:

'Plant mixture that is capable of inducing altered states of consciousness.'

'Altered state of consciousness?' Ben murmured.

He spent the next two hours reading forum posts, articles and looking at images. There was one story about a former soldier, who had served in Iraq and suffered post-traumatic stress disorder known as PTSD.

This soldier had gone to Peru and engaged in an Ayahuasca

ceremony, before returning home. As a result of this, a TV crew had accompanied him back to Peru to do a documentary on the effects of Ayahuasca.

"Mr. Ben," Anna knocked on the door, jarring Ben from the screen. Dinner in thirty minutes, ok?"

"Yes, excellent."

Ben leaned back and locked his hands behind his head, just looking in a defocused state. His mind was trying to do what he was good at doing at work which was assembling bits and pieces of information to arrive at a coherent likely outcome. But this was different; there were just so many thoughts going through his mind.

This type of thinking was uncomfortable for Ben, as it left him with a feeling of no structure or control.

He was just about to push the off button on the screen when he remembered that he had not talked to the IT department at work about access to his computer for a guest.

He quickly created a guest account with no admin rights in the name of Christina and turned the screen off.

Christina was already seated at the dinner table when Ben walked in.

"What's up? Tough day?"

"No, no. I was just thinking about all this stuff we have talked about, and it - " Christina cut him off mid sentence.

"It messes with your head, eh? Well, that's what it did to me."

Anna served them both, accompanied with the usual chit chat and went on her way back to the kitchen.

"I need to ask you something, and please be honest with me?" Ben asked.

"I'll try."

"There is no trying to be honest. There's only honest or dishonest."

"What I mean is I will unless it would hurt me."

"Ok, fair enough. So here it is. What do you know about something called Ayahuasca?"

Christina's fork froze half way to her mouth. She placed the fork down on the plate and said.

"Ok, so you do know something?"

It was like a kaleidoscope had just been turned in Christina's mind as she panicked as to what response to give. She needed some time.

"Yes, I do know about it, but tell you what... how about we finish dinner and go to the lounge and I will tell you what I know."

Ben nodded in agreement and started to eat at twice normal speed. He rang a bell for Anna to bring dessert and finished that at the same rate. They had not spoken while eating which suited Christina, as she worked on what to say.

"OK, all done. Shall we go?"

Christina grabbed her crutches and walked smoothly on them to the lounge.

"Hey, you are pretty good on them."

"Yes, not bad eh? Maybe I had to use them in a past life."

They seated opposite one another; Ben was leaning forward like an interrogator. Christina still hadn't worked out what she was going to say and needed more time.

"Just a quick question Ben... The picture above the fireplace. What was it with the masks?"

Ben looked up at the picture and exhaled audibly through his nostrils. Christina read it as frustration, and she was not wrong.

"It was just kids having fun... A mask is a mask; it doesn't have to mean anything, does it?. Now Ayahuasca, what do you know?"

"Ok, first hear me out on this, as I want to tell you first about my mask."

"What has a paper mask on a picture got to do with Ayahuasca?"

Ben's lips squeezed tightly together, and his breathing was now solely through his nose, making it even more audible.

"Will you just relax and hear me out? I promise I will get to it, ok?"

Ben leaned back on the sofa and dropped his shoulders.

"Ok, fire away."

"When I set off traveling, I wanted to find something, but I had no idea what that something was. I suppose you could say I was lost, which is ironical when you think of it, as I then went off and got lost traveling through different countries and cultures."

"And you ended up in Peru?"

"Look I don't know how you have tied this to Peru, but you said you would hear me out. If you're not going to do that, then I'm off."

"Ok, I just googled the name Almedio, and it grew organically from there. That's all I did."

"Ah, Ok, I get it. Now I understand where you're coming from."

"Just off topic for a moment. Almedio was interpreting one of my visions — "

Ben cut in loudly

"Visions, what do you mean visions?"

Christina threw up her hands.

"That's it! I'm off."

Ben jumped up with is hands outstretched, palms down, moving up and down like he was pressing air to keep Christina seated.

"Sorry, I'm sorry. I will not interrupt again."

Christina leaned backward, and Ben sat down but still on the edge of the sofa.

"You look uncomfortable. Lean back and let's just chill out."

Ben leaned back as if on an acceptable command.

"You were talking about Almedio," Ben started.

"Yes, well... it was just one thing that jumped into my mind, as we were talking about trying to find out information, as opposed to allowing that information to come to us.

Almedio explained how most people had lost the ability to observe and listen correctly. I naturally wanted to know more about that, and he then started to talk about what he called modern loneliness.

He said that technology has great potential to bring people together - a bit like your google search - but at the same time, it can cause us to become more disconnected than we have ever been.

He said that if one pauses and looks inwards at loneliness for a few moments and then quickly thinks of ways to solve that loneliness, one can instantly see a solution in technology.

You can check your messages, jump on the Internet, check some promoted stories and pretty soon the Internet has logged our search pattern and starts delivering what its algorithms are saying about what we want to know.

The internet search results are an attempt to connect with the searcher at an emotional level."

"This Almedio guy seems to me to be pretty westernized for someone living in the jungle - " Ben interrupted.

"Well, that's another story for another time. But getting back to this modern loneliness."

"Yes, sorry I interrupted again."

"Ok, so Almedio was saying that modern loneliness is a more serious problem that we believe it to be.

'Loneliness causes us to live our lives wearing masks.' This is why I suppose I mentioned the mask on the picture' which started this off. I didn't mean that particular mask or that person. It was like just a mental prompt that caused us to be having this conversation now."

"Sorry, I am wavering again."

Christina gave a little chuckle to which Ben returned a warm smile and said: "It's ok, we all waver from time to time."

"Modern loneliness is the result of the withdrawing of empathy and compassion. We no longer feel these things with the same intensity. Our feelings are shielded by what society now tells us is more connectivity, when in truth much of technology interns of human contact, allows us to hide behind our virtual world of social media.

Much of today's media plays fiddle to the hyped world of connectivity and how we can instantly see and hear about what is going on the other side of the world but then fails to explain why we don't know the person working next to us.

The difference here is that in the case of the person on the other side of the world, we are perhaps getting to see a reaction to some event in their life. Their reaction does not tell us who this person is, what their hopes and dream for the future are, etc. What we have is a superficial connection with this person, that is a direct contrast to the opportunity we have to know and engage with the person standing next to us.

We might ask why is this? What is it that causes us to connect with the person who is far away and not connect with the person in the next booth? I thought that was an interesting question. What about you?"

Ben's eye focus indicated that he was internalizing. He then came back and said.

"Let me guess that one?"

Christina jumped in - "Well, I'm not saying I have the answer. Connectivity to me would be to know someone's life; not to be like an imposter or anything but to have a connection to say that person's problems and concerns. What makes them happy, what they like doing, dislike doing, etc. But above all, being a person that other people could talk to and vice versa."

Ben bit his lip and rolled his head right back into the soft sofa. It was silent in the room for a few moments.

"What were you thinking about?"

"Nothing."

"Yes, you were. I could see it. Some thought was going through your mind, and I bet it was related to someone you know."

"OK, it was two people. The first was my father and the second was Mary, my secretary."

"Do you have feelings for this Mary?"

"No, she's in a relationship."

"Ok, what about your father then?"

"Not open for discussion."

"Not open for discussion, but something that apparently bothers you?"

Ben leaned forward and pierced Christina's eyes. Christina quickly put her hands up.

"Sorry, I didn't mean to pry or anything."

Ben leaned back again.

"Ok, let's get back to Mary as an example," Ben said.

"Today, I told her a few things about that we had talked about. She seemed genuinely interested, and then without notice, she asked for the rest of the day off, as if something in our conversation had touched her in some way.

I remember feeling that I wanted to ask her why, but didn't feel comfortable doing that. This is not the type of relationship we have, although I like her company and love to listen to her logic as she calls it, regarding other people."

"So, it was not like you were being nosey or wanted to invade, but rather you felt what? " Christina asked.

"I wanted in a way I suppose, to console her."

"So she was upset?"

"No, not visibly, but I could just tell something was going on inside that was important."

"Ok, that is exactly what Almedio was getting at. He said that the root of modern loneliness was not responding in ways that we intuitively know we should.

You had a feeling that you wanted to console her. For you to feel that, you must have had, by default at that moment, a connection with her that then resulted in the feeling you experienced.

What happened is that you ignored that feeling because you logically thought it was inappropriate. This must have been what Almedio meant when he said that modern loneliness causes the sense of disconnection, of being lost and alone.

These feelings can result in frustration and anger which can manifest to the point of us wearing permanent masks to cover up who we really are.

We have the fear that says if our loneliness in discovered, it could be seen as an ailment or weakness of character that one wants to hide."

Ben reached up and dragged his fingers down his cheeks as his hands came together with his chin resting on his fingertips.

"You're deep in thought," Christina said.

"Mm... I suppose I am trying to take all this in, against a life-time of skepticism or rather a lifetime of just being who I am."

"Being whom we are was one the messages I received in one of my visions. Remember, you wanted to know about that?"

"Yes, tell me more."

"Ok, so after meeting the boy and his girlfriend on the boat, all I had was the name Almedio.

That was all he told me, and remember he said that he spoke to me for no other reason than he felt it was the thing to do. Anyway, the boat landed, and they just gave a wave and off they went. I did what I always do when I land somewhere new. I like to get into the heart of the place and find somewhere to stay."

"You mean you don't book anywhere before you arrive?"

"I used to, but then after two or three booking mistakes and wasted time, I decided just to wing it and see what happened."

Ben's eyes widened.

"Besides, Christina continued, "You sometimes meet the most interesting people on your travels that you would usually never even speak to, which....

was exactly what happened when I arrived and found a back-packers that was nice and centrally located.

As I stood up after unpacking some essentials, I nearly fell over and knew instantly that I had not been drinking enough water. One thing I have found out on my travels is to watch the water. I grabbed some money and locked the door behind me.

As I turned to go, a voice called out

'Hey, are you going to the shop by any chance?'

I peered into the opposite room and there, sitting on the bed holding a small stone against his forehead, was a guy in rainbow trousers."

"Rainbow trousers?" Ben said.

"They are just trousers with all the colors of the rainbow in them."

"Yes, I know what you mean now - I call them hippie pants."

"Ah. Now here's a thing — before I continue. Tell me — what do you think about the wearers of hippie pants?"

"Just that hippies, no place to go and living in a dream world that is a drain on society, generally a waste of time."

Christina smiled.

"You know. that's pretty much what I thought, but that was all about to change with the wearer of these particular rainbow trousers."

"You mean there are different types of rainbow trouser wearers?" Ben laughed.

"So it turns out. Anyway, he introduced himself as Henry and asked again if I was going to the shop. It turns out there is a shop right across the road that he said sold everything from anchovies to zippers. If I was going, could I grab him a bottle of water?

'I'll give you the money when you get back, he said.

Henry was still sitting on the bed cross-legged when I got back, but now the stone was just hanging from his neck. He must have noticed me looking at it as he touched it and said — "For meditation, I use it for meditation.

I handed him the water, and he drank half of it straight down.

'Dehydrated.' he said.

'You'll be ok now?' I said

'No, I meant you. You are dehydrated.'

'Oh' not that bad.'

'Actually' more than you think. Sit down and drink at least a liter.'

He moved over on the bed and motioned for me to sit. I felt a little uncomfortable, but there was something quite calming about him.

'Dehydration always gets you like that; you don't think it's as bad as it is and then bang, you're down. We were trained to monitor each other for that.'

Over the next couple of hours, I learned that rainbow trousers used to be a special forces soldier. He had served several high conflict areas around the world. He was 36 years old and was absent without leave but was not being pursued, due to suffering post-traumatic stress disorder.

This was his second time in Iquitos and was waiting for a film crew to go with him into the jungle together with some other soldiers, who also suffered from PTSD. They were going to record a documentary about an Ayahuasca ceremony.

He had on an earlier occasion taken part in a ceremony, and the PTSD symptoms had vanished. When he went back to Denmark, he met other soldiers and this is how it all came together for him to be back in Iquitos.

'So....,' he said after telling me all that.

'Are you going to do a ceremony?'

'No, I didn't come here for that.'

Henry laughed. 'Really... That is exactly how I arrived here and exactly how I bumped into Almedio.'

'That's the second time I have heard that name today.'

'Tell you what, why don't you come with us tomorrow to the village and you can see if you are meant to meet this guy that you have heard about twice today?'

'No, I don't think so.'

'I tell you what — don't say no now. Wait until tomorrow and then decide.'

I remember shaking my head from side to side to gesture no, but at the same time the word wouldn't come out. Anyway, I went back to my room and just crashed out on the bed.

Next thing I knew, there was a knock on my door.

'Chrissy…'

It was Henry. Apparently, my name was now Chrissy, and it was going to stay that way.

'I have made some soup. You hungry?'

'From the moment I heard the word soup, I realized how hungry I was.'

'Great thanks, I'm coming now.'

We met in the kitchen with one other person called Jim, who was traveling with Henry - rainbow trousers. Jim was not a soldier but had met Henry in New Zealand; they became good mates and ended up traveling together.

Jim was very different to Henry, and I instantly felt at ease with him. He was the same age as Henry but very different. Whereas Henry would internalize at lot, for example, you could almost always see some processing going on behind those bright blue eyes, Jim would openly speak about pretty much anything that came to mind.

We were just finishing up the soup when Jim suddenly looked at me, undid a necklace he was wearing, stood up and walked around the table behind me and put this necklace on me. Before I could say anything, he said 'I am a believer in karma or just going with my thoughts. I was just thinking about that necklace, and I knew it was meant for you. Someone gave it to me yesterday, and I never felt comfortable with it.'

He laughed out loud. 'Don't worry' it's not expensive nor is it an engagement gift or anything.'

I protested a bit, but both Henry and Jim stood their ground and made me promise to keep it.

We shared four beers between us and said good night.

Jim was already in the kitchen the next morning when I walked in.

'I made you some toast,'" he said

He turned around and handed me the toast and then dropped another two slices in.

'So you're coming to the Bora village with us this afternoon?'

'E... I said I would sleep on it.'

'Yes, Henry told me you said that, but he told me you would be coming anyway' as he said curiosity would not let you stay away. I reckon he was right.'

Jim pointed at my neck.

'Nice necklace you have there. Must have been some real high flyer to give you a bit of an old tree root.'

I just shook my head as we both laughed out loud.

I caught a flash of some rainbow trousers out of the corner of my eye as Henry appeared.

'Jim, you have made me toast already?'

The toaster popped. Jim grabbed the two slices.

'Not this time matey, put your own in.'

Henry dropped two slices in and turned to Jim and me.

'Ok, it seems like the film crew has been delayed in Lima for a few hours due to some hold up with customs and camera equipment. They will be here tonight; well, early evening. I have sorted the boat ride, so we just have to meet up at the boat ramp at 5:00 pm. Chrissy — the boat ramp is about a kilometer from here, across town.'

I hated being called Chrissy, but there is something that is kind and gentle about this special forces' soldier that speaks from the heart. I almost thought that he would have been offended if I objected to Chrissy, so I just let it go.

We chatted a while before agreeing that we would meet as planned at the boat ramp.

I then spent the rest of the day looking around Iquitos, trying to achieve the impossible task of avoiding what seemed to be street sellers from a world convention event. I was offered everything from crystals to live tortoise for dinner later on…

I was only carrying my mini pack, as I had left my main pack in a locker at the backpackers. I had everything I needed, so started to make my way to the boat ramp which was about 2 kilometers from where I was. It was 4:00 pm, so I decided to take a taxi. Well, taxi is what they call it, but it's a motorbike cut in half, extended, and then two wheels and a bench seat placed on the back.

Riding one of these is quite frightening due to the speed they go and the weaving in and out of traffic, most of it on-coming.

The driver then shouted back to me 'No further miss, no further. Ten dollar miss ten Dollar, feria Miss, party day. Ten Dollar Miss.'

I held two dollars in one hand and five in the other and looked him dead in the eye. 'five dollar Miss, five dollar. You hard lady Miss, you hard lady.'

$2.00 was the real fare, and we both knew it, but that was ok.

I grabbed my mini pack and started walking in the direction he pointed me to.

It was a nightmare to get anywhere. The street party was wall to wall with people; everyone had to push and squeeze to make any headway. I started to get concerned that I was going to be late and miss the boat but then I thought that unless Henry, Jim, and the film crew were already there' then they were going to have the same problem.

I pushed on, and by 5:00 pm I was still at least half a kilometer away. The light was starting to fade, and I was not happy to be in this situation at all.

There was no way I was going to make the boat before it left but on taking stock of things, there really was no way back. I had come this far, so I might as well continue.

I figured that when I got to the boat ramp, I could probably find a backpackers close by to spend the night.

It was 6:00 pm when I finally pushed through the last of the crowd and could see the boat ramp ahead.

I scanned around, and there were at least fifty boats all looking the same. They were long and thin, with small engines and very long shafts that extended a long way out the back of the boat.

As I got closer, everyone was calling and waving to me to get in their boat.

For the first time in a long time, I felt very alone and vulnerable, and it started to show.

Just as quickly as I sensed this feeling, I knew I had to stop it. I raised my voice and stopped smiling at everyone. I gave the outward impression I was in control and knew where I was going and whom I was going to meet.

I moved off to the side where a few women were sitting and sat beside them. As soon as I did this, the men on the boats stopped calling out to me, and I relaxed a little."

"Sounds like a bloody nightmare to me," said Ben.

"Yes, but you can't show those feelings in a situation like that. However, it got worse before it got better.

After about five minutes' I noticed there was a lone boat some distance from the others. As I looked, the man in the boat waved for me to come. I ignored him. A few moments later, I looked again, and yet again he beckoned for me to come. I decided not to look again and turned slightly, so my back was to him.

About a minute later, I felt a tap on my shoulder.

'Miss, taxi boat?'

'No, thank you.'

'Miss taxi boat, camera, camera?'

Just then' one of the women interrupted the man and spoke rapidly to him. She then turned to me.

'Camera film people Miss. You are waiting for them, Miss?'

'Yes,' I said, 'yes I am waiting for them.'

'They go early Miss because of Feria party. They arrange for this taxi to take you to the Bora village.'

Saved! I thanked the woman and headed to the boat with the man.

The boat pushed away from the shore.

'Fifteen dollar, Miss.'

I had no way of knowing if this was a fifteen dollar ride or a two dollar ride and as I was now in the boat' I had to hand over the fifteen dollars. Soon as he had the money, he turned the boat towards a platform that was well lit up about two hundred meters out into the river. We pulled up alongside, where the money for fuel exchanged hands which was passed over in large coke bottles. He tipped two of these into the fuel tank on top of the engine.

By now, it was getting dark, but I didn't realize how dark until we moved away from the fuel platform.

Within minutes, we were enveloped in complete darkness. It was so black that you could not see a hand's distance in front of your face. All I could hear was the rush of water and the steady chugging of the motor. Then out of the darkness, another chugging sound. It was another boat coming towards us; the noise got louder and louder until it passed right by us. The only thing I could see was a faint red glow from what I assumed was an exhaust pipe as it passed by.

I started to think about a possible collision, as another boat passed us. This time I could feel on my face the push of air that it caused, and yet, we were still in total blackout darkness. I started to panic and thought about what I would do if we collided with another boat. There was no life jacket, but what use would that be anyway? What about the piranhas, the snakes... everything that would be in the night water.

I remember taking a deep breath and telling myself to shut off all such thoughts.

The driver of the boat lit a cigarette, and for a moment the flash of light lit the boat up.

"All good Miss, nearly there.'

I looked out front and could see something that resembled a candle burning off in the distance.

Eventually, as we got closer, it turned out to be a single light bulb on a landing platform.

'Here, Miss.

We pulled up, and I climbed out. It felt good to be on solid ground again and to be able to see my surroundings.

There were a few tables and chairs dotted around on the platform, which turned out to be a waterside cafe area that had long since closed. Over a makeshift bar, hung a sign saying, Bora.

The driver started the boat and pushed away. I called out to him 'Where do I go?'

He shrugged his shoulders and turned into the blackness. He then shouted.

'Light out at ten Miss, light out at ten.'

Three things I always carry with me, even in my small pack: a multi tool, a head torch and a tiny digital alarm clock, little bigger than a postage stamp. I have learned from experience that these can be the most valuable items.

I checked the time. Ten to ten.

I assumed that I had ten minutes to lights out."

"Christina' I just have to stop you here a moment and ask you something."

"Ok."

"Are you mad? You are a beautiful young girl on your own—

Christine cut him off mid sentence. "Really, when did you notice? She said flicking her hair back and stroking her face."

"Look, all joking aside — "

"So you were joking about my looks?"

Ben exhaled deeply. "Look, let's be serious for a moment. Why did you put yourself in this situation? You didn't know where you were going; who, if anyone, was going to meet you and nobody knows where you were. Weren't you afraid?"

Christina mentally placed herself back in that situation.

"Yes, I suppose I was a little nervous."

"A little? I would not have been happy, and I am a Man."

"And being a Man makes it different?"

"Well yes."

"So the fairer and gentle sex is more vulnerable, you're, saying?"

Ben paused and cleared his throat, giving Christina time to defuse the conversation.

"Look, I do get what you're saying, but things are not always like that. Once you get over the initial irrational fears of traveling on your own in different places, you quickly become tuned to where you should or shouldn't go. And remember one important thing that is often overlooked, which is the vast majority of people are inherently good when it comes down to the wire."

Ben leaned back on the sofa, ready to listen again.

"I reckoned I had ten minutes of light and then I would be in that solid blackness again. Way off in the distance I could hear the low thudding sound of an engine running which I assumed was powering the light bulb, so I decided to head towards that noise.

It was a good choice because as soon as I started to walk up the bank, I could see another bulb glowing.

I followed the light, and pretty soon there were more lights, and then I saw a few houses. Some of them were of solid construction;

others I assumed more traditional, being wooden with thatched roofs.

People were sitting outside the houses, and most of them had one single light bulb. Most of them were either packing things away or placing candles.

'Miss, you want to sleep?' I heard a voice call out.

It came from a young boy about twelve years old with a huge smile.

'Miss I know sleep place, good place Miss.'

He pointed further along the street and beckoned me to follow. There was a sign outside saying: Clean beds, spelled with a Z.

The owner came rushing out to meet us. I instantly liked her.

Within minutes I was shown a small room with a single bed. There was a toilet and shower area shared with the owner. $15.00 a night with breakfast sealed the deal."

Chapter Twelve

"I love the light of the next day. What I mean is that when you arrive somewhere at night and then you wake in the morning, every impression that you had at night is almost always way off from how things really are.

The Bora village was not at all like I expected. I thought we were to be going into the jungle, but there were some narrow concrete roads. Some of the houses were of solid construction, but many of them were shack like with thatched roofs made from palm leaves.

I later found out that roofing iron was expensive and made the house like an oven in the summer.

Breakfast was fruit with some bread toasted over red embers of an open fire.

Have you ever tried toast from an open fire?"

"No, I think I'll stick to Anna's toast." Ben smiled.

"You should try it someday; it's a whole different experience."

"Anyway, so Pablo…"

"Pablo?"

"Pablo was the young boy who took me to where I was staying. You often find a child like this in these places. They learn a little English, and then they start directing tourists to earn commission from vendors. In most cases, they are completely trustworthy and can be relied on. They have long since learned backpackers recommend to other packers and pretty soon, word gets around. They are handy to know.

Pablo was no exception. His clothes and shoes reflected a higher standing than the average twelve-year-old in the village.

Anyway, so after coffee, again brewed over red embers, I agreed with Suzi $15.00 a night to stay with her. Although Peruvian, Suzi was actually her real name, she managed a little English, enough to get by with tourists anyway."

"When you say tourists, was this Bora place a tourist resort? I mean do a lot of people go there?"

Christina chuckled.

"A resort... no... Maybe only fifty to a hundred people a year and they will be backpackers, who either stumble across the place or who are told by other packers it's a place to go.

Pablo appeared with the trademark ear to ear grin. Something he had probably learned was the best icebreaker possible. But you could tell with Pablo that his smile was real.

He said that one day he was going to get a backpack and walk to America. Logistics had not been thought about, but I sensed that somehow he would likely make it.

Anyway, I asked him if he knew Henry, he did and also Jim. He told me that they had arrived early last night and left early this morning with the film crew. He could take me to catch up with them, but he was not sure exactly where they were heading. He then paused a while and said

"Maybe you want to meet Almedio?"

It now started to feel a little too well organized, but I decided to go along with it.

'Yes, if you like,' I said.

The next moment I heard 'Is Chrissy here?'

The tone of the voice tricked my mind into thinking it was a young man but when he appeared clearly, he was over seventy years old.

He had silver gray hair and beard, and he ducked under the doorway. He was over 6 feet tall with a body of a much younger, stronger man.

'Ah... Chrissy, but that's not your real name is it?'

'No... it's — '

'It's Christina, right?'

'Yes, Christina.'

'And you prefer that name, yes?'

'Yes.'

'I spoke to Henry last night, and he told me he had met you. Also, you met a couple on a boat trip here, I believe?'

As you can imagine this all started to seem a little spooky, not in a bad way or anything, just spooky how all this seemed connected."

"I would by now be one very suspicious guy. But no doubt you will remind me that is not a good thought?"

"I wouldn't say it was a bad thought, but I think we have to try not to accept our first impressions as truth. If we believe our first impressions are all there is to know, we may well miss the essence of opportunity that is right before us.

Suzi then appeared.

'Almedio, entre, entre. Venga, tengo cafe,' she said.

Which roughly translates to 'Come in, come in, I have coffee ready.'

"So, finally you get to meet Almedio," Ben said.

"Yes and looking back, I can now see that this was the beginning of a transition into an entirely different outlook on life.

Meeting Almedio was a strange experience. When I say strange, it was not in a creepy way or anything, but there was that underlying feeling that somehow this was all orchestrated.

Looking from the outside, it seemed like it started with the meeting on the boat trip with the couple who told me about Almedio but as I later came to learn, this was only one dot in an ocean of dots."

"Dots? What do you mean dots?"

"Mmm… I probably mentioned them too early in this conversation, as the understanding of them came later on. Let's just say at this point that a dot is like an ethereal byte of information. I'll try and make that clearer later on."

Ben gave a little yawn and stretch, then looked at his watch. "Jeez, it's nearly ten thirty."

"Shall we continue tomorrow?"

"No, please go on. I am interested in this Almedio fella."

"Well, not much happened that day. Almedio convinced me to walk around the village with him and then visit a butterfly farm that had been set up."

"They farmed butterflies for sale?"

"Yes, that was what I thought. A bit strange, eh? But what they were actually doing was trying to get some mainstream tourism to the village, and this was one idea to come and see butterflies.

Anyway, so after a few hours walking around, we sat down on the grass, and I realized that there had been a pattern to our conversation.

Almedio would be talking a lot and then listening a lot. The very moment I become aware of this pattern, he said

'What do you know of the ceremony?'

'I told him that the only thing I knew was that Henry had got involved for his PTSD and I was not sure why Jim was there. He stroked his beard a little longer than normal.'

"The ceremony is like opening a gateway or revealing a path to a place that can give a person understanding regarding the most important question in life."

He paused and gave me a soul-piercing gaze.

"Do you know what that question is, Christina?"

Now I will say at this point, that I had not thought about or at least I was not conscious of having thought about my reply. The words just came out.

"'Probably, deep down, we want to know the answer to the question, but the rational side of our brain likes things just as they are, and enjoys the comfortable status quo of our lives.'"

"So what was your answer?" Ben asked.

"Why am I here and is there a purpose for my life?", Christina replied.

Ben sagged forward; his body looked like someone who had just let a little too much air out of a balloon, to the point where it showed wrinkles.

He turned for a brief moment towards the fireplace and the picture hanging there, before turning back to Christina, saying

"I think we had better call it a night."

Christina didn't want to end here and came right back.

"As soon as I answered 'Why am I here and is there a purpose for my life?', Almedio pointed to the necklace I was wearing.

'Why do you wear that? I sense that you don't like jewelry' he said.

It's true that I don't like jewelry and I don't know how he managed to work that out, but anyway, I told him that Jim had given it to me while telling me that he felt it was the right thing to do.

Almedio jumped to his feet and started to walk away. It was like I had offended him in some way, but then he turned his head as he was still walking away and gave me a lovely warm smile.

sweet dreams, tell me tomorrow about your plans.'

And just like that, our conversation ended, and I was left just sitting there, feeling like this whole day was once again not a random event."

"Bed time," Ben said.

Chapter Thirteen

B en pulled into the underground car park at the same time as
Jake. They both parked and Jake made straight for the
elevator.

"I'll hold it for you," he called back.

The garage attendant walked towards Ben to get the car keys.

"Morning, sir."

Ben dropped the keys into his hand, saying "Good morning to
you also" He then walked towards the elevator. After three steps into
that path he stopped, turned and walked back to the attendant, who
straightened to attention as if something was wrong.

"Sir?"

"I was just wondering. You have worked here for a very
long time?"

'Yes, sir. Is everything Ok sir?"

"Yes, but it just came to me that I — "

Jake called out from the elevator.

"You can always take the stairs, buddy."

Ben turned back to the attendant.

"It just came to me that in all the time you have worked here, I
don't even know your name."

"Sir..?"

"What is your name?"

"Bill, sir."

"Good morning, Bill."

Bill turned his head slightly and flashed a set of gleaming white teeth.

"You have a great day, Bill."

Jake called out again, and Ben made a quick pace to the elevator.

"Jake, do you know his name?"

"Who? The garage man? Yes, of course, it's the garage man."

"It's Bill."

"Bill?"

"Bill is the name of the garage man."

"What are you on man? Who gives a crap what his name is. He parks the cars for us; someone's got to do it. Fred, Bill, Joe… what's it matter?"

"I was just wondering… when you think about it, how many people work in this building, even just on our floor and we probably don't know the names of more than a handful of them."

"Ben… what the hell is going on in that head of yours this morning? You're all over the place."

"Oh, it's just something that Christina said that got me thinking."

"For Christ's sake, Ben. You banged her while the plaster was still on. You're one —"

Ben cut him off with a deadpan stare.

"Cut the crap; it was nothing like that at all."

"Whoa!! buddy, sorry to stoke the fire."

The elevator doors opened, and the noise was deafening. A trader sprinted over to meet them, looking straight at Jake.

"Jake, your shorts on the Canadian dollar are three million out of the money. What do you want us to do?"

Jake's face turned white, and his voice crackled like an off-tuned radio station.

Ben looked at Jake for a response.

"Fuck, Ben... I felt it was the right thing to do."

"So you just felt it, and you went with your feelings? Is that what you are telling me?"

Every blood vessel in Jake,s face had now donated its contents to the rest of his body.

"Jake and... you... what's your name?" The young trader replied "John, Sir. John". "Pay attention to me now. I am going to my office. I do not want to be disturbed until lunch time."

Jake's shaking wrist came up to where he could see his watch face which he steadied with his right hand.

"But Ben... three million off. What shall I do?"

"Do nothing and do not disturb me until lunch time."

"Fuck' Ben... this is —"

"ENOUGH!" shouted Ben and left Jake and the young trader staring at each other.

Mary met Ben at his office door.

"Everything ok Ben?"

"Yes sure, are you free for a while this morning?"

"I can be in five minutes."

"Great, I'll meet you in the garage in say ten minutes."

Mary's eyes popped wide.

"Garage?"

"Yes, we are going for a walk."

"Er... walk... ok."

Ben took the elevator to the garage. Bill left his booth to greet whoever arrived in the elevator.

"Car, sir or limousine?"

"Limo, please Bill."

Bill signaled back to the booth for a driver and pointed to the limo. A driver opened the rear door.

"Where to, Sir?"

"We're going to Central Park."

"We, sir?"

"Mary will be here shortly."

"Mary. Very good sir."

"My name is Ben, Bill."

"Yes, sir. I know what your name is. Day one on the job we have to learn everyone's name. I can name everyone who passes through the garage."

The elevator doors opened and out stepped Mary.

"I bet you have nicknames for everyone upstairs, eh?" Ben said to Bill.

"Yes Sir. We have a few." Bill chuckled.

"What's mine?"

"You, sir?"

Ben gave a smile, knowing that he would not hear his nickname.

"Tell you what Bill, when you think the time is right, you can tell me my nickname. We have a deal?"

Ben thrust his hand out to get the automatic response that he knew would come. They shook hands as Bill's face changed to a slack expression, but broke into a smile again to match Ben.

Mary was just approaching them.

"Hi Bill, what's going on?"

"Morning, Mary. Don't see you down here too often."

"Well, I'm still working on getting that car space," she laughed.

Ben motioned for Mary to get in the limo.

The driver turned the key.

"Central Park, was it, sir?"

"Yes please."

Mary shifted in the smooth leather seats and turned to Ben.

"Not a date, is it Ben? You know you're way too late on that front."

Ben slowly turned to face her.

"Mary... are you happy with your life?"

Mary bit her lip and took a deep breath.

"Where is this going Ben? What are we doing in this limo and why are we going to Central Park at 10:00 am in the morning?"

"I just wanted to talk, that's all, Talk."

"Couldn't we have just done that in the office, instead of all this malarkey?"

"So are you happy with your life?"

"What's happy Ben? Happy is a very subjective thing. I am happy with some things and not so happy about other things. Surely that is true for everyone."

A short while later they arrive at the park.

"Shall I wait for you, sir?

"No, I'll call,"

They both stood on the sidewalk for a moment as the limo pulled away.

"So are you going to tell me what this is all about, Ben or is this going to be some self-discovery as we go process?"

"Self-discovery... how apt," Ben replied

"Look, Ben, you are freaking me out a little, are you ill? Something serious going on? Are you in trouble?"

"Come let's walk."

They walked in silence until they were amongst the lush green of the park.

"How long since you have been here, Mary?"

"Can't remember..."

"Me neither. Things seem to get away from us without us even realizing it, don't you think?"

"Ben, it's a lovely day and every girl likes a walk in the park but what is going on here?"

"The girl with the broken leg, you know, Christina."

"Ah… so it's a relationship problem, and you think I can give you some help with that? You bring me out to Central Park to walk with you, while you talk about another woman? Very charming."

Ben looked at her, and they exchanged looks of appreciation. Ben was the first to jump in.

"You see, you and I would have been good together>" Ben laughed.

"Ok, so what is going on with Christina?"

"Nothing is going on in that sense, that's not to say I don't like her. I do but remember she is just a girl."

"So you have developed feelings for a girl that is way younger than you, and you're confused about that? Am I getting this right so far?"

"I've never met anyone like her before. I sit and listen to stories she tells and can't comprehend how a girl on her own can have traveled so much and done so many things."

"Well, some kids just do that today, that's the way things are."

"Yes, but others don't. Why is that?"

"Who knows… maybe the ones that do are looking for something and the ones that don't have found what they're looking for or don't have the courage to leave home."

"There you go, that's it," Ben said.

"What's what? You're not making any sense."

"Courage"

Ben reached out and took Mary's hand and pulled her into a different direction.

"Come on. We are going shopping."

They reached the edge of the park and hailed a cab.

"Hat shop, on Bleecker Street."

The cab pulled out into the traffic.

"You really know how to treat a girl, don't you Ben? A walk in the park and then shopping."

"Bleecker Street; the hat shop is four stores down from the corner." Ben handed over a twenty. "Thanks, sir, you have a nice day now."

The shop had one of those old bells that rang when you opened the door… It was a taste of old world simple functionality. If there were a power cut, then probably this would be the only shop in Bleecker street that still had the means to alert them to a customer arriving or leaving.

"Oh, so we're shopping for you? How charming."

Ben walked over to the men's section.

"Choose me a hat," he said to Mary.

"Ok, how about the Filmore Slim?" It was a bright blue narrow brimmed hat that was on the top seller's list. She placed it on Ben's head and tilted it sideways.

"Very trendy Ben suits you to a tee."

Ben looked in a mirror.

"Now here is the thing… you know it, and I know it, this hat no more suits me than it would suit you."

Ben placed the hat on Mary.

"Wow I take that back, that is YOUR hat, Mary Lou," said Ben.

"Mary Lou? So now I have a new hat and a new name… Mary Lou?"

She removed the hat, took hold of Ben's arm and pulled him towards her.

"What's this all about Ben? What are we doing here?" She said in a soft low voice.

"Need any help guys?" said a zealous commission driven young salesman.

"No, we are all good." replied Mary.

"Ben, talk to me. Why are we in a hat shop?"

Ben reached up and took down a hat called Henry Jones.

"This hat," said Ben. "Is an Indiana Jones hat. I know it, you know it, and the staff probably know it. It's called Henry Jones and that is no coincidence of itself."

Ben called over the hovering assistant.

"Sir?"

"Tell me, out of twenty guys my age coming in this shop, how many try on the Henry Jones hat?"

"Er... probably fifteen or so."

"And how many end up buying this style of hat?"

"Very few... I've always wondered why that is; they typically end up buying one of our top sellers."

"Thank you; we can manage now."

The assistant shrugged his shoulders and went back behind the counter. Ben put the hat back on.

"So what I am getting at is that guys come in here and want this hat. They want this hat not because of the hat, but because of what it does to them inside. How it makes them feel. Then before they can buy it, this little voice comes in saying... 'don't be ridiculous, you look like an idiot, who do you think you are, some wild adventurer?'

They then take the hat off and buy what's trendy. This gives the warmth of conformity, and Henry Jones crawls back inside."

"So you were saying something about courage in the park?" Mary said.

"Yes, this is it, it's all about courage... it's all about Henry Jones being Henry Jones. It's about Henry Jones having the courage to walk out in the street and crack a bullwhip if he feels like it, as he rides off into the sunset."

"My God, she has got to you, Ben. I would like to meet this young lady."

Ben placed Henry Jones back on the shelf. "Let's go have some lunch."

Chapter Fourteen

It was 2:00 pm by the time the elevator reached the trading floor. Jake was the first to notice and tentatively raised his hand in acknowledgment. Ben nodded and pointed to his office.

"It's been a beautiful day Mary. We must do it again sometime."

Mary laughed and continued shaking her head as she walked towards her cubicle.

"Sit down, Jake."

Jake's throat thickened as he tried to hide a reflex swallow.

"So a good day for you, Jake?"

"Er… sort of."

Jakes' eyebrows pinched together, matching his lips.

"Well… yes. It came good in the end but not as good as it could have been."

"Explain."

"Well, the market turned and came on strong in our favor; in fact, there was twelve million on the table."

"And you took off the table..?"

"Three."

"You took three... Why? Don't worry, Jake I'm trying to help here. You need to understand why you ended up with three."

"Well, the truth is I panicked when it moved against our position, and I covered seventy-five percent of it to reduce our exposure."

"And how soon after you covered did the market start to move back in your favor? Don't answer that, I will. No more than fifteen minutes, right?"

"You were watching?"

"No, I never saw a thing."

Jake leaned forward with both hands on top of his head.

"Then how — " Ben cut him off.

"It's not a how Jake, everyone looks for a how. How's are on the outside of what is going on; it's the inside of the minds of men where the truth lies."

Jakes' face was screwed up, and he was shaking his head from side to side.

"We look at charts, lines on fucking screens... How the hell is that getting inside minds of men? You've lost me," said Jake.

"No... you have lost you and the reason you have lost you is because you read those lines instead of what causes those lines."

"Ben, I read the prices like a hawk watches a rabbit before it makes the death swoop."

"Yes and you're good at it, that's why you run the rest of the team and why you're not one of that team. But you are missing a fundamental element that would place you in a cage of your own."

"Well, for Christ's sake tell me, buddy... jeez, we've known each other long enough, just tell me."

"Come to think of it, why the fuck haven't you mentioned this before?" continued Jake.

"I can't answer that, Jake. It just came to me today while looking at a hat."

"You were shopping for a fucking hat while we were seven million in the hole? Jesus Christ Ben, what the hell is going on with you?"

"Do you know why you don't wear an Indiana Jones Hat, Jake?"

"That's one thing I do know. I would look ridiculous."

"Actually, you would look like a man with a hat on. Only you would make it ridiculous."

Jake threw his hands up in the air.

"Ben, I don't know what's going on here. Mate. I am totally lost as to what you are saying and where this fucking hat thing is going. If wearing a fucking Indiana Jones hat will give me your trading skill, then fuck mate, I'm all for it."

"It's not the hat. Jake. It's what you gave the hat when you said ridiculous. A hat is an innate object; you associated a belief you had about wearing the hat to the hat.

The hat was still just a hat, but you gave it something outside of itself, by saying what you told me you would look like wearing it.

Wearing it or not, it's still just a hat."

Jake blew out a breath loudly.

"Mate... we are going to Scaggys tonight for a serious session of looking into the meaning at the bottom of a few cocktail glasses."

Ben continued

"What you gave the hat was a belief; the belief changed the hat in your mind, but it was still a hat. The lines and charts on your screen are just lines and charts; they are just like the hat. It's what's behind them that matters; read what's behind them, and you get to sit in a cage all of your very own."

Ben picked up a few papers and dropped them into his briefcase.

"Scraggys later?" said Jake.

"No, I have a meeting with a young lady."

"Ah, you son of a bitch... that's what all this is about. You're doing that chic with the backpack."

Ben slowly turned, looked at the floor and then raised his eyes to meet Jake's. He held that gaze until Jake felt it.

"You just did the hat thing again, Jake. Think about it."

Chapter Fifteen

"Mr. Ben, you're home again early. Is everything alright, Mr. Ben?"

"Yes all good Anna, it's been a fabulous day. I'll be in my office for a while. Can you bring me a coffee, please?"

"Yes, of course. Coffee in the office."

Anna turned to leave.

"Oh…. Anna, where is Christina?"

"I think she is still with Marcello. They have been walking and talking all day. Nice to have someone her own age to talk to, I think. Marcello is a nice boy. Mr. Ben. I get your coffee now."

Ben's left hand went up behind his neck, and he pulled hard as his head tilted back.

"Yes, coffee. Thank you."

Ben sat down in his office. The screen saver was bouncing bubbles.

"Anna… Anna…"

A few moments later, Anna appeared.

"Who's been in here today? Anyone from the office?"

"No, Mr. Ben. No visitors all day."

Ben moved the mouse and the bubbles disappeared, showing the guest login window.

"Ah, ok Anna, sorry to have called you. I'll have that coffee when you're ready."

Anna's tongue pressed against the inside of her face, revealing a misshapen cheek on the outside as she turned away.

Ben shuffled some papers and then spun around his chair to take in the full view of the garden. He could see Marcello in one of the flower beds some distance off. He squinted slightly to help with the longer vision required.

"Hi. How's it going?"

Ben spun around to see Christina on one crutch, holding a coffee.

"From Anna... I would not be waiting on you as she does but I thought no harm to bring it for you."

Ben returned a half grimaced smile.

"What's up? You look grumpy."

"Have you been messing around with my computer?"

"Well, if you think reading my email is messing around, then probably yes."

"I said I would get it sorted for you."

"I came in here looking for a pen, that was all. I must have moved the mouse, and I saw the guest login window appear. I assumed you had set that up for me?"

"Er... yes."

"Well, what's the problem then?"

"You could have asked."

"Asked what? You set up access, I came in and saw it. Now you're having an anal episode."

"Well, I would have given you the password..."

"You didn't need to; it was easy."

"What do you mean easy?"

"You left it on your desk, there."

Christina pointed to three question marks that had been doodled on the back of an envelope.

"I don't remember doing that…"

"Well, I tried it, and it worked. I also changed the screen saver to bubbles. I hope that pisses you off as well."

Christina flipped him the finger and hobbled off.

"Shut the door, please."

"Shut it yourself."

Ben got up and kicked the door shut.

"Yes, and I know what your thinking Christina," Ben yelled back as the door slammed shut.

Anna appeared all flustered.

"Christina, what is happening?" "Mr. Ben, where is Mr. Ben?"

Christina nodded her head towards the office door.

"In his own little world in there. He accused me of … Oh, never mind, it's not worth it. The sooner I get out of here the better."

"Christina, Christina, don't say that. You are welcome here, it's good for you to stay and Marcello, he would miss you."

"Who? What?"

Christina shook her head as she hobbled to her room and closed the door.

Christina opened her eyes on cue from a rumbling stomach. It was 7.30pm, and dinner was normally around 6.

She grabbed her one crutch and went into the entrance hall. The doors to the dining room were closed. She could hear some classical music coming from the lounge and made her way there.

Ben was sitting with his back to her, wearing headphones. There was a plate of covered sandwiches on the coffee table.

She moved closer until she caught Ben's peripheral vision. He jumped slightly and removed his headphones.

"Headphones and speakers on? Sort of defeats the purpose, doesn't it?"

Ben looked at the music system and shrugged his shoulders.

"Anna left something out for you," he said, pointing to the sandwiches.

"About earlier –" Christina cut him off.

"About earlier, I was wrong. I should not have flipped you the finger and used your stuff. I'm sorry about that, I apologize."

"Err... ok. So you had a good day?"

"Yes, not bad."

Ben pulled the film wrapping off the sandwiches and grabbed one.

"I thought they were mine" Christina smiled.

"You'll have to be quicker than that, sweetie."

"Sweetie! the last time I heard that was from my mother."

Ben's face flushed red.

"So you had a good day with Marcello?"

"What is this? First Anna, now you. What is it with the Marcello thing?"

Ben grabbed another sandwich.

"Told you, you gotta be quick."

Christina sat down and pulled the plate away from Ben, laughing.

Ben looked at her.

"Sweet dreams, sweet dreams."

"Uh!"

"That was the last thing Almedio said to you as he walked away."

"You remembered that?"

"Of course, I want to know what happened next on your crazy adventure."

Christina signaled for him to wait as she polished off another two sandwiches. She used the time to think about how she wanted to approach what might be a delicate subject.

"How do you feel about drugs?"

"Drugs?"

"Don't tell me you are into drugs?"

"Whoa, hold it right there," Christina replied.

"Before we go any further here, let me put this in another way. Do you think there are good drugs and bad drugs?"

"Yes, of course."

"Ok, so give me one of each."

"Heroin."

"Yep, that is the standard conditioned response for the bad. And for good?"

"Oh, I don't know… er.. aspirin."

"And believe it or not, that is the standard reply to that question."

"These replies show how we have programmed ourselves or allowed others, like the media, for example, to arrange mind programming for us."

"I can go along with that to an extent," said Ben.

"Ok, so let's look at some facts."

"Each year, 15,000 people die as a direct result of taking aspirin, and over 100,000 are hospitalized.

In 2013 there were 8,000 deaths attributed to a heroin overdose.

So statistically speaking, you are more likely to die from taking aspirin than you are from an overdose of heroin," continued Christina.

"I'm not trying to justify this; there are other issues around heroin that have devastating effects on those who use it and people around them. What I wanted to do was to just bring a sense of rationalization to what we are going to talk about next."

"So, back to the story."

"After Alemedio left me, I felt pretty lost and alone. I had come to the village for I didn't know what. I had not seen Henry or Jim again, and as far as I knew, they had gone off into the jungle to make this documentary.

I decided to go back to where I was staying, as there was not much else to do. As I reached the backpackers, I could see Pablo was walking towards the place with three tourists in tow."

"Sounds to me like wee Pablo is going to end up a wealthy young man," interrupted Ben.

"For sure! Anyway... the three tourists consisted of two guys and one woman. The woman was in her fifties and did not look well. Her skin was gray and her face and body quite gaunt. She looked like life had drained her. One of the guys held back with her, as she was not walking as fast as the guy in front who was about thirty-five years old. He was a large man, wearing camouflage trousers and jacket. He was a million miles from Henry's rainbow trousers.

We all converged together and met Suzi, the owner, at the front door of the place. She took over from Pablo, and everyone was fitted in and sorted with the efficiency of a well-oiled machine.

I went to my room to update my journal that had been lacking for a few days. I like to keep track of people I meet and odd things that happen on my travels, as looking back they can be kind of interesting.

"Do you remember the discussion we had about the radar and the dots?"

"Yes, actually I have been looking out for them." Ben laughed.

"Ok, so I went to my room and spent an hour or so writing. Then I got a whiff of something cooking. Suzi appeared at my open door.

'I have extra food prepared. Chicken with rice and vegetables $3.00.'

"I said yes because of A. I was hungry and B. $3.00 is a pretty good deal.

It turns out that Suzi had had the perfect amount of extra for all four guests at $3.00. She was one enterprising lady.

We all sat down to eat and got chatting. Camouflage man's name was Jeff; turns out he was not in the military but had been brought up in a military family. It had rubbed off on him. He also had the strongest New York accent."

"Ah' a home boy," Ben said.

"The woman, Mary, was from the UK and the other guy was from Russia. His name was unpronounceable, so he went by the name of Mick, or Mick the Russian, as he liked to be called.

Turns out the reason they knew each other was because even though they all arrived in Lima on different flights, they somehow hooked up in the airport. They all discovered they had one thing in common. They were coming to Peru to experience a Ceremony. They had either read about it, heard about it or knew someone who knew someone who had done it. It was all quite wishy washy random if you know what I mean."

Ben's brow furrowed, and he said…

"So let me get this right. These three previously had no contact with each other. They arrive from different corners of the globe, they meet at an airport, and now they are buddies, traveling with each other to the same place to do the same thing?"

"Yes, pretty much."

"That has gotta be like the radar and dots story," said Ben, leaning back to take it all in.

"Anyway, we all ate and chatted until Suzi set out some candles in preparation for the electricity to go off like it did every night. As she lit the last candle, the lights went out as if on cue. We each had a candle to take to our rooms.

Jeff and Mick the Russian made a move to head off to bed, but Mary stayed and as tired as I was, I knew she wanted to talk.

As soon as we were alone, she asked me what I knew about the ceremony and was quite disappointed that I had nothing to tell her.

She then started telling me what she knew about it.

It takes place at night in the jungle, in a hut called a Maloka, with a shaman who conducts the ceremony.

The participants drink a foul tasting brew that looks like muddy water, and then they wait for something to happen."

"That was it? That was what she had traveled to Peru for?" Ben said

"Yep, that was it," Christina replied.

"Why? I don't get it. You told me she looked ill and yet she wants to come and drink the muddy water?"

"It's called Ayahuasca," Christina replied.

"Yes, I had figured that out by now from what I read on the internet."

"You have been researching?"

"Let's say I stumbled on it and a few stories about it. Did you know it makes you vomit and the onset of diarrhea is rapid?"

"Not as quick as they say, actually."

"Jesus, don't tell me you tried some. You didn't take part in a ceremony, did you? You did, didn't you?"

"Are you going to let me finish?"

"Christ yes, I want to know what happened."

"I'll get to that in a minute but back to Mary."

It turns out that Mary was, as I suspected, not currently a healthy lady. She did not want to go into it but hinted that life in the future was going to be a challenge.

She had come to do the ceremony after reading about how some people had been cured of quite a range of ailments.

This upset me a little as I have seen how sick, desperate people can be exploited. I mentioned this to her, but she came right back with the cost of this. It was $70.00; so, this was no elaborate healing scam. She said she had been in communication with someone called Almedio."

"He's a well-known guy around town, eh!" Ben quipped in.

"She told me that she felt comfortable with what she had learned from him. She also said that he had told her that the money went towards the village and that if she could not pay, then there was no problem with that at all."

"So, Mr. Almedio is not in it for the money then? I suppose that at least means something."

"We chatted for a while longer and then turned in for the night. I don't know if it was the food, but I had dream after dream that night, anything from snakes to spiders, and being chased through the jungle. You name it, is seemed to crop up. The one where I was being chased woke me up. It was the weirdest dream I have ever had. It was frightening and at the same time exhilarating. I was running through the jungle being chased, but it was not a thing or an animal. I came to a cliff edge that dropped into blackness; it was so deep that I knew that if I had fallen over, I would have died.

I stopped right at the edge and turned around to face the jungle and my pursuer, whatever it was.

The leaves and branches were moving like a wave, getting closer and closer. I stepped back, and my heel dislodged some small stones which tumbled into the blackness below.

The wave through the branches now slowed, as whatever was coming sensed that I had nowhere to run.

I was terrified; the terror was so bad that I considered jumping into the blackness so that I did not have to face whatever is was that was coming for me.

I looked back at the blackness again and then turned back to the jungle. There were hundreds of people, all pushing out of the jungle towards me. As they came close, they all held out their right hands like they wanted something.

As they got closer to me, I knew that unless they stopped, I would be pushed from the cliff.

I planned to grab one of them and then if I fell at least someone would be going over with me."

"This is one spooky dream," Ben said as he blew air through funnel shipped lips.

"When they had almost reached me, I felt a presence behind me. I turned and saw Almedio standing out in the blackness. There was nothing under him; he was floating there. He beckoned for me to come to him, to step off the cliff edge into the nothingness.

I felt the hands of the people start to touch me and stepped backward. My heel sank about two inches into the blackness, but it was firm enough to stand on. I kept moving back until I was standing side by side with Almedio. The people had stopped on the cliff edge and looked at us standing there with their hands outstretched.

Almedio beckoned them to come forward, to step off the edge. They would not come. He then nudged me to beckon to them as well.

We were now both beckoning for them to come towards us.

They surged forward, and as they did, they plummeted over the edge, like a waterfall into the blackness.

They kept coming, more and more of them until they were all gone. I was in tears at what had happened.

Almedio put his hand on my shoulder and pointed to the jungle. There was one small boy left, and he was walking forward. Then I recognized him; it was Pablo.

I shouted to him not to come, to stop but he looked confused and kept coming. He then stopped right at the edge. I looked at Almedio, who smiled and then beckoned for Pablo to come.

Pablo stepped off the edge and sank a little as I had. As he came closer, he started to sink further and further into the blackness. I held out my hand to stop him falling, but Almedio pulled my hand back. Pablo disappeared into the blackness. I turned to Almedio to ask him why; he shrugged his shoulders and walked off. I looked down at the blackness, and it collapsed... I was falling to my death. I woke up, covered in sweat and shaking all over.

I laid there until dawn, too afraid to go back to sleep."

"That was one hell of a dream or rather nightmare I would say," said Ben.

"Sarah had again prepared extra breakfast for the same $3.00 for each of us. It was rice with an egg stirred through and fried. I liked it, but Jeff and the Russian were not impressed. They wanted bacon, beans, and mushrooms.

Mary still looked gaunt and weak and only ate a few mouthfuls.

It was about 10 o'clock when we all finished up and cleared the table when the conversation turned to the pending ceremony. Nobody knew what was going to happen, when or how. It was all very random.

Pablo's head popped round the doorframe.

'Almedio coming now,' he said

A few seconds later, Almedio came in.

'Ok, so we're all ready to go?'

Mary, Jeff, and Mick all said yes in unison.

Almedio turned to me.

'And you?'

It was a simple question when you think about it, but I felt confused by him even asking it. I blurted out something like I am a tourist looking around and did not come for a ceremony.

'Really?' he said.

'You didn't connect why you are here? With these people?' He gestured a hand towards Mary, Jeff, and Mick.

They looked at me all confused waiting to see how I was going to respond.

'I....I don't know about any of this.' I blurted out.

Almedio's eyes focused on mine with the strength of steel rods.

'Young lady… it is time to learn why you have to step off the cliff into what you perceive as blackness.'

He turned and walked out. Mary looked at me and shrugged her shoulders then grabbed her bag and followed Almedio, as did Jeff.

Then Mick the Russian looked at me laughing and said.

'You can't pass up jumping off a cliff, can you?'

I grabbed my bag.

Almedio told the four of us that we were going on a walk to prepare for the ceremony that evening. If anyone decided that they did not want to take part, that it would be ok."

"So you had not committed at that point to do it?" said Ben

"To be honest I had, because of what he said about the cliff. The way he looked at me, it was as he knew about the dream. Hell, I don't know, maybe he even knew he was in it.

We walked around the perimeter of the village and out to areas where the jungle had been cleared. I remember thinking how lush and green everything was. Anyway, after a short while, we turned off into the jungle.

What was surprising to us all was how within a hundred yards, it was impossible to tell direction.

We followed narrow paths. Soon these crisscrossed, adding to the loss of direction.

Almedio carried a machete, which he would swipe away at anything blocking his path."

"Did it bother you walking, through the jungle like that?"

"How do you mean?"

"Well, the jungle is a hostile place, isn't it?"

"I suppose it is, but there is also something else about it that is also calming and even rejuvenating at times. Ok, I am pretty sure that if Almedio had not been there, then the four of us would soon be in trouble. But for now, it was a walk, and although it was humid as hell, it was interesting.

We must have been walking for a few hours, and Mary was feeling the strain. She stopped for a moment and pulled the last of her water.

Almedio said 'No, not this time.'

We all looked a little stunned because he came to each one of us and took our water bottles. He stacked them on the side of the path and cut several small sticks to leave a marker.

'Is that so we can find them again?' I asked him.

He paused before his reply, which by now, I realized he always did to some degree or another.

'No, we will not be coming back this way but others might.'

'But I need some water,' Mary said as she looked pleadingly at Almedio.

He touched her on the shoulder and said 'Everything we need is here, right around us. I have brought you all here today to get you to look at your environment.

When you are thirsty, look for water; when hungry look for food, but you must look for the language of your environment. Understanding this language allows you to walk free from the jungle.'

I had this flash of terror that he was now going to leave us in the jungle to find our own way back.

He spotted that fear in me in about a millisecond and laughed as he said to us all.

'Fear will sap your strength and straight thought. Listen to your minds now as I say don't worry, I'm not going to leave you. Notice how that welcoming thought enters your mind without question.'

He walked about 3 meters away from us and reached out to a vine that was three inches in diameter. He beckoned for Mary to come over and started tapping several of these vines with the back edge of his machete. They made different hollow sounds and then one sounded solid.

He put the point of the machete into the vine and twisted; water started to come out. He showed Mary how to put her thumb over the hole and get her mouth ready for the water.

He then reached as high as he could and made a small nick in the vine. The water was now under pressure from Mary's thumb.

'Now,' he said 'drink what you need.'

We all took it in turns, swapping thumbs and drinking. It tasted wonderful; it also had a hint of sweetness about it.

When we had finished, Almedio took a drink and then released the rest of the water.

He then put a hand either side of the vine and thanked it.

Jeff said laughing 'You're what we call a tree hugger back home, Almedio.'

Almedio kept one hand on the vine and turned to us all.

'If we had been thirsty on this path today and had come across someone with bottles of water and they had given us water, likely we would have thanked them.

What difference is the vine that has been growing here all its life, so that this day it could provide us with water? There are millions of vines like this in the jungle, but today this one gave us its life blood so that we could drink.'

I could tell that we all felt something when he put it like that.

'It's time for us to move on, but apologize to the vine for the injury we caused it and thank it for its gift as we pass.'

Mary was the first up to touch the vine. I was surprised how long she placed her hand on it. We exchanged glances, and as I put my hand on it, I noticed there was some color in Mary's face that I had not seen before.

'Anybody hungry?' Almedio called out.

He stepped off the path a few meters and hacked away at another vine but kept looking up. He then jumped back, and there was a thud as something heavy fell.

He cut off five pods the size of small melons and passed them back to us. A quick swipe with the machete and they opened up in half.

'Smell,' he said.

We all smelt the most beautiful aroma which intensified as we put them close to our faces. The center of the fruit was a black jelly like substance with seeds in it.

Jeff made a move to taste it.

'No!' shouted Almedio, which was such a contrast from his usually calm demeanor.

'If you eat the seeds, we will have to carry you out of the jungle. On the way out of the jungle, your face will swell and then your throat, so that no air will pass. If we do not find medicine before we leave the jungle, you will become part of the jungle forever.' Jeff's eyes widened as he swallowed hard. Almedio laughed 'But don't worry,' he said as he plucked a leaf and wiped out all the seeds, leaving soft white flesh.

'This is all good.' He pushed his fingers into the fruit and ate a mouthful of it."

"What did it taste like?" Ben asked.

"It was a cross between a vanilla custard and butter melted over potatoes; like the main course and dessert all in one go."

'We could sell this in Russia and make a fortune,' Mick said.

Almedio tapped the fruit that he had not yet cut open. It was already discolored. 'It gives up its life once it falls from the mother; profit is not its aim in life.'

We spent the rest of the day walking and stopping to eat and drink when we wanted to. Suddenly, it started to get dark, and I say suddenly because it was like that. One minute there was light and the next it was fading fast. The path started to widen out into a clearing and in the center of the clearing was a circular hut.

This was the Maloka, a single circular room where the ceremony would take place.

There was a fire pit out front which Almedio got a fire going. He directed us around the back of the Maloka were there was rainwater on tap and a pretty basic toilet and wash area.

He told us that once it got dark, the only way to get around would be by memory. We should map out in our minds where everything was so that if in the night we needed the bathroom, we could find it.

The fire was now heating a large metal pot of water. Almedio got up and walked off into the jungle.

I felt fearful as soon as he was out of sight but twenty minutes later he came back with an armful of what looked like tree roots.

He washed them off and then proceeded to bash the hell out of them. They turned into a fiber like mash. He then dropped them into the boiling water.

We all sat around the fire.

Jeff was the first one to ask the question we all wanted to ask, 'What is it you're brewing?' Almedio lingered a while in his now customary way of answering any direct question.

'Some call it Ayahuasca, others Earth Mother. There are many names it's known by. He reached over to give the mixture a stir, which wafted a foul smell into the air.

It's the root of a particular tree. This tree is found all over the jungle; there are millions of them for all we know. It is said that in the jungle there are more than forty thousand plant species. But there is a curious thing with this' He tapped his stirring stick on the boiling pot.

'We could brew this mixture for years, and nothing would come of it. That is, it would not become Ayahuasca or Mother Earth or any of the other names it is called by unless we add this to it.'

He opened up a small pouch around his waist and pulled out a few freshly picked leaves. He held up one leaf for us all to see, gave the customary thought pause and then said.

'I have a question for you all.

What do you think the chance would have been for my ancestors to discover that this one leaf was the only leaf from over forty thousand species, that when combined in the right quantity with the root of the tree, it would release the mother earth spirit for us?'

We all just stared into the fire.

'And there is another variable to this story,' he said again tapping the pot. 'How much do we need to drink? Some need to drink more than others.'

I could see the reflection of the flames in his eyes as he looked directly at me. My stomach rolled over at the thought of drinking any of what now looked like steaming muddy water.

He then threw in a handful of the fresh leaves and started stirring, while repeating over and over a prayer-like chant. We all sat there looking at the flames again.

After about 10 minutes of stirring, he took the pan from the fire and raked out the ashes. Mick the Russian went to put on some more wood, but Alemedio stopped him, saying 'The spirits from the jungle do not like the light. They will come when the embers fade to the color of the night.'

I looked up at the sky and exhaled a breath of wonder. 'I have never seen so many stars in a night sky. It's a lonely place this earth; imagine we are the only living beings on all the stars that we see tonight.'

He looked at us all while nodding his head with a wide grin.

I could never be sure with Almedio if he deliberately used words in a way that reflected that English was his second language, or he used them the way he did to emphasize things he wanted us to think about."

"So you now get to drink the magic potion?" asked Ben.
"Not yet. Almedio said it had to be left standing to cool.
He told us to now decide if we were going take part in the cere-

mony. If we were, then we were to go into the Maloka, get a mat and find our space."

"Find your space?"

"Yes, what he was saying was just to go in and see where we felt most comfortable. As it turned out, comfort was not going to happen.

Inside the Maloka were some old exercise mats, you know, the ones about five millimeters thick.

I took one and placed it on the floor. As it was a round building, there did not seem many choices of placement anyway.

Jeff put his mat to the right of mine, then Mary, then Mick. We had fanned out like the petals of a flower but with room for Almedio.Mick pointed to some pots and said

'I wonder if we are going to need those?'

Almedio appeared at that point with a single candle and placed it in the center of the room. He then passed one of the pots to each of us.

He told us that if we get sick to use them. We all looked at each other, but it was now hard to make anyone out in this light.

'Ready in about one hour,' he said as he left us by ourselves.

Mary was the first one to raise a concern to us all.

She said she had heard that we drink different amounts according to what the holder of the ceremony thinks is appropriate. She said that it was between half and a full half of a coconut shell.

She wasn't addressing any of us in particular, so nobody spoke for a moment until the pressure to respond got to the point where you feel compelled to speak.

Jeff was the first to comment. He said
'Well, we don't know, so we just have to go with it.'
Mick responded with a straight 'Yes.'
Even in the dark, I could sense that Mary was worried, so I looked towards her and said 'Don't worry, after today with Almedio, I am sure he will know how much we should have.'

The truth was, I was every bit as nervous as she was but it's not in my nature to show that, and I guess that helped in this situation.

Almedio came back. I was nearest to the door and could make out that he was carrying a small pail and a half coconut shell. Mary had been right on that part.
He was also carrying a bunch of leaves, like a small bouquet. He then kneeled in the center of the room by the candle. I could see these were dried leaves.

He then pulled out a pipe from his waist pouch and filled it with what looked like tobacco. Nobody said a word. It was like a reverence had come over the place. He lit the pipe, and as he did, his face lit up. His features were different his face looked soft and kind in a way I can't describe.
He then approached each one of us in turn, put his hand on top of our heads and pulled forward gently.

He then circled the room again, blowing smoke onto the top of our heads while tapping us with the leaves. It had a calming hypnotic effect. I remember thinking how relaxed I felt but that feeling gave way to fear, as he dipped the coconut shell in the pail.

He took a tiny sip for himself, then filled it and passed it to me. All this time, he was singing softly in Spanish. I could translate some of it to be saying 'Mother Ayahuasca, come to us, come to us.'

The shell was full.

I took a deep breath and then gulped it down. To me, it did not taste too bad. Maybe because I was expecting it to taste worse than it did.

He then made his way around each of us in turn and gave the same amount. All this time he was still softly singing and rustling the leaves as he wafted the smoke around the room.

When everyone had drunk, he went back to the center of the room, dipped the shell again and passed another full cup to me."

"You didn't drink another one did you?" Ben said.

"Well, think about it, I had no idea what was to be drunk by anyone."

"No, I suppose not," replied Ben.

"This time I knew what was coming; now I could smell it. As I did, I could tell that this was not something that was natural for my body.

My stomach rolled, you know, like you taste something and you know it's off and not fresh.

Almedio was waiting for me to drink, so I went for it and tried to gulp it down. No way, this time I had to have three attempts until it was all gone. I could now tell that this was not going to be relished by my body. In fact, nausea wafted over me a few times.

Almedio then went back to the center of the room, picked up the pail and placed it by the box of mats out of the way."

"So you had two shells, and the others had one?" asked Ben.

"Yes, that was exactly what I was thinking myself.

Almedio stopped singing and said to us all.

'You are here tonight to meet with the spirits. The spirits of the world are neither good nor bad; they will be who you are.'

He then instructed us to lay down and wait. He blew out the candle, and it was pitch black. Everything went soft and mellow. It was the calm before the storm."

Chapter Sixteen

"How were you feeling?" said Ben, his voice revealing signs of nervous expectation.

"I felt nothing. I was just laying there, thinking that this was all some elaborate hoax or something. I grew restless and found myself looking upwards. I started to make out specs of light, like tiny stars almost.

I started to question why this night sky held so many stars that were all the same size and radiated all the same light.

Then it dawned on me."

"What?" asked Ben.

"This was not the night sky, as we were under a roof. It was like a light show was going on with these little sparkling effects. I watched them for a while but then become bored.

The moment I became bored, they changed to multi colors and again, I watched them until I felt boredom coming on again.

I then started having a conversation with myself and asking questions:

Why was I here? What was this all about? You idiot, what are you doing in the jungle with a bunch of people you don't know, drinking something that might kill you. My head was full of noise like this.

I started to grow angry and frustrated with the light show. I was now shouting in my head. Fuck this. I've had enough of your stupid light show. I didn't come here for this nonsense. I want to know how the universe works and what is my role in it?

In that instant, all hell broke loose with the lights. They grew larger and formed into a mosaic glass ceiling above me.

The same words went off in my head.

'I want to know how the universe works and what my role is in it.'

In that instant, my body shot up and through the glass, shattering it everywhere.

You understand this is going on in my head and no glass is actually in the Malocka, right?" Christina asked Ben.

"Yes, yes of course," Ben replied.

"As the glass shattered, it went into slow motion, and I could see every fragment at once, and everything was a perfect shape.

Now a very strange thing happened in my mind. Somehow, I knew that the perfect shape concept was if you like a message. It was knowledge being passed to me that everything is perfect, nothing is random.

There was nothing random about anything."

Ben leaned forward with arms resting on his knees.

"So what happened next?"

"I looked up again, and there was another glass ceiling, the same one as before. Again my body broke through it and again it shattered into thousands of pieces of every color known to us and a thousand more.

'How could there be more colors than we know?'

I thought about that afterward and remembered seeing a documentary about how limited human vision is and how we only see a small number of actual colors that exist. I can only assume that the ceremony was opening my mind to a wider spectrum so that I could now see and experience things at a higher level.

After that shattering, I knew that each of these most beautiful glass ceilings were levels of human consciousness."

"How did you know that?" asked Ben.

"It was like when you discover something as a child that becomes instant understanding, even though it might be shaky at first, like learning to walk for example. One day you can't walk then you can, you know you can. You just know it to be pure truth.

So now there was another ceiling above me, even more, beautiful than the one I had just broken through. I was preparing myself to go through it and then realized that I was going nowhere. I was stuck at this level, hovering.

The next thing that happened was weird. My arms floated up in front of me so that the insides of my upper and forearms were visible.

The first thing my mind said was hey, this is impossible because I know I can feel my arms are flat out by my sides.

That conscious understanding had no effect. In fact, my awareness of my free-floating arms became stronger than my real arms."

"But then which was real?" Ben asked.

"Exactly what went through my mind and in that instant, they were more real than real.

As I was looking at my left arm," she continued, "I saw a tattoo start to appear. I don't get it with tattoos. It's not something I would ever have done. I can't see the point of marking yourself for life in that way."

"No, me neither."

"As the tattoo was being drawn, I asked: 'What is this?', 'What does it mean?'

These were all conversations in my mind, you understand? Nobody was making any noise in the Maloka at all. Well, they could have been I suppose, but as far as what was happening to me goes, that was just the way it was.

Anyway, so the tattoo when completed had a vertical line with a sloping line to the left and three lines that came together in a river like a pattern."

Christina yawned.

"It's getting late; maybe we should continue tomorrow?"

"No, at least show me what the tattoo looked like."

"I can't because I can't draw, which is a real problem if I have to get a tattoo of it."

"How is that going to work out then?"

"I have no idea at this stage."

"Do you know that it means, though?"

"Yes."

"What is it, tell me."

"Ok, but first I need to tell you what happened next."

Ben was like a man running for a bus that was already leaving the stop. "Sorry, ok, go on."

"As the tattoo completed on my arm, I received a message."

"A message?"

"Yes, remember how I said that these messages were like bytes of information? Something you know to be the answer, the truth."

"Yes"

"Right, well, that is what they are like."

"So you had lots of them?"

"Way more than I will have time to go over with you. In fact, I was still writing them in my journal today, as I have flashbacks to them.

"Ok, so the tattoo completes, and I instantly know what the message is: that I will have to have this image tattooed on my left arm."

"The physical tattoo you are talking about here?"

"Yes… and there is no way I will agree to that."

Ben looked at Christina.

"In my book, there is nothing worse than a beautiful young girl covered in tattoos - "

Christina's cheeks then became slightly pink, which Ben noticed.

"Sorry, I didn't mean to interrupt you."

"That's ok.

So I am now looking at this tattoo on my arm, which extends from the upper arm to near my wrist. As you can imagine, it would cover almost the whole length of my arm.

I ignored it and tried to move on, but nothing happened. I was stuck in this place, underneath the glass ceiling.

The more I ignored it, the stronger its presence became. I then received the message that unless I agreed to this physical tattoo, I would remain floating where I was now.

I can't tell you how frustrating this was. I sensed that the answer to my question: 'How does the universe work and what is my role in it?' was above this next glass ceiling.

Everything I wanted to know about my life was on offer here, and the only way I was going to get to learn about that was to agree to have this tattoo placed on my arm."

Christina looked directly into Ben's eyes.

"So tell me, what would you have done?"

Ben instantly replied.

"Go for it. For that knowledge, I would go for it in a heartbeat."

"Well, I thought for a moment and then said to myself: 'Well, it's only one tattoo. I guess I can live with it.'

I had been too hasty because the instant I mentally agreed, a mirror image of the tattoo appeared on my right arm and I again received the understanding that this deal had to be honored.

Two tattoos, both arms. Agree to this and what I want will be given.

I agreed… and I will tell you what happened tomorrow."

Chapter Seventeen

"Good Morning, Bill."

"Morning Sir, going to be needing the car again today sir? We had someone coming to repair the mark on the front from the damage the young lady did that day."

"Oh, I think the real culprit there was myself, Bill don't you?"

Ben tipped his head to one side and looked at Bill with a smile, waiting for an answer. An unsure smile came back.

The walk from the elevator was a quiet one. Ben was early, and only a few heads acknowledged him. Mary would not be in for another hour, an hour which he wished he didn't have to go through.

As he walked into his office, he stopped and looked around. The furnishings cost as much as it would have to furnish an entire home. Something had changed in the office, he could not put his finger on it, but something was different.

He sat down and flicked on the screens. Red, blue and green flashing prices appeared. He looked at them for a while and then flicked them off again, just looking at the blank screens. He then reached forward and powered them on again.

He repeated this several times, each time leaning back and thinking about what he was doing.

After about fifteen minutes he shook his head, rubbed his face and did a drum roll on the desk with his hands.

He powered on the screens again, picked up his usual pen and slid over a yellow legal pad. A smile came over his face as he touched the pad with the pen point.

'Creatures of habit,' he wrote.

He tapped the pen on the pad while looking at the words and then shook his head again as he put several lines through the words.

"Enough. Time for action," he said out loud to the empty room.

Mary came into his office as the page on the yellow pad reached its capacity of prices, lines, and arrows.

Mary knew exactly what each symbol meant and would have these typed up into instructions in less than 10 minutes. The team out front would then make them their business for the day.

"Good morning Mary. Two questions for you today. First, don't you think it's a beautiful day? And two, how the hell did I let that fiancée of yours steal you from right under my nose?"

Mary was walking towards him as he tore off the top sheet from the pad for her. He handed it to her but did not let it go.

"Well?"

"Good Morning and yes, it is a lovely day."

She tugged at the paper which Ben held firm.

"And?" He said.

Mary gave him one of her all knowing pauses.

"What makes you think you ever had a chance?"

Ben smiled and released his grip on the paper. Mary turned to leave.

"Lunch later?"

"What makes you think you ever had a chance?" She said as she closed the door behind her.

Ben chuckled to himself and leaned back to see his market predictions setting themselves up as he knew they would be.

His office door cracked open.

"Creatures of habit?" Mary said.

"We are indeed," Ben came right back.

"Yes, but do you want that to go out to the team?"

"No, I was just doodling."

Mary closed the door again.

Jake was next in.

"Benny Boy, Are we in for a good one?"

"Mary will have the details for you as usual, but I left off quantity."

"What..why?"Jake gave a quick high-pitched laugh, the one he always did when nerves got the better of him.

"You make the call Jake on what you feel is the right leverage. That's all I'm saying."

"That's not very fair, Ben. If we have the plan why not tell us how far to leverage it?"

Ben spun his chair around to look out across the cityscape.

Jake walked around to get his attention.

"Ben."

"Nice view, Jake?"

Jake gave a quick glance and then back to Ben.

"Yes but why not the leverage amount?"

"Because you would like this chair; because you would like this view.

Ben gestured a sweeping arm at the view.

"I don't know what the fuck has got into you, mate."

Ben stood up and tapped Jake a couple of times on his shoulder.

"Opportunity Jake, opportunity."

He then turned and walked Jake to the door.

"Mary will have it ready for you now." He opened the door for him and gently pushed him over the threshold, closing the door behind him.

—

Christina, Anna, and Marcello were eating breakfast.

"Anna, do you think I could get a bus into town today?"

"Why, no. Marcello has a car; he can take you. Can't you Marcello?"

"Yes, I can take you."

Mary knocked and entered the office.

"Yes, lunch would be nice."

"Errr, great."

"What's up, you're not so keen now?"

"No, no. I was just thinking about something else."

"Something else or someone else?"

"She is an amazing young lady Mary, she really is. She could wear the Indiana Jones hat, and it would be true."

"You can tell me over lunch."

Mary closed the door and returned to her cubicle.

Ben leaned back in his chair, closed his eyes and replayed how far they were into the tattoo story, the jungle walk, and Almedio.

"Ben, Ben..."

Mary pulled on Ben's shoulder, and he woke. Mary's eyes were wide open.

"Sleeping on the job, Ben? You gotta be kidding me."

Ben lifted his shoulders up high and then let them drop back with a small yawn.

"I don't know what came over me. I was looking out at the city and then the next thing you're here. What time is it?"

Ben looked at Mary noticing she was holding a small clutch bag.

"Oh, that time." Ben checked his watch.

"Let's go; I'm starving."

Jakes' eyes followed them to the elevator while his head remained focused on the screen in front of him.

The limo was waiting.

"Where to sir?"

"It's your call," Ben said turning to Mary.

"Ok… What's the most expensive place near the park?"

Ben made a deliberate and emphasized slow head turn.

"What's this deal, then?" He smiled.

Mary turned to the driver.

"Just take us to the park for now."

The Park was busy with lots of people on their lunch break, sitting out and chatting.

"Here, this will do," Mary said, taking Ben's arm and pulling him towards a food cart.

"You probably don't want any more meat today if you're tired."

Ben looked at the cart vendor and shrugged his shoulders as he turned his palms to the 'go figure' position. The food vendor returned the same body actions and laughed.

"Two of the salad rolls, please."

The vendor handed them over, and Mary gave him a $20.00. Mary handed one over to Ben.

"There you go, lunch on me today. Let's go sit on the bench."

Chapter Eighteen

Marcello had just pulled up at Seven Oaks Hospital.

Christina was now very adept with the single crutch and was soon at the reception desk.

She gave her name to the receptionist who checked the screen.

"Yes, Miss I see you booked in online. The doctor will be with you shortly. You can wait here or in the lounge."

She pointed off to the right.

Christina and Marcello walked towards the lounge, but before they reached it, the Doctor appeared and called her name.

"Good afternoon, Miss."

Christina turned around to see the doctor walking towards them.

"Hi, I was wondering if I could have a chat with you about this."

Christina motioned towards the plaster cast.

"Yes, of course, Miss."

The doctor motioned to an examination room.

Christina looked at Marcello and motioned her head for him wait in the lounge.

The doctor said as he closed the door of the examination room.

"I read your request Miss when you booked your appointment. It's most unusual. I mean this cast has to stay on a while longer yet."

"Yes I know Doctor, and thank you for your concern, but I would like you to do as I ask."

"Yes, of course. I will arrange it now."

He picked up the phone and pressed a single button.

"Reception."

"Have a porter with a chair come to room 2, please."

"It's quite a way to the X-ray room; the chair will be better for you."

———

Mary smiled and motioned for Ben to look at two young children. One was just walking age, and the other was maybe a year older.

"Do you ever think about having kids, Ben?"

"No. Too much trouble, too much money, sleepless nights and diapers. Kids, yuk. But on the other hand, I suppose they could be alright in certain circumstances."

Mary punched his arm, and they both laughed.

"So, why did you ask me for the afternoon off the other day and then tookoff pretty quick, or is that none of my business?"

"It was that story you told me."

Ben pulled on his ear. "Story?"

"Yes, the when story, the prison visitor."

"Oh, yes the prison bars of when. I have thought about that a few times since myself."

They both took another bite of their lunch. Ben methodically chewed his while Mary took a second bite.

"So what did it make you think about?" Ben asked.

Mary continued chewing as Ben put the last mouthful in.

She lifted her hand to her mouth and signaled for Ben to wait until she swallowed.

Christina hopped up on the X-ray table. A nurse placed a mat under her ankle and went behind a screen.

"All done miss, they will be ready shortly for the doctor to see. I will have the porter take you back to the waiting lounge."

The porter wheeled Christina back into the lounge where Marcello was waiting.

"All done? Can we go now?" He said.

"Not long, we just have to get the results."

A short while later the doctor appeared holding a large folder.

"I have the results, miss. Shall we go back to the room?"

The doctor wheeled Christina into the same examination room. He slid out the X-rays and hung them on the light box on the wall.

"I don't understand this; it's very unusual."

"It's healed, yes?" Christina said.

"I have never seen this before. It's not been long enough to repair like this."

"You will be able to remove the cast now?"

"Remove the cast no, no, we can't do that. This is most rare a bone cannot repair itself this quickly."

"If the bone has repaired then I don't need the cast."

"But Miss, we don't know why this has happened, maybe something is wrong."

"Or something is right." Christina gripped the crutch laying it across her legs.

"I can't say."

Christina got up from the chair and stood with the one crutch then held the crutch out, so there was no support.

"Take it off."

"No miss, I can't agree to that."

"Then when will you take it off?"

The doctor looked at the images again and stroked his face.

"Come back in a week, and then we will take another X-ray. If then it looks ok, we can put on a strap and let you walk on that for support."

Mary swallowed the last of her lunch. Suddenly, it just came over me. I wanted to see my father. He is in a home now and has Alzheimer's. Sometimes he recognizes me, sometimes not.

Mary's eyes dropped toward the ground as she tidied the sandwich wrappers.

"Sorry to hear that, I didn't know. If you need time to go and see him, then just say."

"Well, that was the thing that got to me the other day. I do have time, but I had justified not going so much because of the times when he doesn't recognize me.

It's a terrible thing to justify like that and when you told me the when story, it came home to me how I used that word over my father."

"How do you mean?"

"When I go to see him sometimes he does not recognize me."

"Yes, you just said that."

"Yes I know, I was making the point of how I was using the when word, not just to push something off into the future but to justify going less and less often."

Anyway, that day I went straight to see him and spend time with him."

"Did he recognize you?"

"No, not even for a moment; we smiled and chatted about anything that came into his mind. But it was different for me."

"Different?"

"I was there with him, and I mean not just doing something out of a sense of duty. I was really there."

"By being there, you mean giving all of your attention to it?"

"Yes, exactly and you know what happened? As I went to leave, I kissed him on the cheek like I always do and I could see in his face he was surprised that a stranger would do that.

As I was about to leave he beckoned for me to come close, then took my hand and kissed the back of it and said 'Oh, my… kissed by such a pretty young girl. When I was a younger man, I would have proposed to you.'

He laughed like I had not seen him do in a while and there was that word when again in his words.

It was the best visit in the last three years, and it was because I was really there."

Ben took the sandwich wrappers from Mary to stop the crunching noise she was making with them and then said:

"So, why are we sitting in the park talking about a word?"

Mary burst into laughter, followed by the same from Ben.

"Christina, you know, the girl staying with me?"

"Yes, this young girl who is making you do weird things."

"Weird things?"

"Ben… come on. We are sitting in the park eating sandwiches. Yesterday we were in a hat shop talking about Indiana Jones. It may not be weird for most people but you, come on… you don't do this stuff. I think it's all centered around this girl. This girl, by the way, I would like very much to meet."

"Ok, why don't you come over and meet her one evening?"

Mary thumbed the soft bag she was holding. "I would have to talk to Michael about that. He might not be too happy for me to have dinner with another man."

"Sorry, that was a bit of a dumb suggestion. Don't worry, I will think of something."

"So, are you going to tell me why she has messed with your head?"

"Messed with my head?" Ben laughed.

"She has not messed with my head; she has just made me think about a few things."

"In my book and with you Ben, that's messing with your head.

"Ok?" Mary nodded for Bens acknowledgment.

"Ok, messed with my head."

———

Christina and Marcello arrived back at the roost. Marcello went back to the garden and Christina went into the kitchen where Anna was preparing food.

"Hola, Miss Christina. Would you like a drink or something before dinner tonight?"

"No, thank you. All good."

"Did you have a nice time with Marcello? He is a nice boy, eh?"

"We went to the hospital, that was all."

"Why? Are you not well? Tell me what is the matter with you, your leg is hurting you?"

"No, no, everything is fine. My leg is almost healed, and soon the plaster can come off. The doctor said everything was perfect and the plaster can come off any day now. Soon I will be able to leave."

"Where are you going? No need to leave for a while yet. Mr. Ben says you can stay as long as you want. He told me this only the other day."

"I have to be on my way; I have things to do and places to see."

"Where you want to go that is better than here? Charlie, I think you are a little crazy."

They both laughed.

"I like to travel and see new things."

"My Padre used to say to me that people who travel are looking for themselves and one day if they do, then they soon find themselves back where they started."

"Your father sounds like a wise man Anna."

"Yes, he is in heaven a long time now, but I know he still looks after me."

"I'm going to check my email. Ben said I could use the computer in his office."

"Si, si. Yes, he tells me this is fine."

—

"The thing is," Ben said. "I am mesmerized by the experience she had in Peru. I find it fascinating that anyone, let alone a young girl, would just go and do the things she has done. And I suspect she is going to carry on doing stuff like that".

"Didn't you ever want to travel?" Mary said.

"I have traveled all over the world."

"No. You've traveled in a limo, to an airport lounge, to a first class seat, to another limo, to a boardroom or the like and then back again by the same route. That's not the type of travel I meant, and what about the hat?"

"Oh, that's just a bit of fun."

"Is it?"

Mary waited for Ben to process that.

"Maybe you should buy the hat. You could always wear it to sleep in. No one would ever know the adventures of Indiana Ben as he sleeps in his hat."

Mary smiled, and Ben laughed at the vision he created of himself laying in bed with the hat on.

"I don't know," Mary said. "Who the hell knows anything about this thing we call life. What are we here for? What is the purpose of it all? Are we meant to spend our lives sitting in a cubicle, waiting to type up reports?"

"You see there it is; that's it!"

"What's it?"

"Those things you have just said. They are the things that are going on in my head."

"Everybody has those thoughts, Ben. You are not special in that department."

"Really? I can honestly say that until she moved in, I never entertained such thoughts.

"Maybe that's because you have everything that money can buy but does that include happiness?"

Ben inched along the bench a little to assist in changing the direction of the conversation.

"Last night, she, I mean Christina was talking about walking in the jungle and being supplied with food and water by Almedio - "

"Almedio?"

"I think they call them Shaman or something."

"Yes, that's right."

"You know about them?"

"I have read a little but carry on with what you were saying."

"Ok so there we were, sitting in this huge house and grounds and she is telling me about walking in the jungle with a guy who is taking what they need and no more."

"Ben, get real. How can you compare your life with that?"

"I'm not comparing; I just got this nagging question come over me as she was telling this story. It was the same question you said a few moments ago. Who the hell knows anything about this thing we call life? What are we here for? What is the purpose of it all?"

"Well, they are good questions to ask, don't you think?"

Ben rubbed his chin.

"No, actually I don't. Because you can't answer them unless you know and if you know, then asking the question would be irrelevant."

Mary shook her head.

"What?" Ben said.

"There you go, that is why you are in the position you are, that is why you made it to the top of everyone else. It's called cold hard logic with no room for the heart. You have used people and circumstances as stepping stones to ever higher levels. There, I have said it and one more thing, you're not a very nice person."

Ben's mouth fell open.

"Jeez, I wish I'd bought lunch now."

"When I said to go to the most expensive place for lunch you believed it and the reason you believed it is because that is the world you live in."

"Jeez, Mary I had no idea you didn't like me."

"You idiot! Do you think I would be wasting my time sitting here talking to someone I didn't like, someone I didn't care about?"

"Uh!"

"Look I care about you, Ben. I like you a lot and who knows what might have been, but you have never shown me who you really are. Never!"

"Sorry."

"You're not sorry."

"Yes, I am."

"No, you're not, and the reason you're not is that you are not aware of what you are meant to be sorry for. So there is nothing to be sorry for, so I forgive YOU."

Ben shook his head then looked at Mary, who had turned a shade of red. Ben waited until the red turned to a mild pink and said

"Michael has one hell of a special lady."

He then leaned forward and kissed her on the cheek.

"Let's go," He said.

It was late afternoon now and easy to get a cab. Mary gave the driver the address of the office. It seemed like a long walk across the floor with so many heads not moving but looking.

Mary turned into her cubicle. Ben signaled for Jake to come to the cage.

"Close the door, Jake."

Jake shifted his weight from one foot to the other.

"What's up, you've not done well while I was away?"

"Not as good as what you would have done but we are up 3.5 million on the day."

"Great, tell me how much would I be up on the day if I had been here?"

"I don't know, probably - " Ben cut him off.

"Jake probably is a word and state of mind to use when we are working out the why and where a market might go to a certain price or stay in a certain range of prices. Probably is a good word for this, a good state of mind to be in. However, when the chips are down, and the deals are running, probably guesstimating what another trader might or might not have done is of no value."

Jakes' head rocked slightly as he tried to process what Ben had just said but then he gave up.

"So where to from here, Ben?"

"That is up to you to work out, but I will give you something to work on. It comes in two parts. I've mentioned them to you before, but you never noticed. Now I suspect you may take it on board. Here it is. Part one is that the markets from the outside looking in, are an ever changing ocean of prices. On that, we can agree, yes?"

153

"Yes."

"Part two is that to succeed in trading the markets, one must understand what is behind every one of those changing prices. If I tell you what that is, then you will not absorb it. You must discover that part and feel it for yourself."

Jake gave the self-absorbed nod again.

"Ok that's all, see you tomorrow."

Ben grabbed a few papers and left Jake motionless in the office.

Chapter Nineteen

A fter dinner, Christina and Ben took up their now familiar seats in the lounge.

"So as I recall, you had agreed to the tattoos. So what happened next?"

"Well my body, let's call it my spiritual body, started to rise and broke through another glass ceiling. Just like before, as the glass shattered, I could feel a sense of perfection. Nothing was random, every shard of glass was the most perfect of perfection.

I rose again and again; the same thing happened with the same thoughts and understanding of this perfection.

Then it sped up, and I rose higher, shattering new glass levels."

"How many?"

"I don't know for sure, anywhere between six and nine. Then I went to the final level."

"How did you know it was the final level?"

"I can't say, it was like I knew it.

Anyway, so as I pass through this last level and I get this feeling of intense peace and calm.

This place is the serenity of mind and body. I could say a thousand words of this place and not one of them would be able to convey what I was experiencing.

Suddenly, I felt the presence of something. I looked up and saw what I thought was a skull. I only thought this because of the qualities regarding what it seemed to hold.

I reached up and touched it. IT had the most incredible smooth surface, but more importantly, I knew I was in the presence of universal consciousness."

"Wow, that is a big statement to make."

"Yes, I suppose it does seem that way when I am explaining it as I am now. The problem that you or any listener will have is that I'm trying to convey a feeling, an experience that I felt on a knowing level. I am trying to do this with only words to your ears."

"Tell me more about this universal consciousness," Ben said.

"Ok, I will try. It's important to remember that I am relaying what I felt and experienced. Much of this was through a sense of knowing. I cannot prove it is the truth, but I believe it to be so. For me, it's truth in pure form.

Universal consciousness is through all and in all, it is all. Everything that we are, everything that is the planet, emanates from this consciousness.

To be conscious of and connected to universal consciousness is our path. To evolve to a level of awareness that we are part of the one is our path.

To be conscious of universal consciousness and to understand that the one singular consciousness is our own consciousness.

If we really understood and accepted the singular consciousness, we could not interact with any species on the planet in a negative or destructive way.

We could not be destructive in thought or deed because as we are connected to the same consciousness, we would be impacting our very selves. It would be like self-harm on a universal level.

Ben... I do have to say at this point that a lot of what I am saying here came after and as a result of the completed ceremony. So things I am saying to you now carry the conviction of truth based on what I experienced. These things did not exist in my mind before the ceremony. It's important that you understand that."

"Ok, I get what you're saying, but I am confused about how one knows about universal consciousness. Well, when I say confused, it's more like an intense interest."

"That's good and let me tell you why. You can't have an interest in something that you are not aware of. Even at this stage, I would hazard a guess that something in you, a deeper part of you, knows that universal consciousness exists. I have a theory about that if you'd like to hear it?"

"Yes, please."

"Well, it's not a researched theory or anything like that. Let's just say it is one the messages that I received in the ceremony. A sense of knowing something to be true.

There is a term used that goes something like 'movers and doers.'"

"It's actually 'movers and shakers, ' but it's the same principle," Ben replied.

"Ok, so movers and shakers. When you look at the lives of these people, often they come from humble beginnings. They have a passion and a purpose but in many cases, no fixed future direction. However, that interpretation is often in direct contrast to how the world perceives them. The world sees them as movers and shakers, as focus driven individuals that rise to the top by sheer driving force of will and desire to conquer.

I don't mean to be derogatory to you here Ben, I don't, but I looked into currency trading. I found out what you do, and I saw money moving around the planet, profiting from other countries.

Looking around at your wealth, you are indeed a mover and a shaker but not the type we are talking about."

"Christina, I do understand what you mean. If one uses money as a means to measure a person, then it's not a very accurate measure and almost superficial. Maybe you have used that on me once or twice since we met?"

Ben's smile was returned; Christina carried a shred of guilt.

"So, movers and shakers with a passion…"

"As I said, often these people have no direction. In the beginning, it's like they are drifters with an unknown purpose. Having an unknown purpose means that most people experience an unlived life, but that's a whole different story."

"Story or message?"

"Yes, it was another message but not for now."

Ben leaned back on the sofa and the color drained from his face. He put his hand up over his mouth; saliva had built up in his mouth, which he had to swallow hard to get rid of. Christina leaned forward and put a hand on his knee.

"Are you Ok? What's the matter?"

Ben was now swallowing hard; he placed his left hand on his stomach.

"Sorry, I felt the most intense stomach churning sickness. I thought I was going to vomit."

They sat there a moment with Christina resting her hand on Ben's knee, waiting for him to recover. After a few moments, the color came back, and he leaned back on the sofa.

"It's ok; I am all good now. God knows where that came from?"

"Where it came from is a good statement, as I experienced the same feeling when I was with Almedio one day, and it came out of nowhere as yours did. He explained to me exactly what it meant."

"And it's the same for everyone?"

"Well, yes the same place but not the same reasons. You remember a while ago I mentioned how most people live an unlived life?"

"Yes."

"And how I said that it was a whole different story and for another time?"

"Yes."

"Well, that time is now, and the reason it's now is because of what just happened to you.

So… you have a choice. I can carry on telling you about the rest of the ceremony or I can explain what Almedio had to say about the experience you just had."

Ben put his hands up and shrugged his shoulders.

"Whatever you think."

"No, whatever you think and as you are processing that thought, think about what makes this the decision it does."

"Are you sure you weren't Almedio in a previous life?" Ben said with a chuckle.

"It's serious business. So what's your decision?"

"Ok, let's go with the here and now."

"Ok but first, tell me how you felt about deciding to leave one story and go to another?"

"That's interesting because I know what you mean. I don't want to stop the ceremony story. I want you to carry on with that now. I thought that and then the sick feeling started right at the base of my stomach. Not like before, but I was aware of it.

Then my mind jumped to talking about that feeling, and it went away. Then my mind jumped away to the ceremony, and it came back again."

"So it was like another part of you was telling you the decision to make?"

"Yes and that was when I remembered something my father used to say over and over to me when making decisions. 'Go with your gut boy, go with your gut.'"

Christina laughed out loud. "So your father was a gut thinker?"

Ben smiled. "Yes, I guess he was."

"OK, let's get on with the story before you start going all pale again."

"Good idea." Ben relaxed back into the sofa.

"This is what Almedio said to me.

'The life we live is a life of limited awareness. This limited awareness gets us through the day, through work, relationships and all the other myriad of things that make up what we call our lives.

But there is a whole other life, a life that dwarfs the life of limited awareness.

This higher awareness gives us direct access to the essence of who we really are and what our purpose is.

The limited awareness life is, for the most part, the presentation of our ego. These two levels of awareness are in conflict. Both want to shine, both want to be dominant and express themselves, but the ego is a very powerful force to bring us to conformity.

Since you know the life you are living now, you know what you are presenting as you to the world, so there is little need for us to go into that. However, this higher awareness is something that we all need to get in touch with, to draw out, to offer encouragement too. We need to nurture this awareness as we would an infant. We need to offer every encouragement and show faith that it will become the light that illuminates the path of our natural lives.

You see, while this higher awareness is much higher in quantity and meaningful content, it's a side that has been continually put down, placed little value on and left out of our lives.

If we were living our lives through our higher awareness, then our lives would be in balance and harmony with all aspects of our environment.

We would lead lives that provided us with fulfillment, which would lead to satisfaction. We would have no voids in our lives, and we would be aware of a feeling of completeness.'

He then went on to say that what prevents us from living this life is not so much that we are not aware of it but more than that, that we cannot see a way where we could achieve it.

He then surprised me, as I had assumed that he had spent his whole life in the jungle. He told me that looking back on his life he could see how he had spent years trying to obtain financial freedom so that he could do what he wanted to do in life. He gave up the jungle for the city. He gave up the teachings of his mother and father for the teaching in concrete buildings.

He then went on to say 'the truth is that I exchanged 30 years of my life trying to work out how to live. When all the time that freedom was within me. The harder I worked, the more I buried the freedom. The harder I worked, the further away I got from understanding the most important part of whom I am.

As I was I working towards freedom, I was pushing myself further and further away from it. Ironical when you think that most of us tread the same path: We go to school, get some good grades, go to university, get some more good grades, get a job, get into debt, work for the next 35 years to pay off the debt. And all this time we are carrying the false social dream that this is the way to freedom, this is the way to a happy life.

All this time we are busy burying our unlived life. We are selling our souls, selling our very life 'time' to somehow try and get that time back in the future. We believe that one day we will suddenly be doing what we really want to do and living out who we really are.

The real question we need to be asking is 'How do we live our lives in freedom now?"

"I would have loved to have been there when he was explaining all this to you." Said Ben.

"It was kind of intense and very moving at the same time. I asked him how one can make even a start connecting with this higher awareness. He paused for a moment, and I could tell that he was processing what he was about to say. He then said.

'The first thing we must do is some nurturing. We must dig deep down inside and look for that weak and damaged side of us that we have ignored for so long. No matter what age you are now unless you have nurtured this side of you, then you will discover how weak and vulnerable it is.

However, the good news is that no matter how weak this side is, no matter how damaged and repressed, it can be brought back to full health.'

He said to make a start would be to create a list of everything that is important in your life. Imagine if you had no concern for money, what you would be doing with your life; whom you would be sharing your life with, etc.? After you have done this, study the list a while to make sure that this is what's crucial to you.

The next part of this is not quite so easy and maybe a little uncomfortable, but nevertheless it needs to be done.

Now imagine that one day has passed and on this day, you had an unexpected medical visit. As a result of this visit, you discover that you have only six months to live.

Now pull out a second sheet and make another list. This list is going to be in two parts. Part one is going to be a list of things that you wish you had done in the past because at the time they just 'felt' like the right thing to do.

Part two is going to be a list of the things that you want to do before your body leaves this place in six months time.

When you have completed this second list, pull out the list you made earlier and compare them.

Chances are that many things you thought were crucial on the first list are now of no value. The reason for this change in value will be in direct relation to what is your essence.

You see, faced with death at a particular date and with only a short time before that day, we are forced to focus on what really matters to us. That meeting you have to attend. That possible deal that you might get that raise that you are after are all of a sudden of very little value. The things low on your list, things that you would have previously 'liked' to have done or wanted to do, are likely moving up that list fast. With the time of the six months ticking by, everything takes on a different structure of meaning in your life.

What you will discover from this is that this change in the structure of your life has suddenly become much more focused on you.

Now what makes you happy has moved way up the value scale and in doing so, it has pushed many of the seemingly important things like money, job, positions, way-way down the list.

This emergence of the important things in your life is the emergence of your unlived life; that life that has for so long been buried under the life you have been living.

Now, of course, we have given this a hypothetical cut-off date for your life, based on a diagnosis which sort of softens this whole exercise. However, there is an exercise worth doing to place a little more perspective on this.

Imagine for a moment that you are standing on some railway tracks and you can see way off into the distance. Right on the very horizon, you can see what looks like a train coming towards you. There is no way that you can judge the speed of this train or how far it is away, or how long it will take to reach you.

This train represents time and where you are now standing represents your death. There will be people before you and people after you, and that is their life timeline.

We can't stop the train, but we can fool ourselves that there is plenty of time left to enjoy life before the train gets here. We can delude ourselves that it is better to work now at something we don't like, with the dream that one day we can do what we do like.

It's not uncommon to hear of people who are given months to live and instantly quit their jobs and engage in something they have always wanted to do. Not only that, everyone encourages them to do this. Not one person would say 'Oh, you can't do that, what are you going to do for money? How will you manage? I am not sure that that is a good idea.'

No, no one will say such things because what will be going through their mind is what they would do the same thing if they were in that person's shoes. And you can be sure that what they come up with will be the life they have not lived; it will be living the essence of the life they know they were meant to live.

What does all this tell us?

That we are more than we are; in fact, we are way more than we are and deep down we know this to be true. We have more love to give, more happiness to share and more life to live.

We have something inside us that tells us who and what we are. This something is the most beautiful accurate guide if only we would give it the chance to surface in our lives.

And here is a strange but true thing. When you are living a life that is centered on your essence, it is the most un-selfish state possible. When you are in your essence, you will be radiating out peace, love, and happiness. These radiations are picked up on, and people move towards you because we are all drawn to people who are living out the essence of their lives.

This is why you will find that people who are living their essence have no concern for things that are so important for people who are not living their essence.

'Why is this? Why can people who are living their essence be so free of thought and concern for the future?'

It's simple; it's because when you are living your essence, you have accepted the train; you know the train will pass over you. You know that nothing outside of you matters other than your radiant self. That degree of self-acceptance is contagious to others; others will seek you out to learn your way of living.

The greatest gift you can give to yourself and others is to live YOUR essence; to live your life as you know, it was meant to be.

Your essence was yours at birth; you have either nurtured this essence or buried it under a career or life path that conformity has provided for you.

Your unlived life is calling out to you.'

Well, that was pretty much what he had to say but now, while I'm thinking about that, maybe it could be related to that stomach churning sickness."

"How?"

"Maybe for a moment, the essence of who you are and what your core purpose in life is came bubbling up to the surface of conscious awareness.

Even in that awareness though, you weren't fully aware of what your life purpose is. However, your subconscious was not only aware of it but flipped you temporarily into the full experience of it.

That flipping into the full experience of it caused the sensations you experienced.

You might wonder why the thought of living your unlived life should make you feel sick. Surely, if it were something that was the real you, then it would have been an exciting and rewarding experience and not the one it was? I suspect from other things Alemedio talked about, that the reason for this is fear.

Fear is a debilitating force on the human body. Fear triggers the fight or flight response. Fear triggers massive amounts of adrenalin into the body, to deal with this fear. Blood is drawn from the extremities of the body and routed to the heart, lungs and muscle tissue.

If the situation is not a genuine call for physical fight or flight, then all this adrenaline and response in the body has nowhere to go. With nowhere to go, it can only be dispersed back into the body, causing a temporary system overload resulting in nausea feelings."

Ben leaned forward, rubbing his fingertips up and down on his forehead. When he looked up, Christina saw eyes that could have very easily burst into tears.

"So as I understand this, as we were talking earlier about unlived lives, that triggered something in me?"

"Yes, that is exactly what Almedio said."

Ben got up from the couch and walked away, not looking at Christina.

"Sorry, we need to call it a night."

Without another word, he left the room and climbed the stairs. As the bedroom door closed behind him, his eyes burst.

Chapter Twenty

"Mr. Ben, Mr. Ben, you're late this morning."

Anna was knocking on Ben's bedroom door, something she rarely had to do in all the years she had been a housekeeper.

"Alright, Mr. Ben, alright?"

Ben stirred, the curtains had long since automatically opened and the light was streaming through. He lay there for a moment, listening to Anna as if some time difference existed between them. All of sudden the knocking caught up and jarred him to the present moment.

"OK ANNA" He called out.

"Mr. Ben the office called, so I come to disturb you."

"Anna, return the call and tell them that I am not too well and will not be in today."

"Are you not well Mr. Ben? Shall I call the doctor Mr. Ben?"

"No, no. Return the call to the office and tell them I will not be in today."

Anna went downstairs to make the call.

Ben showered, dressed in jeans and a t-shirt and then made his way to the kitchen. As he entered, Christina was sitting at the center island eating toast.

"Mr. Ben, you go to the table and I will bring you breakfast." Ben stood there and looked around the kitchen. It was not a room that he was familiar with. He then pulled up a stool opposite Christina.

"It's ok; I will just have some toast here this morning."

"But you're not well, Mr. Ben."

"Not well?" Christina repeated, "what's up?"

"Both of you, I'm fine, ok? I just decided to take a day off without having to explain the reason."

Anna passed Ben some toast.

"Anna, could you please fetch my watch? It's beside my bed."

"Si, Mr. Ben."

Anne left them eating toast together.

Ben reached into his pocket and pulled out his watch.

"Christina looked at it and then at Ben.

"I wanted to ask you something in private," he said.

"Would you come with me today to visit my father?"

Christina slowed up on the mouthful of toast.

"Err, not sure of the point of that or if I want to get that close."

Ben smiled. "It's ok; he's dead."

Christina swallowed hard.

"Mr. Ben, it's not here," Anna called out.

Ben got up and walked to the doorway to call upstairs.

"It's ok Anna, sorry, I have found it."

He moved back to the island.

"Well, will you come? I did not want Anna to hear where I was going as she goes on about things a lot. I don't want to start another explanation."

Anna came back into the kitchen.

"Sorry, Anna, I had it in my pocket all the time."

Ben put the watch on as he looked at Christina.

———

Ben and Christina met in the garage. Ben selected the keys for the Mercedes Cabriolet Roadster.

"It's a beautiful day; we can have the top down on the drive."

They drove further away from the city for about two hours until they came to a small township called Allamuchy. They turned down Springbrook Road until they came to a sharp right turn and pulled over on the grass verge which was overgrown, besides a small iron gate.

"Ok, we're here."

Ben was first to the gate and had to pull back the branches and wrestle to get the gate open. He held the branches back while Christina squeezed through.

"Wow... not what you'd expect," she said.

Ben pulled the gate closed.

"No, I like to keep it this way. Well not me personally of course. I have a gardener come and tend everything."

"Why is the gate so hard to get in, then?"

"Some vandals came in once and messed the place up, so he suggested we should let the gate grow all over and make it hard to get in. It worked, we've never had a problem since."

There were about twenty headstones; each one immaculately tended for with neat borders surrounded by lush short grass.

"All your family?"

"No, just Dad."

"Your Mother?"

"She took off when I was very young."

They both sat on a covered bench facing the headstones.

"I don't come here very often, but I have everything maintained like this so that I know all is good here."

Ben's voice croaked, and with thumb and index finger, he rubbed either side of the bridge of his nose. Christina became aware of the change in voice and tried to lighten the mood.

"So all these other people get a good deal, then?" Christina put her hand on Ben's back and patted lightly.

"So why here?"

"This is where I grew up. There used to be a small house behind the garage and general store. I lived there with my father for most of my younger years."

"So, if you don't mind me asking, how did you get from this start in life to where you are now?"

"Dad always had sayings that he would repeat over and over. One of them was 'Our ship is round the corner, and it's coming our way.'"

"Not likely here, unless it was an airship." Christina looked up at the sky.

"One day, Dad was working out back of the store. We didn't own the store; he just did odd job sort of things. Anyone in town needed something fixing; Dad offered to do it.

When I got home from school this particular day, Dad told me this story.

About 3:00 pm that afternoon, two guys pulled up, went into the store and asked if they could get a sandwich. He said they were dressed in expensive suits and were driving a Cadillac.

The store didn't sell stuff like that, and the store owner whom I always remember as being a real grumpy old git was never very helpful to anyone.

Dad heard them ask but didn't give it much attention. He then came through the store and noticed that the car they had pulled in had a semi-flat front tire. He went up to one of the men and pointed out the tire to him.

Yes, we know, the guy said and then ask dad if he could sort it out. As always, my dad was straight on the case. He went to the trunk to get the spare, but that was flat. He then went back to the other suit and told him.

The first suit went off like a rocket. Started saying how the a..hole at the last place wouldn't make them a sandwich as they had arrived 10 minutes outside lunch time and he was closing up. Nobody had any air, and so on…

Anyway, my dad told the other suit that he could take off the tire and repair it in no time. They drove the car around the back of the store to the front of our house.

Dad told them to sit on the porch out of the sun while he repaired the tire.

Dad went inside and said that he made the fastest sandwiches he had ever made, poured two glasses of cold milk and went back out front, placing them on the porch table.

The two suits instantly smiled and started munching on them while dad fixed the tire.

He said he offered to fix the spare, but they did not have time.

All finished up they asked how much the bill was. Dad said to give him what it was worth to them.

He said they both laughed and the older one gave dad a $100.00 bill. As he handed it over, he said "I want to give you a tip as well, on one condition.

I want you to go down the road to the place we stopped at

earlier and tell them what tip you got for the sandwich. Do you promise you will do that?' Dad agreed. The guy took out a checkbook, wrote it out, folded it in half and handed it to dad. Dad took it, but the guy held onto it and asked dad again to promise to tell them about the tip.

Dad promised, and they got into the car and drove off.

Dad told me that a few weeks later he saw a picture of the older man in the paper. He had died from liver failure."

"How much was the tip?" Christina asked.

Ben looked at Christina and paused a while as if he still could not believe it.

"Twenty-five thousand."

"twenty-five thousand dollars for a sandwich? What did your dad do?"

"He thought it was a practical joke but he had his $100.00 so didn't care. About a week later he went to the bank and paid in the cheque. It cleared, and the money was in Dad's account."

"Did he go and tell the person about the tip?"

"He would have done, but dad was never one to gloat over something like that.

So anyway, we moved into the city, and after that, dad got a job running tickets on the stock exchange floor. That was strange as well as he had no experience, but one day he saw a picture in the newspaper of the other guy in the car that day. He wrote to thank him, and in some roundabout way, he ended up with the ticket runners job.

The rest is, as they say, history. Dad ran tickets and then climbed the ladder. He turned that twenty-five thousand into three million in two years, trading on the stock exchange. Dad kept that all very quiet, not even I knew, but every night, he would sit with me and tell me about stocks and what was going to happen the next day.

He used to say over and over:

'The world thinks that prices move a stock, but it's the minds of men and dreams of the future that are behind every price change.'

It was like he was driving that into me.

Soon dad was given a top job trading for the firm. I started off as a trainee but we argued a lot, so I was moved over to currency trading.

We carried on like that for a few years and then Dad suddenly died, without us ever really getting to know each other."

Ben's voice cracked again.

"That is some story. You know, if I had one person I would like to share that with right now, it would be "Almedio.""

"Almedio. Why him?"

"He would have connected the dots for you. He would have led you from one event to another and not missed all the dots that we miss connecting when we are part of the story."

Ben laughed. "Maybe I should go and see him."

"Stranger things have happened. Hey, your dad got twenty-five thousand for a sandwich and look where that led you."

"I don't know why I brought you here today."

"Does that matter?"

Ben got up and walked to one of the headstones. Christina wanted to stay seated but went with him.

They both stood there looking at the headstone.

Christina read the inscription out loud.

"William Williamson."

She touched the top of the headstone. "I would have liked to have met you, Willy."

"How did you know he was called Willy?"

"E..r I guessed it, I suppose. William, Willy, it followed on."

"The one thing we argued over was kids. He wanted grandkids, and I never did. There was no way I was having kids."

"Why?"

"I suspect it was to do with my mother leaving us. I never wanted that to happen to anyone else."

"So you stopped yourself having any kids in case your wife might have run off and left you with a child, the same as what happened to you?"

"Yes, pretty much. That's about it."

"And as compensation for that, you spend your days making millions of dollars?"

Ben's jaw dropped.

"Where the fuck did that instant psychoanalysis come from? Jeez, you sure have a lot of answers for a youngster."

"Sorry, I don't know where that came from. It just came into my head, and I said it. Sorry, that is a bad habit of mine now."

"Now?" Ben looked straight at Christina.

"One-day Almedio was translating one of the messages for me, and he said that the intuitive response within us is more times than not, the truth to listen to.

Instead of thinking before I speak, I tend to blurt it out sometimes. Sorry, I didn't mean to spoil the trip to see your dad."

Christina reached over and stroked the headstone again.

Ben followed with several taps.

"Oh, I don't think we'll disturb Dad too much."

"Come on, let's go back to the city for some lunch."

The drive back took a little over two hours. They managed to find the last available parking space near to where Ben had recently spent time with Mary on their park visit.

"There is a food cart further down this side of the sidewalk. Are you going to be ok walking that far?"

"Yes, I told you, I have no pain, and it's pretty much healed now. It's harder to walk now because of the plaster more than anything."

Ben walked; Christina did the same but with a twist of the body with each step to allow her other leg to step out in front.

After about a hundred yards, Ben noticed that walking was uncomfortable for Christina.

"Look, that bench there coming up, you get to there, and I will go onto the food cart and bring us some lunch, ok?"

"Yes, all good."

Ben's pace quickened towards the food cart. Christina reached the bench and sat down.

The walk had taken more out of her than she thought it would. It was the unnatural body twisting that did it.

Ben was on his way back with two rolls and two bottles of water.

"I got you salad."

Ben handed the roll and water to her, and they both started to eat.

"So why did you want me to come with you today to see your dad?"

"I don't know, when I went to bed last night, I got thinking about things and decided to have the day off today. I could not get my dad out of my mind so I thought I would take a trip up to see him. Sorry if it was a bit morbid."

"No, being up and about is great. I can't wait to get back on the road again."

"Where are you going, London?"

"Why London?"

"Err… no reason. I… err, don't know why that came into my head."

Ben's blood flow to his face increased a little, and he could feel the heat building.

"Lovely day, isn't it?"

Christina ate the last of the roll without saying anything.

"So back on the road to wherever. You do know that it's no trouble you staying for a while with us, don't you?"

"I don't like to be in one place too long, but thanks anyway."

"Now don't get all defensive when I say this but I would like to give you something when you head off, as a way of saying sorry."

Ben pointed to her plaster cast.

"By something you mean money, right?"

"Yes, if that would be ok?"

Christina smiled. "I'll let you know, how's that?"

"Fair enough, we'll leave it at that."

Ben got up and took the roll wrappings and water bottles to the bin a few feet away. While his back was still turned from Christina, she called out:

"So the unlived life got to you a bit, then?"

Ben came back to the seat without saying anything.

"What I mean is, it affected you?"

Ben shifted on the bench.

"Yes, I suppose it did."

"Suppose, what does that mean?"

"Jeez, you like to dig, don't you?"

"I thought we were having a conversation about that, which got cut short when you went off to bed. Look, I was just interested as it had a big effect on me and I am curious if it had the same effect on you, that's all. If you don't want to talk about it, that's fine."

Christina folded her arms and looked out across the park.

"Nice day, isn't it?"

Ben didn't answer, his head was forward and eyes defocused on the area in front of the bench.

"I don't think it's going to rain. It could do of course, but I don't believe that it will. Then again, I suppose it could snow but probably not this time of year."

Ben's mind let go of the grass.

"Ok, I get it, we can leave the weather alone."

Christina said nothing, keeping the pose with her arms crossed.

"Yes, it did get to me," Ben said.

Christina's arms unfolded, and she turned towards Ben.

"How?"

"What's this, an inquisition?" Ben smiled.

"Well, you wanted to talk about it, if you have changed your mind again, fine."

Christina maintained eye contact, and she tipped her head slightly to one side.

"Well, let's not beat around the bush eh," Ben said.

"No point in that" Christina came right back.

Ben leaned back on the bench.

"Well, I suppose it got me thinking about my youth a bit. I was thinking about you and your travels. Then the bloody prison bars of when re-surfaced again and the whole lot sort of overwhelmed me."

"Did you cry?"

"What?"

"You heard me, did you cry?"

"I don't see what that has got to do with anything."

"So you did cry. Carry on."

Ben rubbed his hands up and down to his knees and back.

"As I said, it got to me, and it did stir a lot of stuff up in my head. Ok, and yes, I had a few tears."

"There, that wasn't so bad, was it? What the hell is it with men and the crying thing?" Christina broke a smile that would have melted an ice cap, as she reached over and rubbed Ben's forearm.

Ben's chest raised high as he leaned back again, filling his lungs up before slowly exhaling.

"It was tough for me as well, and I am a lot younger than you."

"What has that got to do with it?"

"Pretty logical, I would have thought. Well ok, to be honest, this was how Almedio put it.

The longer you live an unlived life, the further you get away from who you really are. The further away you are from that; you have a longer and harder journey to find yourself."

"Suppose that makes sense," said Ben.

"But, he also said that time and the journey are sometimes wiped away in an instant. It often happens when people suddenly find out that they only have a short time to live. Some of these people, he said, almost go immediately into a higher level of consciousness."

"Higher consciousness, that sounds like something my Dad used to talk about."

"Really? Tell me more."

"Well, nothing much; he used to say that most people are caught up in the act of living to be alive."

"I wouldn't say that wasn't much Ben, far from it when you think about it."

"I remember him taking me out on the weekends to a green area, near water if possible. He said he was a self-confessed people watcher but liked the solitude of mind that it gave him. I never really got that. I mean a people watcher with solitude of mind at the same time."

"Mmm, I see what you mean. The problem is of course that when people explain to someone else things like that, it can be difficult to explain in a way that can be easily understood.

After the ceremony, I spent a lot of time with Almedio, who helped me understand some of the messages I received, but some of them he stayed away from. I could tell he knew what they meant, but it was like a no go area for him.

I tried many a time to lead him into an explanation of a message that I wanted to understand, but he would side step it and go elsewhere.

I know why he did that and I knew why I was not getting the understanding of that message."

"The tattoos, right?"
　　"You see, how did you know that?"
　　"You told me about them."
　　"Yes, but how did you connect that? What I mean is that yes, you knew about the tattoos but that was just knowledge. The connection you made was intuitive. Something bubbled up out of consciousness that you knew to be true."

"It's how I do my w… " Ben went silent and profoundly deep inside himself.

"You see, it happened again," Christina said. I can see it in every part of you. What is it? Finish what you were going to say."

"Work, I was going to say it's how I do my job. I have never really thought about it before, but I just got an insight into how I can do things at work that I can't explain to others.

When I first got promoted, the top bosses wanted to go over my analysis of markets. They wanted to know what I was basing my decisions on. They wanted graphs and reports. They wanted to see charts and check everything.

I couldn't do that, and they were very suspicious. I was sure to lose my job almost immediately after my promotion.

I was called into the board room one day after a big deal had gone wrong that I had said would go wrong. The USD against the GBP was forecast to rise substantially. I sold the market as high as my limit at that time allowed me to.

The news came out, and against all expectation, the market plummeted. The company lost millions of dollars on their long positions. But I made millions for them on my short positions."

"So one canceled out the other?"

"Not by a long shot, the company as a whole had a much larger position than mine. They lost forty-eight million, and my position made eighteen million."

"So they were thirty million out of pocket?"

"Yes and that was why I was now sitting in the boardroom. It got real heated in there, voices were raised, and there was a lot of finger pointing. All they kept saying was 'How did I know?'

The more I said I just knew it, the more infuriated they became. I was pretty convinced that at any moment I would be fired, but then my commission on the deal I did was a little over two million so not too shabby."

Christina shifted from side to side on the bench.

"So you're telling me that you earned over two million dollars in a day?"

"Actually, about 24 hours."

"Don't you find that obscene?"

Ben shrugged his shoulders. "Not really, why would it be?"

Christina looked at him and shook her head from side to side.

"What?" Ben said.

"Nothing, carry on with the story. I want to know if you got fired that day."

"Well, obviously not, as I am still with the company."

"Ok, so what happened?"

"On the boardroom table, there was a single phone. I had seen it before but never paid attention to it. The finger pointing, questions, and raised voices were pretty full on when the phone gave one ring, and then a light flashed on it.

Everyone fell silent as the chairman picked up the phone. All he did was listen. He never said a word. Not a hello or a goodbye, as he put the phone down.

With the click of putting the phone down, all eyes were on him. He looked straight at me.

'Do you want a cage, Ben?'"

"A cage? What is that?" Christina asked.

"It's a name we have for the glass offices that overlook the dealer's floor. If you have one of these offices, you get a team of traders to follow your instructions."

"So this office is as far as you can go?"

Ben looked at Christina, opening his palms, questioning.

"This is all very boring. I'm sure you don't want to know about my work."

"No, please, I am interested in what happened. Where you now at the top?"

"No, I was in the primary cage, as they call it. The difference between that cage and one five cages away was that the top cage could call on the whole floor to trade any position they wanted."

"You're now in that top office, aren't you?"

"Yes."

"How long did it take you to get to the top office from the one they put you in that day?"

"Less than a year."

Christina put her hands together, interlocked her fingers and tapped them against her chin.

"That day in the boardroom," she said, "they never got you to tell them how you did it, did they?"

"No."

"And tell me, was it because you wanted to hide it from them?"

"No, the truth is that I don't know how I do what I do. I look at the markets, and I get a sense of something.

The words of my father come to mind sometimes about how prices are driven by the minds of men, but that's about it. I just have an overwhelming sense of knowing what the masses are thinking and how they are going to react."

"I know how you do it. Let's go home, and I will tell you tonight after dinner."

Chapter Twenty-One

Anna cleared the table as Ben and Christina moved to the lounge. Tonight they both sat on one sofa, one at each end.

"Today was a great day, wasn't it?" said Ben.

"I would have enjoyed it more without this." Christina tapped on her plaster cast as she lifted it to rest between them.

"Never mind, soon off."

They both leaned back into the soft cushions.

"I just remembered that I hadn't told you what happened during the rest of the ceremony. You know, when I went through that last level, and I was in the presence of universal consciousness."

"How could I forget? But I must admit I have lost track of where we were with that."

"Ok, so I had broken through this next level like before, but this time I knew it was the final one. Don't ask me how I knew, all I can say is that I just knew it. I reached up, not with my physical arm as I was still lying flat on the floor in the hut. It was like I was in another body, a body that was mine but free floating above myself lying on the floor. It's kinda hard to explain, but as long as you get what I mean?"

"I think so, I read a book once that talked about out of body experiences and it sounds similar to what you are saying."

"So I reached up and touched what I thought was a skull, but it turned out to be the shape at the head of the tattoo. I remember thinking, this is it; here I am. I'm in the presence of universal intelligence. I can only say that it was the most intense experience of awe and profound respect.

Then this question came into my mind. 'If this was the source of universal consciousness, then how did we have access to this?' My mind was then directed to the three channels that came out from the skull. I instantly knew that they represented mind, body, and spirit. Universal consciousness flowed down through the channels of mind, body, and spirit into the river of life. Remember how I told you that the tattoos were like an intertwined river?"

"Yes."

"Well, this symbolized the river of life."

"But you said that the tattoo or the river came to an end point though?"

"Yes and that was where it all became terrifying for me."

Ben's eyebrows pinched together as he leaned forward.

"Terrifying?"

"Just like you identified that end point, so did I, and as I did, the question of 'How can a river end like that?' came to mind. The moment I thought that I received the sense of death. When a river disappears like that, it has died. But this river was a representation of human consciousness flowing down through mind, body, and spirit. How can this die?

My mind was then drawn to the point, and I knew this was the point of my death. I nearly freaked out at this point.

I did not come here to know about forecasting my death. This was all too much for me. I wanted to escape the experience.

I had agreed to have my arms tattooed as a constant reminder of my death! You can imagine how this all started to fall apart."

"I can't imagine being there doing that. In fact, I can feel a bit of that sickly feeling again right now," Ben said.

"I then grew calm," Christina continued, "and somehow I accepted it in peace that this was my death point. I started saying to myself 'It's ok, everyone dies at some time, and I am no different.'

Then the next bombshell - this was not my death; this was every-one's death.

This was not my death point but everyone's death point. Every-one; you, me, Anna, Marcello, everyone on the planet, this is the death point.

Now as you can imagine, my fear and anxiety went into overdrive. I wanted none of this, I wanted it all to be over, and I wanted it over now. Then another wave of peace swept over me, and it was communicated to me that — by the way when I say communicated to me, that is like a sense of knowing experience. OK?"

"Like you just know something to be true, you mean?"

"Yes exactly, you know it's truth."

"The wave of peace came about because of the sense of knowing that this point was not representing physical death. This was the death of human consciousness.

It was the death of one level of human consciousness as we leap into another conscious existence. Everything we think we know of this world through our current conscious existent is dying."

"I'm not sure that's a pleasing thought," said Ben.

"I would have agreed with you but the more you think about it, the more you come to realize that maybe this is our only hope for survival as a species."

"That sounds a bit dramatic."

"Yes, I suppose it does, but that comes only from us being able to see the world from our current consciousness.

Imagine the world, for example, where the need to accumulate money, to make a profit from another did not exist."

"Oh come on, how would that work?"

"Well, it couldn't work — thinking from our current consciousness.

This is the whole point, a shift of consciousness is what is required."

"Sounds like a utopian world."

"Exactly, but what is utopia? It comes from a Greek book written in 1516, where a fictional society was created. It was something conceived in the human mind and written as a fictional story. Utopia could not exist, we say but what if we were of a consciousness where that did exist? What then? In that world, it would be the truth."

Ben let out a long slow breath.

"I tell you what, for your years you are definitely showing signs of philosophy."

They both laughed.

"So getting back to your two questions. You remember them?"

"Yes, of course. How does the world - universe work and what is my role in it."

"Yes, that was what you wanted to know when you went into the ceremony, right?"

"Yes."

"So in your opinion, how is that working out at this stage in your experience?"

"Well, I got what I wanted to know.

Dealing with the first one first. How does the universe work?

That was conveyed to me from the basis of universal consciousness. This consciousness is in us, through us and is what makes up this planet. Everything that is now and everything that will be in the future is already here in existence, in universal consciousness. We as humans exist within this as it exists within us. It's all one; everything is this one."

Ben let out another breath, this one almost a low whistle.

"You certainly give food for thought; I'll give you that. And what about your second question, what about that?"

"That was a real shock to me. I don't think I am capable of what I was told. Who is going to listen to me? I mean by what authority do I have - "

"Whoa, hold on. You haven't told me what this thing is."

"Well, as I was looking at the point of the death of the river on the tattoo image, that second question came into my mind.

'What was my role?'

At that moment, golden threads appeared from the point of the river tattoos. They started to extend on both my arms and work their way out to the tips of my fingers and thumbs.

I can't tell you the beauty of these threads. In fact, that is the truth right there in me saying that. I could not tell you of their beauty, as there are no words we have that could begin to describe it. Then my hands rotated down like you would hold your hands over a keyboard.

In that instant, it was conveyed to me that my purpose was to write and speak about universal consciousness and what it means for us all. And here was the kicker.

The Tattoos that I had agreed to have done were to serve as a constant daily reminder to carry out my purpose."

"That's kind of cool when you think about it."

"What, me agreeing to have tattoos?"

"No, the fact that you have this gift and you have to share it with the world. It's pretty cool to know what you have to do in life."

"You may think so, but what right do I have to talk about such things. Who am I to write and talk about universal consciousness and stuff. I have no experience as a writer or speaker, so I interpreted that part wrong."

"So you like everything so far, but you want to run away from your role in all this?"

"It's not running away."

"Yes, it is. You can slice or dice it any way you want. If you don't do it, then you are running away."

"Excuse me, but that's bollocks!"

"No, you want it to be bollocks; you don't want to face up to your responsibilities."

"What, so now you're a fucking psychologist, and this is the analysis couch?"

Ben leaned back and folded his arms across his chest and said nothing. Christina moved the cushion behind her to put her more upright.

Ben rubbed his chin.

"Seems to me like I touched a nerve."

Christina moved to fire back. Ben put his hands up.

"Hear me out a moment. I have run from things in my life that I did not have the courage to face.

I know that my life could have been very different and I have regrets that surface late at night when I am alone in this place."

"But you have everything you could ever want and can buy a million things you don't want."

"Not everything can be purchased."

Christina caught Ben's eyes move above the fireplace.

"So what do you regret then?"

Ben turned his attention back to here and now and laughed.

"Well, we don't have enough time for that list, but let me try and give you some advice.

You say who are you to write and talk. Ok, that might be a valid thought BUT is it the reality of the situation? I don't think so."

"What do you mean by reality?"

"Well, consider the conversations we have had in the short time we have known each other.

Primarily for much of this time, I have been captivated by your life experiences."

"But that is you, and you're easy to talk to, sometimes!"

"Ok guilty of sometimes, but what I am getting at here is that you have held my attention with all this. I find it fascinating, and I am sure other people would as well."

"There are a lot who would laugh."

"Ah ha! So now it's not about your message, it's about you. Imagine this is all true, all this is the truth of the world we live in — by the way, let me interrupt that thought for a moment. I need to ask you a question."

"Go for it."

Ben leaned forward and looked carefully at Christina, pausing long enough to make her focus.

"The question is — do you believe in all this? Do you believe in everything you learned?"

"One hundred percent, every part of it."

"Ok, so back to what I was saying about all this being true. If you believe and you do, then how can you not at least attempt to carry through your part of the deal? You made a contract and contracts should be honored."

"Kind of a big commitment having my arms tattooed."

"That I cannot deny and I don't know how you are going to over-come that. It's something you have to work through with yourself."

Ben looked at his watch.

"Ok, if you are not too tired — was that the end of the ceremony?"

"The end! That was just the beginning."

Chapter Twenty-Two

"Morning, Sir. Didn't see you arrive yesterday," Bill said as Ben stepped out of his car.

"Had a day off Bill; you know, one of those days when you just need to float away."

"Float away Sir? Now there's a thought, floating away."

"What's that then? Something you're planning on doing?"

"Oh, just a pipe dream."

"Tell me, what's the dream?"

"Silly really, me and the wife, we used to dream about sailing around the world when we were young but you know, life gets in the way sometimes."

"Your wife, she still has the dream?"

"Mad as a fish sir, mad as a fish."

Ben laughed.

"I call her mad as a fish because she has this book where she works out everything to sail around the world. Researches it any chance she gets. I bet she could tell you to the dollar what it would cost; the routes, the wind, everything.

I told her maybe when we retire; we can get a small sailboat and take a few trips."

Ben touched Bill on the shoulder.

"I heard a story a short while ago about the word when. I am going to tell you that story one day soon. But right now, I have some work to do."

Ben headed for the elevator.

"You have a great day Sir," Bill called after him.

As the elevator rose, it seemed to go into slow motion as thoughts of Bill in the garage all day parking cars contrasted with his life. The whoosh of the doors opening jarred him back to the here and now.

There were a few traders already at their screens. Like always, eyes acknowledged without heads moving. Heads that had only one thing on their minds - how to get into a cage.

Ben contrasted them for a moment with Bill in the garage and thoughts jumped to Bill's wife and her book. He wondered what the difference or even if there was a difference between their minds and hers.

Once in the office Ben turned on the screens, leaned back, put his hands behind his head and stared. After a few moments, he wrote down some prices on the yellow legal pad and tore off the top sheet.

He then got up and went to Mary's cubicle. She would not be in for another fifteen minutes or so.

He placed the sheet on her desk and could not help notice how she had personalized her cubicle. There were twenty or more pictures of her with a man in various poses - some funny, some serious and some in-between.

"What are you doing in a girl's cubicle?"

Mary gave Ben a gentle poke in the ribs.

"Oh, just dropping off the morning's sheet."

"How many times have you seen the inside here?"

"Ummm."

"Never that I know of, you have never been in this cubicle before, have you?"

"No… I don't think I have. Why, is it out of bounds?"

"Don't get antsy with me Benjamin. I was making an observation, that was all. Let me give you a tour.

This is my wall; I use this to remind myself that I have a family, a man that I love and interests outside of all this."

"First time I have seen Michael. A handsome man a little like myself, don't you think?"

Ben got the second poke in the ribs.

"Not even close, Mr, not even close."

Ben pointed to one of the photos of them both on a boat.

"So you're sailors, are you?"

"He is, he loves being out on the water. I enjoy going out as we spend time together, but I am not into boats as he is. He jokes that we should sail around the world. I told him if aliens land, then it's a deal."

"Funny, that's the second time this morning I have heard this sailing around the world story."

"Well, how about you clear out of here and I get on with the sheet?"

"Ben, you got a minute?"

It was Jake heading towards the cubicle. Ben nodded towards his office.

"So how did you get on yesterday?" Ben asked.

"Nothing spectacular but ok."

"So what was ok?"

"We closed out just under $1,500.000 for the day."

"Upstairs would not be too upset with that; I would have thought. You did well, given the market conditions yesterday.

It was a tough market, and you managed to pull a profit, nothing wrong in that."

"Today's sheet?" Jake asked.

"Mary is typing it up now."

Jake bounced from one foot to the other.

"Great, I'll get the team on it straight away."

"Just one thing, Jake. On the list is one real crapper that I could not make money on today."

Jake started chewing the inside of his mouth.

"I… I don't understand. Why - " Ben cut in.

"Why is it on the list then, you're thinking?"

"Yes."

"It's there to see if you can discover which one it is."

"Oh, for fuck sake Ben, what's with all this shit? What the fuck has got into you?"

"You told me you wanted a cage. I am offering you my cage when I quit."

"Quit! Don't make me laugh; they will never let you go."

Mary tapped on the door and walked in, handing the sheet to Jake.

"There you go," she said.

Ben looked at Jake. Jake scanned the sheet and then looked back at Ben, his shoulders now hunched and head shaking from side to side.

"Something wrong with it?" Mary asked, stepping closer to double check the list. Ben stopped her. "If you typed up what I gave you, then all is fine."

Ben turned to Mary. "What holidays do I have available?"

"Holidays!" Jake interrupted.

"Yes, holidays. Jake, you have a team waiting."

Jake thought about coming back to Ben but decided to leave the office instead.

Ben nodded for Mary to close the door. She then turned back to face Ben.

"So what was that all about?"

"Nothing, just getting him in training."

"Training? I don't understand. Are you going somewhere? You want a holiday?"

"I don't know what the hell I want."

"Mr Control, Mr Organised, Mr Perfection… doesn't know what he wants?"

Ben squeezed his eyes shut.

"Is that what you think of me?" He asked.

Mary's body went into a slight freeze mode.

"I..umm — look I'm sorry, it just came out that way. I didn't mean it that—"

Ben put his hand up and smiled, to release her from her freeze mode.

"It's ok; I recognize some of what you said. Only a little mind."

Joint laughter cleared the air. Ben motioned for Mary to sit.

"So holidays, I have some I'll take it?"

"I don't think you have to ask to take a holiday, but I would imagine you have several weeks of standard holiday available. Where are you going?"

Ben leaned back in his chair; hands interlocked behind his head and put his feet up on the desk.

"Maybe I will let the universe decide."

Mary looked at Ben's feet up on the desk and then his hands behind his head.

"My, oh my, she has got under your skin. Careful Ben, careful."

"She is an amazing girl, Mary. I'm telling you, she is amazing."

"And twenty years your junior, Ben."

Ben's eyebrows pulled in together.

"What — No, not like that for god's sake. You think I am thinking — Look, she is amazing, yes she is beautiful, and I have come to really like her. Not that you could ever show her that as she has a fuse, the length of a postage stamp and any remote attempt to help is met with some fierce independence."

"Really... fierce independence, she'd have a match in you then, eh?"

"Jeez, Mary, you sound like her more every day. What the hell is happening to me here?"

Ben swung his feet off the desk and swiveled the chair to stare out at the cityscape. Mary stared at his back.

"Sorry, that was rude of me."

Ben swung his chair back around.

"No. It wasn't. It was a truthful observation — tell you what. How about you come home for dinner tomorrow night?"

"Like I said, not sure Michael would be happy with that."

"No, I meant for you to bring Michael. I would like to meet him and that way, you get to meet Christina."

Chapter Twenty-Three

Christina and Ben had moved to the lounge for what had now become almost ritual like positions, each sitting at the end and turned inwards.

"How would you feel about some company tomorrow night for dinner?"

"What, you have someone coming over?"

"I invited Mary over from the office."

"That's ok, I will have dinner in my room and not bother you."

"No… it's not like that. She's coming over with her fiancée Michael; it's just for dinner. They will probably stay over, so they don't have to drive back into the city at night."

"Ok, I would like to meet this Mary of yours."

"Great, she is looking forward to meeting you."

Christina's eyes narrowed.

"I hope you have not set this up to get me involved in something. I am not a circus act, and I don't want to discuss the things that we have talked about with strangers."

"It's not like that."

"I think I'm better off in my room if you don't mind."

Ben rubbed his forehead for a moment realizing this was not going well.

"Look. I'll be honest with you. I have never met Michael. Mary, yes I have spoken to her about some of the things we talked about. I did tell her the prison bars of when story and that did cause a reaction in her life. Since that time she has said that she would like to meet you."

"You could have checked out with me first though, couldn't you? Last night we even talked about how I felt about speaking about this with other people. I am not up to that."

"You have an amazing story to share." Ben leaned forward and paused long enough to pull in Christina full attention. "And what's more-" Christina cut him off.

"If you had not hit me in the car that day, we would never have met, and you would know nothing of any of this."

Ben reached out a hand. Christina looked at it and then looked back at Ben.

"Take my hand," he said.

Christina placed her hand in his.

Ben focused intently into Christina's eyes.

"If I had known about you on the day of the accident and I knew about our talks, I would have run you over on purpose."

Ben kept a deadpan expression until Christina's lips started to twitch at the ends.

Christina pulled her hand away from Ben's, slapping it as they came apart.

"So you did do it on purpose then?"

The twitching lips expanded into a broad smile.

Ben leaned back again.

"Ok, so it's all good then? We have dinner together?"

"But you're not going to put me on the spot over anything. I would not like that. It makes me feel uncomfortable."

"No, I promise, it's just dinner, and you and Mary get to meet, and I get to meet Michael."

"I'll strike a deal with you," Christina said

"Ok, what's the deal?"

"I want you to tell me about somebody."

"Well, I will if I can."

"Ok… it's her."

Christina pointed to the picture above the fireplace. Ben turned to look and fell silent.

"Why do you want to know?" he said, his voice dropped a tone.

"She was someone I used to know. We were kids messing about in face masks, that's all."

"What's her name?"

"Why do you want to know? It's a girl I had a crush on. We were young things, it didn't work, and that was it."

"But you still keep this picture of her?"

Ben rubbed the top of his thighs.

"I remember it as a great day, we were at the fair having a good time, and that's all there is to it, ok?"

"Ok, Mr touchy, we had a deal that was all, didn't mean to strike a nerve."

"So back to last night when I thought it was the end of the ceremony, you said it was only the beginning, remember? Can you tell me more about that now?"

"Sure, you don't want to save it for after dinner tomorrow?"

Christina cooked her head to one side and pulled her earlobe.

Ben sensed this was not an innocent remark.

"No, be serious. I promised I would not put you on the spot or any awkward situation ok? I understand how you feel."

Christina filled her lungs and exhaled slowly.

Ben jumped right back in before the breath finished.

"So you were telling me more about the ceremony."

Christina's eyes defocused as she traveled back into the experience.

Ben leaned back, waiting for Christina to start but decided to prompt her.

"You were saying that you had agreed to the tattoos and that your purpose was that you were to write and speak about your experience; to spread the word so to speak."

"Well, yes but not the actual ceremony."

Ben's eyebrows did that familiar pinch when he was internally processing something he didn't understand.

"But I thought that was what this was all about?"

"Yes and no-" Ben cut in.

"The tattoos were to be a permanent reminder of the ceremony and to tell others about it. That's what you said."

"Hold on a minute will you, you are racing ahead here."

"Sorry."

"Ok, so… Yes, it is about the ceremony, but the ceremony is not the thing of itself. The ceremony was the tool to open the mind so to speak, to access and communicate with universal intelligence. What came out of that communication was what I am to speak and write about."

"Ok, so what came out of that?"

"The best way to describe them are as messages in bite size pieces. What I mean is that you get a bite size piece of information that then fills out to something that is understandable."

"This sounds very difficult to comprehend."

"Ok, I will try to explain it another way."

"You remember the dots and the radar screen and how I explained that?"

"Yes."

"Ok, so think of each message a bit like a dot, but this dot is like an ethereal byte of information - a message, but... it's encoded, and you have to decode it. I'll give you an example.

Laying there in the pitch-black, a pattern not unlike all the broken shards of glass came into vision. As it came into vision, I instantly knew this message was about fear."

"And now you have to decode that message to understand it, is that what you're saying?"

"In the case of fear, no-"

"Sorry, you are losing me. Can you tell me what you mean? You instantly knew what the broken shards meant. How could you, for example, work out that it meant fear?"

"Look, I am trying to do my best here. This is not easy to break down like this, especially when you keep interrupting."

"Sorry, I didn't mean to make it difficult. I will shut up and listen."

"No, it's ok to ask a question but when you have the urge to do that, just hold back and ask it when it's relevant to the point I am making."

Christina burst out laughing.

"What's up? What's so funny?"

"Honestly, you couldn't make this stuff up, here I am talking, you keep interrupting, and then I say hold back and ask it exactly at that point.'"

"What's funny about that?"

"Just that —hold back and ask when it's relevant is a message of itself."

"But better I understand about fear first — right?"

"Yes, let's deal with that first."

"So you instantly knew."

"Yes, I call it a sense of knowing. In my journal, I just write it as SOK for short, and I am finding myself writing it more and more frequently.

This sense of knowing or SOK is something that just comes to you as truth. It's something that you know to be true that you suddenly become acutely aware of. I will try to give you an example.

You can tie a shoelace, right?"

"Yes, of course."

"Ok, so you know you can tie your shoelaces, that is a sense of knowing at an unconscious level.

Now go back to when you were learning how to tie that shoelace. Likely you struggled quite a bit. Then you got it and were likely mildly surprised how it all came together. Right about now, you would have experienced a moment where you simply knew and you momentarily became aware of the knowing that you could now tie a shoelace.

It is that momentary flash that is called a sense of knowing. It happens to us all the time, but we give it little attention as it happens so fast.

Here in the ceremony, the sense of knowing was slowed down so that I could fully appreciate the value of knowing something to be true that was true."

Chapter Twenty-Four

"**M**orning Bill, how are you on this fine and sunny day?"

"Don't see too much of the sun from the garage, sir" Bill smiled.

"Well, think what it will be like when you and your wife are out there on the high seas."

"I don't think I will see the high seas sir, more like a sedate river."

"How does that tally with your wife's vision?"

"She wants to feel the salt spray on her face and the wind in her hair."

"And that's not for you Bill?'

Bill rubbed his chin. "I don't know how I would feel about not being in sight of land."

"I am told that most deaths at sea are within a very short distance from land — maybe the open sea is safer than you think with some right planning?"

"I'll ask the wife on that one and get back to you sir, ok?"

"It's a deal Bill, don't forget it. Also, don't forget that fear is more often than not based on what we imagine to be true, rather than what is true.

Ben headed toward the elevator but paused after a few steps, which Bill noticed.

"Left something in the car, sir?"

"No, it was something that came to mind, something that someone told me last night. They said

'Be on your guard for the thief that would sneak up on you at the moment of victory and steal everything from you in the names of safety, security, and risk of loss.'

I felt like sharing that with you."

"Could you repeat that, sir, if you wouldn't mind."

"Be on your guard for the thief that would sneak up on you at the moment of victory and steal everything from you in the names of 'safety, security, and risk of loss."

Ben continued towards the elevator.

Bill raised his voice to reach him.

"Sounds like my wife talking, sir. I will tell her that one tonight."

The elevator doors opened; as always the heads that were there remained fixed but eyes acknowledged. Jake wasn't in yet.

"Good morning, guys!" Ben raised his voice for all to hear but only one gave a stifled good morning in return.

Ben stopped, turned to face the brokers and clapped his hands.

"Guys. GOOD Morning!"

A stronger response came back.

"It's a great day, guys. I have a message for you all this morning."

Every trader in the room now had their full attention on Ben.

"It's a message that contains power for you. Pens ready?

Be on your guard, for the thief that would sneak up on you at the moment of victory and steal everything from you in the names of safety, security, and risk of loss."

Ben repeated the message then paused. The brokers looked up at the pause.

"What, you expect more? I give you the keys to a cage, and you want more. What more is there?"

Ben resumed his path to his office. Spun his chair around, hands behind his head and looked out over the city and watched a passenger jet making a trail across the sky.

"How long have you been watching that?" Mary jarred him from his thoughts.

"I can't wait for you to meet Christina tonight. Is Michael all ok for coming?"

"Yes, all good"

"I'll have a car collect you so that you can arrive about 7:00 pm. How's that?"

"We can make our own way."

"I'm sure you can, but please let me treat you both to a ride."

"Ok, I'm sure Michael will enjoy it."

"Oh, just one thing. Christina seemed nervous about meeting anyone, and I promised I would not mention any of the things we have been talking about together."

Mary shrugged her shoulders

"Ok, whatever works. Are these the numbers for today?" Mary said, picking up the yellow legal pad.

"Er... no..."

Ben realized his numbers were late this morning and grabbed the pad back from Mary. He went to flip over the top page and then paused.

"Mm, I don't remember doing that. I must have done it when I first came in."

He scanned down the pad and cross-checked against the screen, which he hadn't remembered turning on.

"Yes. All good that is the sheet for today."

He peeled off the sheet and handed it to Mary who reached over and patted him on the shoulder three times.

"Ben, I don't know what's going on in your head, maybe it's one of those mid-life crisis things."

Ben looked up from the pad where he had started writing again.

"Not in a bad way, I hope?" He said and smiled before continuing to write.

Mary turned to leave.

"Hold on. Can you type this up and make about 50 copies and place them on the table next to the elevator?"

He handed her the page. She read it out loud.

"Be on your guard for the thief that would sneak up on you at the moment of victory and steal everything from you in the names of safety, security, and risk of loss."

"A philosopher this morning?"

"A little something like that -" Mary cut in. "That Christina came up with? You've got it bad Ben, be careful."

Chapter Twenty-Five

Marcello tapped on the French doors that led to Christina's room. She signaled for him to wait while she shut the door to her room, then she let Marcello in.

"You are a crazy, this is dangerous."

"Have you got one?" Christina asked.

"Yes, this is the smallest one we have."

Marcello pulled from his pocket a folding pruning saw, shaped like a banana. He opened the blade.

"Be careful; it's very sharp. Don't tell Anna I gave you this or she will not feed me for a week."

"Don't worry; she won't find out."

Christina propped herself up on the bed as Marcello returned to the gardens. The saw kept snagging in the soft bandage on the underside of the cast, making it difficult to cut. Twenty minutes later she cracked the back of the cast, as it opened up like a clamshell. Freedom. She raked her nails up and down where the plaster had been and was in heaven.

She wiggled her ankle, and it felt good. 'Time to clean up this mess,' she thought. She stood up full body weight on the leg and there was no pain. It just a little odd without the plaster, that was all.

A few test paces away, and back to the bed; all was good.

The small chips from the saw she flushed down the toilet and the cast, she folded together with the saw and went back to the French doors. Marcello was riding the mower away from her, so she waited for him to turn and waved her arm up high.

About half way back towards the house, Marcello returned the wave but kept on the same straight moving line. Before he got to his next turn, he got off the mower and jogged up to Christina.

"You are one crazy girl for sure," he said, looking from Christina's foot to the cast she was holding out to him.

"Can you get rid of it for me?"

"Sure, don't tell Anna, though."

"Don't worry, our secret is safe." Christina put her hand on his upper arm as she said: "Thank you."

Ben looked up from the screens as Mary turned to leave.

"You may be right, I should be careful but on the other hand, you have not met her yet."

Jake and Mary crossed paths at Ben's door and exchanged good morning greetings.

"Morning. Buddy."

"Good morning Jake and how are you on this bright and beautiful day?"

"Definitely… my friend, definitely."

Ben's eyebrows pinched together.

"You have definitely got a severe hormonal problem. What's her name? Please don't tell me it's that young girl you have staying with you."

"You mean Christina?"

"That's it; that is what is going on here. Playing with fire you are Benjamin, playing with fire."

Mary came into the room.

"Sorry to interrupt boys' talk but four directors have shown up and are in the boardroom asking if you could meet up with them, Ben."

"Sure ok, when are they thinking to meet?"

"Soon as you can, I'd say, by the way, they asked."

"Tell them I'll be there in five."

"Looks like it might be bonus time for you again," said Jake.

"Who knows, Jake. I have asked Mary to type something up and put them on the elevator table. Don't mention that to anyone, leave them there and see what happens."

"You mean this?" Jake handed Ben the note.

"Young Jimmy has stuck this to his trading screen when I saw it. He told me where he got it. I was going to ask you about that."

"You didn't take it off his screen did you?"

"No, I just wanted to ask you about it, so I brought it with me."

"Will you do me a favor and make sure you give it back to - what did you say his name was?"

"Jimmy. He started a few months ago as a trainee."

"Is he any good?"

"A spark but no fire."

Mary came back.

"Ben, they're waiting for you in the boardroom." Her voice was a little flustered and Ben sensed that they were waiting.

"Good morning, gentlemen," Ben said to the four directors as he seated himself at the table.

"We'll get right to it Ben," said one director.

"Your stats are down from normal and we noticed that you have not been your usual self, what with leaving early and at other times away from the office. As you know, we don't condone any office relationships, and we are well.... wondering if we can do anything to help?"

Ben glanced around the table at all four of them.

"Can you repeat that? I- I don't follow what you're saying-"

Another director cuts it.

"Do you want us to re-assign Mary to another job?"

Ben pressed his palms on the table.

"What's going on here? Why on earth would you think I would want to get rid of Mary? She has been with me for years and we are a great team."

The first director came back with:

"So it's just a team thing and not a relationship?"

"No, I don't have a personal relationship with Mary, she has a fiancée. I am sorry, gentlemen I am bewildered as to why we are having this discussion."

The boardroom phone rang. The director who had started the meeting with Ben picked it up. He listened for about fifteen seconds and then said 'Yes, sir' and hung up. Turning to Ben, he added

"Ben, you have not been your usual self. Your routines have changed and as a result, your returns are down.

One particular case, Jake was forced to make decisions without your back up. You let him wing it. What was that all about?"

Ben's flat hands turned to fists on the table.

"Gentlemen — let me recap here. You invite me in here to see if I am having a relationship with Mary. You then offer to get rid of her for me. Then you say my returns are down and finally; you don't like the idea of me offering some help to Jake. Is that all?"

The other three directors looked at the one who had opened the initial conversation.

"One more thing, what's this about?" He slid over a piece of paper. Ben read it.

'Be on your guard for this thief that would sneak up on you at the moment of victory and steal everything from you in the names of safety, security, and risk of loss.'

"What is that all about?" he said.

Ben's fists unclenched. His palms were flat back on the table. He leaned back lifted his hands about five inches from the table, before slapping them back down.

"Gentlemen, if I may say something?"

The directors leaned back in their chairs as Ben leaned forward.

"Fuck you. Yes, fuck you. Now I am going back to my office and you can do whatever you want to do."

Ben pushed the chair away from the table with the back of his legs as he stood up.

At the door, he turned around to face the stunned directors.

"And just to be sure,"

"Ben, don't be hasty here. We are only trying to help," said the director that had kicked this all off.

"Like I said. Fuck you."

Part Two

Chapter Twenty-Six

Anna tapped on Christina's door.

"Christina, the guests will be here in about an hour. Mr Ben asks if you will meet him in the lounge terrace before they arrive."

"Yes, ok, I'll be there in a few minutes."

Christina put on a pair of jeans and thick walking socks. They felt comfortable in the absence of the plaster cast. She had been practicing walking around her room for the last thirty minutes and had just about trained her body to finally let the plaster cast go and flex her ankle normally.

Ben was sitting at a table, watching the sun sink with a glass of orange juice. There was a second glass for Christina.

She approached Ben from behind.

"It's beautiful, isn't it?"

Ben half turned around.

"Hi, how are you doing?" he said.

"Fine, I feel like I am walking on air. It's been a beautiful day. How was your day?"

"So, so, you might say. Just changing the subject for a moment. The sunset- I don't know why I felt this urge, but I am going to ask you anyway. Does it mean anything? Ok, that is a weird question, sorry. What I think I mean to say is- did Almedio ever talk about sunsets?"

Christina sat down, and Ben pushed the orange juice towards her.

"It's strange, isn't it, that once you start getting into all this stuff, you experience how things seem to change around you- and how you, yourself, are almost forced to change with them."

Ben turned away from the sunset to look directly at Christina. The glow from the sunset lit her face and hair, which caused a sharp intake of breath that didn't go unnoticed.

"What's up?" You seem tense and on edge; something wrong?" she said.

Ben rubbed his hands on top of his thighs before rubbing them together.

Christina responded to his question.

"Yes, he did talk about sunsets but not in the context of one of the messages I received. More like a general metaphor for life."

"That's what I was thinking about when I asked the question, although I have no idea where it originated in my head."

Christina took another sip of orange juice.

"He said sunsets should serve as a reminder that today has been washed over and tomorrow we start anew, but he then added that tomorrow is now. I just didn't get it at first, but when I did, I realized the power and freedom that offered, if one could accept it in their life.

I will try to explain it as he explained it to me.

It was a couple of days after the ceremony, and I was thinking about leaving. I had found this spot on a large log that was high up on the bank, at the edge of the village. From here, I could look out across the river. It was a huge expanse of water, and I was thinking how tiny the boat I came to the village was compared to it.

I remember thinking how nervous I would have been if I had arrived in daylight and had been aware of the flow and current.

Then the sunset just overtook my senses, and a feeling of profound gratitude passed over me.

I then felt the presence of someone behind me and immediately sensed it was Alemedio."

"Mr Ben," Anna called out.

"Mr Ben, your guests have arrived."

Ben looked at his watch and then at Christina.

"Have you ever noticed that when we are talking about messages and your experiences, time just seems to disappear?"

"Mr Ben."

"It's ok, Anna I'm on my way.

I'm pretty sure you'll like Mary. In a way, she reminds me of you. I'll get Anna to serve some pre-dinner drinks in the lounge before dinner so that I can introduce her and Michael, her fiancée."

Christina shifted in her seat as she drank the last of her orange juice. Ben left to greet his guests.

Christina took a last look at the sunset and went into the lounge. She could hear the guests' voices.

She didn't know whether to sit down or stand as she was, but then a woman appeared and walked towards her.

"I guess you must be Mary?" Christina held out her hand.

Mary came up close, ignoring the extended hand and instead embraced her with a quick hug.

As she broke away, she said.

"Handshakes are for business. A hug is so much better, don't you think?"

Mary turned to Ben.

"Ben, you told me she was pretty-"

Mary turned back to Christina and said

"Typical Ben. No idea how to tell the difference between pretty and beautiful."

Mary stroked Christina's arm.

"So, no need for introductions then, other than Michael. This is Christina; Christina, this is Michael."

Michael nodded with a smile towards Christina, which was returned by her.

"Come on, let's sit and have a drink before dinner," Ben said.

They all sat down as Anna appeared with a large jug of sangria. She poured a glass for everyone.

"Dinner in about half an hour, Anna? Is that ok?"

"Half an hour, yes, Mr Ben."

Anna left the room.

Mary turned to Christina. "So, how's your leg?"

"It's much-"— Mary cut in. "Oh, it's gone— not the leg of course," she said laughing.

"You didn't mention you were going to the hospital," Ben said.

"I didn't—I cut it off myself."

"What!"

Ben's eyes widened, in unison with his mouth.

Michael leaned forward.

"Now that is my kinda girl. How did you get it off?"

"A garden pruning saw— you know, one of those curved ones."

Michael turned to Mary.

"Hon, when we have kids, we need to make sure they cut their plaster casts off."

Ben interrupted.

"In all seriousness, though, was this a good idea?"

Christina wiggled her ankle and then stood up and got on tiptoes.

"There!" she said, "All mended."

"Are you going to have it checked out by a doctor?"

"Ben, leave her alone. Stop acting like a mother hen."

Ben leaned back on the sofa, looked at Michael and threw his hands up in the air.

"That's it, now that they have teamed up, we are doomed."

"Now that's the truth," said Michael.

Mary and Christina exchanged smiles.

Anna appeared, giving a small cough to get everyone's attention. "Dinner is ready."

"Thank you, Anna."

As they were about to take up their seats, Ben said. "Well, as you have obviously teamed up on Michael and I, it's ladies that side and gents on this side.

Mary and Christina exchanged smiles again.

Michael tapped Ben on the arm.

"I tell you what, if we were all out and about now, and the shops were open, they would probably have abandoned us by now."

"Not probably." Mary came back.

"That's not a bad idea. I think we should arrange that. What do you say, Christina? Some girl time shopping, so I can tell you all the things about Ben that he will not have told you."

Christina looked directly at Ben.

"I think I'd like that."

"It's a date. We'll sort out the details later." Said Mary.

They ate and chatted through the three courses before moving back into the lounge.

"Well, that was lovely. Thank you very much for inviting us over Ben," said Mary. "Yes, really enjoyed it," said Michael.

"By the way, did either of you see the sunset tonight? On the way over this evening, it was the most incredible sight. Michael and I were transfixed by it."

"Yes, we were sitting out on the terrace watching it as you arrived, "said Ben.

Christina felt an urge to be more part of the conversation, as she had not said much all night.

"We were talking about it and how it might affect us." She said.

Mary turned to Michael.

"What did I say to you, Michael? I felt like it was a renewing process."

"Uh- yes, something like that."

Christina turned to Ben.

"Interesting that we all had the same feeling. I might as well finish what Ben and I were talking about if you like?"

Ben shifted in his seat.

"That would be great."

"Yes, please do," Mary and Michel said, almost in unison.

"Well, I don't know if Ben has told you anything about me and my travels, but-" Mary cut in.

"Yes, about your traveling to Peru. He also told me a story about the prison bars of when. I have to tell you, that story had a significant impact on me."

Mary gave an appreciative nod to Christina.

"Ok, so it was on the trip to Peru that I met a shaman called Almedio. I was just sitting on this log by the side of the Amazon river."

"You've been to the Amazon-?"

Michael interrupted.

"Yes."

"So you have been to the jungle, and you cut your own plaster off? Mary, I hope you're taking notes."

Mary laughed as she patted him on the knee.

"Calm down, Mr Adventurer, let's put off sailing around the world until Christina has finished her story, ok?"

"Christina, please ignore any further interruptions," said Mary.

They all turned their attention to Christina.

"Ok, so it was a couple of days after the ceremony-""Ceremony?" Michael cut in. Everyone looked at him and said nothing.

He put his hands up and leaned back.

"Sorry."

"I was just sitting on this log by the river, watching the sun go down when Almedio came to sit beside me. He was a wonderful person to be with; I enjoyed his company. It was always like he had answers to questions that you were only just about to ask, almost like he was a few minutes ahead of your thoughts.

Sitting on the log there, I could look out across the river. It was a huge expanse of water, and I was thinking how tiny the boat I came to the village with was compared to it.

I remember thinking how nervous I would have been if I had arrived in daylight and had been aware of the flow and current.

Then all of a sudden, the sunset just took over my senses, and a feeling of profound gratitude overtook me.

Right at that point, Almedio said that when we are pulled into the sunset, this is a reminder for us that today has been washed over and tomorrow we start anew, but he then added that tomorrow is now.

I was confused and asked him 'how could tomorrow be now?' I hasten to add here that much of what Almedio said, he would leave you to work out for yourself.

Sometimes it was hours after he said something that suddenly 'ping,' something in your mind gets that 'ah, ha' moment of understanding."

Both Mary and Ben nodded in agreement.

"He said that today had existed but was nothing more than now, tomorrow exists in the future but only now."

Then he added that when the sunset overtook my senses, I was at that moment at a time and place that was the only time and place for me.

Many people he said experience these things, but in today's world, few get to walk into that experience with understanding. Unless you walk into the experience fully connected to the experience, then you cannot gain or learn from it.

He asked me what I had been thinking about when the sunset overtook me. I tried my hardest to tell him something, anything, but I couldn't remember.

He then said to describe to him how difficult it was to try and get that memory back.

I don't know where this explanation came from, but I said it was like trying to pull someone free from being stuck in the mud with a piece of cotton thread. He told me to be there with that image and then pull hard on the cotton.

I did that, and it broke, leaving the person stuck in the mud.

He then told me to pay attention to the person trapped in the mud. To look into their eyes and tell him what I saw.

That was weird. As I was looking at this person, their face changed to my face; it was myself in the mud and myself holding the other end of the broken cotton. There were two of me; I was looking at myself.

Before I had a chance to tell him what I saw, he asked me if I would like to know why there were two of me.

I asked him how he knew, to which he just gave a smile before saying that the other me was not me. The real me was holding the broken cotton.

Before I could say another word, he said 'although you thought you were stuck, you felt free, disconnected. However, you also carried a lingering feeling of connection. Hence the cotton thread.

He went on to explain that to live a life free of the stickiness of the mud; we must continually break the threads in our minds that hold us to past thoughts.

It's only when we can be consciously aware of the broken threads that we can be truly free to stand in the moment, neither looking forward nor backward.

He said that this was the feeling I experienced, as I felt washed over by the sunset.

I had previously looked at many sunsets like we all have, but this one was the only one that washed my mind free of all thought.

I now look at all sunsets and walk into them in my mind. It's a wonderful feeling to have peace like that."

Mary reached out to Christina. "Come here." She pulled Christina close, as they both caught sight of each other's watery eyes.

The silence in the room became deafening.

"Michael, it's getting late; we should make tracks."

Ben jumped up.

"No, I have already asked Anna to make up the guest suite for you both. Sorry, I assumed you would be staying to avoid the drive back into the city at night."

Michael looked at Mary and shrugged his shoulders. "I'm good with that if you are?"

Mary looked up at the ceiling for a second as she gently chewed the inside of her bottom lip.

"I really wanted to get into town early tomorrow, but I suppose we can go straight from here-"

Christina jumped in.

"If you're going into town and you were serious about us shopping tomorrow, then I could come with you and make my own way back in the afternoon."

Michael gave a sigh of relief and said,

"That would work, hon as that way I don't have to come shopping with you."

Michael nodded in Ben's direction, who returned a wink.

"Men, anything to get away with carrying a few shopping bags… Ok, it's a date. Can you drop us into the city, Ben?"

"No, I have some work that I just need to tidy up in the office for a few hours, so I will get a ride called up for you if that's ok?"

"Yes, that's fine. Michael? Are you coming with us shopping or not?"

"No, I'm good here. Ben, can I stay for a while in the morning and take a look around the gardens? I have a pet hobby as a botanist, and I've noticed you have spectacular gardens."

"That will be down to Marcello," said Christina.

"Marcello?" repeated Michael.

"Yes, he's the gardener come handyman who works around the place-"

Ben cut in again.

"I tell you what. You girls go shopping. Michael, you stay for as long as you want and then Marcello will drop you back home when you're ready. I will tidy up a few loose ends in the office. How's that?"

"Ben, I am seriously impressed. If only you were so organized in the office."

Ben winked at Mary. "But that's what I have you for."

Chapter Twenty-Seven

M ary tapped on the driver's window.

"Changed my mind; take us to Columbus Circle."

"What's at Columbus Circle?" asked Christina.

"Great shopping and we can take a walk in the park at the same time."

"I have a confession to make," said Christina.

Mary patted Christina's arm, "you're not that much into shopping?"

"Is it that obvious?"

"Don't worry; I only want to get some walking shoes. I have decided to get out of the house at the weekends with Michael and do some mild hiking."

The cab pulled up, and Mary paid.

"Heard what you said about shopping, Ma'am. If you're looking for outdoor gear, you will find a great store one block up, on the corner of McDougal Street."

"Thanks, we'll check that out first."

This was Christina's type of store; she loved all the outdoor gear. Mary made straight for the footwear department.

"Come, have a look at these."

Christina gave the walking boots a quick check over with a nod of approval.

A few moments later, they were in the park ordering lunch from a cart.

"So, what were you going to tell me about Ben?"

"Actually, there is not that much to tell. Ben is a lovely guy, but a bit of a loner in a way. He's excellent at what he does as you have probably guessed. For the most part, he pours himself into his work."

Michael was walking around the gardens as Ben grabbed a pad and turned on his screen. The screen powered up, showing a webmail page with a whole string of emails. Christina had not logged out again.

Ben knew it was wrong but it got the better of him, and he paused to read some of the headers.

He recognized a firm of lawyers in London that he had seen the last time she had left her email open.

He clicked on the email and read.

'We are contacting you again as administers of your mother's estate. The matter is now twelve months old. We realize this is a difficult time for you, but this is something that needs to be completed.

We have strict instructions that we are to execute the reading of the will in your presence, and this is why we are unable to comply with your request to ship the box directly.

We look forward to you visiting our London office as soon as possible. We would again urge you to give this matter your attention at the earliest possible opportunity.

Howe and Horwath Solicitors.'

It was the same email he read before, but now he noticed that there was a string of them with the same subject line.

'Howe and Horwath Solicitors.'

Most of them were unread. He clicked a couple, and they all contained the same message. Guilt overtook him, and he closed the browser.

Both Christina and Mary sat on the same bench that Mary had shared with Ben earlier.

"There is one thing I would like to know about Ben?"

Mary laughed.

"Ok, I'll see what I can do."

"The picture over the fireplace, he seems very sensitive about it. I asked him once, but he avoided a conversation."

"Yes, that would be about right. You know he painted that from a photograph?"

"No, I didn't, it's incredible in detail. I thought it was a photograph."

"He has an incredible skill as an artist and painter.

He told me he gave up painting when she left him."

"The girl in the painting, you mean?"

"Yes, to be honest though, I only picked this up from bits that he has mentioned over the years, in moments of weakness."

"Moments of weakness... he has those?" They both grinned.

"So the girl in the mask, where is she?"

"I don't know, and neither does he. As far as I am aware, from what I have pieced together, they were together all through school and then onto their twenties. She would have been about your age when she left."

"Why did she leave?"

Mary shrugged her shoulders.

"Who knows the complexities of relationships, eh?"

"Well, he must still have affection for her to have her picture there and to have painted her."

"As far as I can piece together, Ben's father got him into the job he is in now. He started making a lot of money very quickly and become obsessed with it.

Their relationship became distant as he made more money and the dreams that she had of traveling the world moved further and further away.

The last thing that happened was they went to a fair ground where that picture was taken. Afterwards, they had a row, and she left. That was the last time he ever saw her."

"Didn't he try to find her?"

"For years, but never any luck. I remember him telling me once that she was out there somewhere, living her dream."

"How sad."

"I don't know why I have to do this, but I want to take you somewhere that Ben and I visited the other day."

The bell rang as the top of the door struck the bell in the Bleecker Street Hat store.

"Good afternoon, ladies. Anything I can help you with today?" Said a man in his 50's.

"Yes, I am looking for a particular hat. I can't remember its name, but it looks like an Indiana Jones hat."

The man smiled. "Know exactly the hat you're talking about; right this way."

The man led them to the men's section where the hat was located.

"What size are you after?"

"We don't know if we want to buy one today. We just wanted to look, is that ok?" Said Mary.

"Of course, madam. If you need any help, I'll be right over there."

He pointed to the cash register area as he walked away.

"So, I don't know why I thought of bringing you here, but it has something to do with when Ben brought me here the other day."

"He came to buy this hat?" said Christina.

"Well, he came to show me the hat and tell me what he thought about it."

Mary picked it up and put it on Christina's head.

"I thought so."

"What?"

"You have got a hat head."

Mary smiled and tilted the hat.

"I bet there is hardly a hat in this store that wouldn't look good on you."

Christina looked in a mirror and adjusted the hat. "Mmm... I had one like this but lost it in the river on a boat ride when I was leaving. Strange, you knew I wanted to buy another one."

"I didn't, that's not why I brought you here."

Christina looked back from the mirror and shrugged her shoulders.

"Why then?"

"As I said, I don't really know. Maybe it was because of what Ben said while we were here."

"So he brought you to this store to talk about this hat?"

"Yes, that was it. He never intended to buy it."

"What did he say?"

"He said that countless men come to this store and try on this style of hat; they look in the mirror, have a smile, and then put it back on the shelf. He even called over the assistant and asked him how many people do that.

Sure enough, the assistant confirmed that that was exactly what happened.

Ben said that the reason so many try this hat on is not because of the hat, but because of what it represents. The Indiana Jones films immortalized it.

The hat became the symbol of swashbuckling adventure. I can't remember exactly what he said, but the overall gist of it was that the hat was like kindling on a fire. You wanted the fire to catch, but before it burst into flames, you pulled off the kindling because of fear of the fire."

Christina paid particular attention to Mary's eyes.

"Did you make that up?"

"No, that was what he was saying."

"Sorry, I didn't mean did you make all that up. I was referring to the fire and the kindling explanation. Did that come from you or Ben?"

"Err- I just made that up. I don't know where it came from. Why?"

"It struck me as strange because Almedio explained something using the same metaphor of starting a fire with kindling."

Mary laughed.

"Sounds like a very smart fellow this Almedio."

Christina was still wearing the hat but reached for another one and double-checked the size.

"Come on," she said to Mary. "I'm ready unless you want to get a hat for yourself?"

"No way. I don't have a hat head like you," she said laughing.

They went over to the cash register. Christina put both hats on the counter.

"Would you like them boxed, miss?"

"No, just put one inside the other and pop them into a bag, please."

"Sure, too easy."

The man bagged the hats and rung up the sale. The bell over the top of the door rang again as they left.

"Let's walk back to the park and grab a cab there. On the way, you can tell me more about the kindling fire thing if you like."

"Doesn't this stuff bore you?" said Christina.

"What stuff?"

"All the psychology stuff; you know, the stories and metaphors?"

"Not at all, why would you say that?"

"I don't know, sometimes people seem interested, and sometimes they seem affected by what I say happened to me; but then I wonder, what next? What are they going to do then, does it make a difference?"

"Is that up to you?" Said Mary.

"What do you mean, up to me?"

"Well, just that. Is it up to you to hold any responsibility for action or non-action, from a person whom you have told these things to?"

"It's just that sometimes I wonder how it will affect them. Will they make changes in their lives as a result of anything I say? What for example if someone left their job and this had a significant impact on their life?"

Mary stopped walking and caught Christina's arm to stop her as well. Mary turned to a shop window.

"Look here at this shop. We can look in the window like we are now. We can go inside and browse, we can buy or not buy, and we can walk out when we like and not give the shop another thought.

This is all our free choice. When you share one of your messages like stories, it seems to me like there is a two stage process to that."

"Two-stage?"

"Yes, stage one is finding the right person. What I mean by that is being observant and discerning. For example, today I have asked you about your experience. I asked you to elaborate more on things you said that interested me. This was my choice to ask and mine alone. My asking had nothing to do with the message or my reaction to it."

"Stage two?" said Christina.

"Oh, that's pretty simple. If you're preaching at people to convert them to your way of thinking and telling them what they should be thinking, then you are the one in the wrong.

In a nutshell, deciding whether or not to share something with someone has to come down to your interpretation of the situation.

For example, can you tell when a person acts interested in what you're saying or if they are just being polite and can't wait to tell you about themselves?"

"Yes, of course."

"Well, there you go; in that case, would you share your time and message with this person?"

"No. Probably not."

"Exactly and that is all this comes down to. Is this person ready to hear your message? Make sense?"

"Yes, I suppose it does."

"There is one other angle to that. Let's say for example that you meet a person in a situation in life where you detect they would benefit from hearing something.

In that case, you are duty bound to at least try."

"Ok, I feel better after thinking about that now."

"Just one other thing Christina, lack of confidence can be a real drain on a person. I am not a confident person, but that part of me I keep in check. I do see an element of that in you. I would add, and this is probably only down to your age, whether you question your age and experience when sharing your messages with others."

"Yes, that's exactly it. Who am I, at my age, to be giving what could be taken as advice to say someone twice my age?"

"As I said, that's only down to you interpreting whether it's the right thing to do or not. Don't fight or suppress what you feel must come out."

Christina held Mary's arm.

"Thank you for talking to me like this. I don't have anyone I can share this with."

"Can I ask you about that?" said Mary.

"Yes, of course."

"Your parents?"

"My mother is dead; she died last year after a long illness."

"I am so sorry to hear that, and your father?"

"I don't know. My mother never talked about him other than telling me his name was William, and he lives in London somewhere; that's all I know."

"So, you're pretty much alone then?"

"Yes, pretty much; you could say that."

They reached the park again. Mary motioned to a bench.

The moment they sat down Christina began to cry.

"Hon, what's up? Tell me."

"I- I left her alone to die."

"Who, your mother?"

Christina was now sobbing. Mary reached and put her arm around her. Between the sobs, she blurted out.

"I should have been there. I should have been there when she died."

"Hon, whatever happened, it was the right thing at the time. It's easy to beat yourself up later on over something that you might have done differently."

"I couldn't put up with it any longer, watching her waste away each day, for two years. It was the most terrible thing to see."

Mary squeezed tight and rubbed Christina's back, letting her know that she was there with her and listening.

"Have you told anyone else about this?"

"No, you are the first person ever."

"Well, I am glad that you felt you could tell me. We all need someone who will just listen to us sometimes."

"I couldn't take it anymore, and one day the doctors told me that it was only a matter of time, but they didn't know when. That was when I took off."

Tears flooded out with a second wave.

"I- I should have stayed with her."

"Christina, you loved your mother and she loved you. That love did not end on the day you left, did it?"

The tears started to subside a little.

"And furthermore, that love still exists today for her, right?"

Mary reached into her bag for a tissue and handed it to Christina.

"But what if I had been there with her?"

"Well yes, circumstances would have been different, but you loved her, she loved you, and nothing changed with her death. Everything still exists the same. It seems to me that in death a person departs in the body, but if we think about that person, they live on in our minds. We can always call up happy memories. Of course, they will be mingled with sadness for a very long time, but we can choose how we want to remember them."

Christina had now recovered from her tears. She put her arms around Mary and hugged her.

"I have not shared this with anyone else in the world. I tried to tell Almedio, but he stopped me saying that this was not something that was right to discuss at that time. I feel a lot better now. Sorry, I cried and got upset."

"Oh, Hon… there is nothing to be sorry about at all, any time you want to, call me."

As they separated from the hug, Mary reached into her handbag to grab something to write her number on. She found an old receipt, wrote the number on the back and handed it to Christina.

"No matter where you are in the world, you can pick up the phone, and we can talk, ok?"

"Thanks."

"Well what a day we've had, eh?" said Mary.

"Yes. We went shopping, bought some hats, and then I cried a lot."

"Sounds like a great day to me," said Mary, stroking Christina's arm.

"There's nothing wrong with a good cry sometimes."

Mary looked at her watch.

"Tell you what, it's not late yet and Michael is probably still pretending he is a botanist around Ben's garden. Our apartment is not far from here. Let's go back to my place and have a coffee and then you can leave from there and go back to Ben's when you're ready. How's that?"

A short taxi ride later, Mary turned the key to the apartment door.

Chapter Twenty-Eight

Michael picked up a petal from what he knew to be the national flower of Nepal, a Rhododendron, and took it to his nose. There was little scent.

At the same time, he noticed another smell that stirred curiosity as to where it was coming from.

He looked up and saw smoke coming from the shed, which was located towards the boundary of the garden.

He made his way over and pushed the door open, which was already ajar. The smell was now much stronger.

All around the walls of the room hung gardening tools. In the center were two old chairs around a pot belly stove.

There was the source of the smell. On top of the stove was an old heavy saucepan bubbling away with what looked like muddy water. There was a wooden spoon in the pot, which he used to stir the contents. It looked like chopped up roots.

He heard the sound of a lawn tractor and went back to the door as it pulled up.

Marcello jumped off the tractor and came straight for the shed. He didn't notice Michael until they were face to face.

"Who are you? And what are you doing here?" Marcello barked.

"Er sorry, I am just looking around the garden."

Marcello sidestepped around Michael's side and pulled the shed door closed, so they were both now outside of the shed.

"What are you doing here?" Marcello barked again.

"I am a guest here, and Ben said I could walk around the gardens."

Marcello's mouth dropped open as his eyes widened.

"I am so sorry, sir. I thought you were an intruder. Please, sir, do not say I was rude to you. Please, sir, do not say that to anyone. I am sorry, sir for my bad manners."

Michael reached over and touched Marcello's shoulder.

"Don't worry at all, no harm done. Hey, you were doing the right thing to find out what I was up to."

"I am very sorry sir; it will not happen this way again sir."

"It's all good, no worries at all. So you take care of all the gardens yourself?"

"Yes, sir apart from spring time when there are lots of planting to do. Then I have some help.

"I came to the shed because of the smell. What are you cooking up?"

"Err...just some roots, sir."

"What for? I have never heard of this before. The smell was pretty strong."

"I think I have made a mistake to do this. I was trying something that my grandfather told me about, how to make a- err- fertilizer

242

like liquid. Yes, an excellent fertilizer but it's not right. I will throw it away in a moment."

There was an awkward pause in the conversation, with Marcello holding eye contact, indicating the end of the conversation.

"Oh ok then; I will have a walk around the garden some more. Is that Ok?"

"Yes sir, of course."

Marcello opened the shed door and closed it behind him, leaving Michael still standing there. He shrugged his shoulders and turned to continue walking the gardens.

Marcello took the pot from the stove and put in into an old sink that was set up in the corner of the shed.

He ran some cold water into the sink to speed up the cooling of the contents of the pot.

He grabbed two old clear glass beer bottles and a small funnel. He then poured off the liquid from the pot into both bottle, taking care not to let any of the root and leaves through. The liquid looked like muddy water in the bottles.

He found a marker pen used to write on plant identity spikes and wrote on the bottles 'Danger – Poison'.

He then rinsed off the remains of the contents of the pot. Tipped them into the sink to drain and then dropped them into the stove to burn. There was a loud hiss and steam as the wet roots hit the hot embers.

Chapter Twenty-Nine

Mary's apartment was small but beautifully decorated and furnished, giving it a much larger feel.

"This is lovely, so much cozier than Ben's place."

Mary laughed. "Yes and a tad more manageable as well. Michael is the designer. He fancies himself as a bit of an internal designer-decorator."

"Have you been with him long? Michael, I mean."

"About four years now. Why do you ask?"

"Oh, just that he seems nice and sort of- well… reliable. Oh! I don't mean that in a bad way or anything. I-" — Mary cut in. "It's ok; I know what you mean. He is reliable; he is a kind and very sweet man. He was not the type of man that I thought I would ever end up with but something happened, and it was like that fatal attraction thing. He moved in about ten days after we met and that was that. We are like a couple of soul mates. Tea or coffee?"

"Tea, please." Mary made drinks while Christina looked about the living room and all the pictures of Mary and Michael out and about, enjoying themselves."

Mary came in with the drinks.

"Seems like you travel a lot, looking at the pictures?"

"No, not really, but we do get out and about most weekends. Michael is a selfi addict since he got one of those annoying sticks that the phone fits in so you can take pictures of yourself. It's a bit of fun, but he does take some nice pictures. I often tell him that he should take it up professionally."

"Yes they are pretty nice shots, they all look so natural."

"Hey, I just remembered about that kindling thing that Almedio had talked to you about; you peaked my interest. What was that all about?"

"He was drawing similarities between lighting a fire and human desire.

He said that an idea in the human mind starts with a spark, but that spark needs fuel to continue. He said this process was similar to lighting a fire, by rubbing two sticks together.

He then said that the average person could rub two sticks together for a month and still not light a fire. The reason for this is because other elements must be present. First, it must be the right type of wood, and there must be a flow of air at the point of friction. With this air and friction combined in the right way only, will we see a whiff of smoke emerge. But still, there is no fire. All there will be is a tiny ember. This ember must then be transferred to some tinder. The tinder is the nurture and care stage. There in the tinder, one has to blow on the ember to make it glow red. One has to keep doing this until the ember spreads to the tinder and a flame is born.

But still the fire is of no use, and it will fail if this is not transferred to some kindling. This kindling needs to be light, dry twigs increasing in size until the fire starts to develop a base of heat When this kindling base is established, then the fire can be used to burn much larger timber.

He said that if one follows those principles, then anyone can start a fire. Like I said earlier, he said that the idea in the human mind starts with a spark, but that spark needs fuel to continue. He said that for the human spark to catch fire, there must be desire present. The desire takes the place of the tinder. Without this desire, the spark will fade.

He said that everyone, at some point in their lives, will have a spark of an idea or enthusiasm about something. But that is as far is it will go, and the spark will fade and die, as they go about their normal day to day lives. The element they did not have at that point was the desire to fan the spark to something greater. That desire was like the spark being transferred to the kindling but without the blowing taking place or occurring in a haphazard way.

But there are some that do have the desire; they see this spark as a way to change their future, to better their lives. This desire starts to create smoke.

Next, he said, came another critical point in the human mind and that was the desire to express and share. This desire could help the spark to fire or extinguish it.

The human desire to share is often at this stage, used to tell others about your spark of an idea, and how good it is.

But there are two dangers at this stage that now threaten the success of this spark becoming a fire.

The first danger is of telling the idea to another who has not had the spark fire in their own mind. This may cause them to throw up some negativity towards this change.

He said it's not like they are trying to be negative, it's more like they cannot see the spark or the burning ember. They cannot see the smoke starting to rise. The first danger then is this person not assisting with the fanning of the ember to make the flame.

He said that there is a saying in the west that goes something like 'pouring cold water on it.'

He said this is what can happen when you tell a person your spark of an idea. As they do not have a grounding or understanding of your spark, their comments are like the act of pouring water on your smoldering ember.

The second danger, he said, was one of dissipation. He said that often the spark grows to a bright ember ready to burst into flame, which would catch the kindling.

The originator of the spark has spent time blowing and focusing on the spark. It's now a bright glowing ember, and instead of staying focused, they start to tell everyone they come across their spark of an idea. With each sharing, the focus fades.

It becomes like holding a magnifying glass, using the sun to focus its rays on a single point, and then moving it around. As this movement happens, the heat is lost, and the ember begins to cool."

Mary came out of the kitchen with two hot drinks.

"I have listened to every word of that, and I know that to be so true, not only for myself but I have seen it in others."

"Yes, it got to me pretty much in the same way, but it gets even worse."

"Worse. what do you mean?"

"Well, unlike the fire that catches the kindling and creates a sustainable fire; the human mind has several more obstacles to over-come before the spark can become a sustainable change in a person's life."

"Almedio told you about these obstacles I assume?"

"Yes and believe me, they are kind of interesting in how they affect different people. He said that some people that get to the kindling stage just about where the fire is starting to take hold of the larger sticks, they panic.

They suddenly realize that things are underway and change is going to happen in their lives. Some will embrace this change and add more fuel, via enthusiasm, to the change. But others, the much larger group, will start to experience a degree of panic as the flames of change start to take hold. Their focus will shift from the fire to the future and what changes will take place in their lives. The secu-rity of the known, the status quo will be challenged in their minds.

If this fire continues to be kindled, then it will grow and mean a completely new foundation of life for them. Nothing is going to be the same again, and this is a significant threat to most people.

Panic now sets in, and they start to think of reasons why it's better to stick with the security of the known. Each of these thoughts is like taking a piece of kindling off the fire before it catches. The stronger the panic, the more sticks of kindling are removed. The fire is still there, but it has no fuel to expand further and take hold.

A fire in this condition can be kept alive but not without some difficulty and danger that the kindling will lose its heat and start to die.

This stage of applying more kindling and then removing some of it before it catches is keeping the fire alive but not allowing it to grow to fruition.

Almedio said that this is where most human unhappiness resides, as the kindling cycle can go on for years.

In many cases, the fire will die out, as it becomes neglected and when this happens, another spark comes along, and the whole process starts over again."

Both Mary and Christina were now sitting facing each other, both holding their hot drinks in cupped hands. Mary took a sip.

"So what happens to those that keep putting the kindling on the spark of their idea?"

"Almedio said that these are the changes of their lives and sometimes the world around them. He cited another saying that says.

'There is nothing more powerful than an idea whose time has come.'

He said this saying referred to the development of a fully built fire that could now offer not only warmth but also the heat that could be transferred to many. This was a fire that took hold in the hearts and minds of others. This was a fire that others would now add fuel to, a fire that could sweep across the globe at breakneck speed.

He went on to say that the secret to this spark and fire making is a sustained and confident effort to maintain and build a fire.

He said the key thing here is a balance.

As you're building a fire, you must at the same time be acknowledging the changes that will happen in your life as a result of the fire taking on a life of its own."

Mary leaned back into the couch.

"You know, I spend my day organizing things for people who are paid a lot more money than me. I don't envy them or feel underpaid, but with the right systems in place, anyone can make a massive difference in how they engage in their usual day to day work.

As you were telling me that story, my mind drifted back to an idea I had about putting together a course on how to create plans and systems in the workplace.

I had ideas of creating this course and then teaching it.

I can now see that I went through the same process, starting with the spark of the concept to the placing and removing of the kindling. I told people about my idea and each time I did; it dissipated until the spark was extinguished and I went back to my normal day to day work routine."

"Maybe now is the time to see if there is any power left in the spark." Said Christina.

"There is, this talk we had today has fired that spark up again in me, and now I know how to fan it into a fire."

Christina finished her coffee.

"Well, I had better start to make some tracks."

"You're welcome to stay longer if you like, but just one important thing came to my mind. I know you have shared some things with Ben and now you have shared this with me. But what concerns me is that these messages, as you call them, should all be written down. Imagine how powerful it would be to be able to read these messages and be able to go back over them if and when needed."

"I have been keeping a journal of my life since meeting Almedio, and each time I have recalled a message or shared a message with someone like we have, I write it down."

"I would love to see that some time, Christina."

"Well, I don't know if I would have the confidence to share that with a wider audience."

"Maybe that is you taking off the kindling from your fire that might sweep the globe? Let me order that taxi for you."

Chapter Thirty

Ben opened up his email. There was a reply from Howe & Horwath Solicitors. His stomach rolled with guilt at having emailed them. The mouse hovered over the delete icon having only read the subject line. He got up and locked the office door and sat again. He read the subject line again.

'Re our emails to Christina Wilkins.'
He swallowed to try and create some saliva to relieve a mouth that was as dry as sawdust. Click!

'Dear Mr Williamson,
Thank you for contacting us. We note that you had accidentally come across an email sent to our client Christina Wilkins and for this reason, you have contacted us.

We cannot, of course, discuss this case with you, and we are only seeking to make contact with Christina Wilkins to finalize the estate of her late mother.

We note that she had been staying with you, but now you say she has left. We would ask if you have any forwarding address for Christina or any other contact details that may assist us in reaching out to her.

We understand that there may be some reluctance by Christina to bring this to a conclusion, as this has been a distressing time. Should you meet Christina in the future and the situation merits, we would be grateful if you could recommend that she contact us.
It is important that we finalize the estate of her mother, Laura Wilkins.
Without Prejudice
Yours Sincerely

Martin Colins

Howe & Horwath Solicitors.'

Ben heard a vehicle on the gravel, a few moments later he heard Anna.
"Hello, Miss Christina, did you have a lovely day?"
Ben closed his email program and logged out. He got up and unlocked his office door, without making a sound, took a deep breath and opened the door.
He looked at the large bag that Christina was holding.
"A productive day then?"
"Oh, not really, just a hat for when I leave. Mary asked me to get the cab to take Michael home if he is still here."
"He has been wondering the gardens all day on and off. Have you seen him, Anna?"
"Si, Mr Ben, He was down near the garden buildings a while ago. I saw him talking with Marcello."
"Let's see if we can find him." Said Ben.
Christina walked towards her room.
"I will just drop this bag in my room and give you a hand, Anna."
Both Anna and Ben were already on their way out of the front door.

Christina dropped the bag on her bed and caught sight of Marcelo on the lawn tractor through the French doors. She opened the door to wave, but he was too far away and didn't notice her.

She ran across the lawn towards him, but as she got closer, he turned the tractor and drove towards the garden buildings. By the time Christina caught up with him, he had parked the tractor and was climbing off.

"Have you seen Michael?" She said.

"Who?"

"Michael. Anna said he was here with you and in the gardens somewhere."

Michael appeared from the side of the building.

"You're looking for me?"

"Yes, there is a taxi waiting for you. Mary asked me to tell you to save some money and get the return ride back home."

"Ok, I'll say goodbye and hope to see you soon."

Marcelo raised his hand as Michael started a brisk walk back towards the house. Christina called out "Bye."

She turned to speak to Marcello as she saw Ben and Anna approaching the building from the other side.

She called out to them. "It's OK, no need to panic, he's already on his way."

Ben waited for Anna to catch up and they both turned towards the house. Christina turned back to Marcello.

"Might see you at breakfast in the morning?"

"Yes, if Anna invites me."

"Somehow I am sure she will." Christina smiled.

She started to walk away and then stopped dead, tipped her head back and breathed a deliberate long breath through her nose.

She turned back to Marcello.

"Have you been cooking something?"

Before Marcello could say a word, Ben called out. He was waiting for Christina to catch up.

She turned back to Marcello again. "I'll be back later."
She left to catch up with Ben.

"You had a good day then?" said Ben as she caught up.
"Yes, Mary was great to be with."
"Listen, I don't mean to pry, so please don't get upset. The other day when you left your login on the computer, I didn't realize it was your email until I saw something from some lawyers in London. By the time I realized it was not for me, I had read that they wanted you to contact them."

"Yes, it's something I must get around to, but there is no rush. Don't worry; I will not leave the login open again. Anyway, I will be leaving soon."
"What? Why? You don't have to leave yet, do you?"
"Yes my leg is all good, and there is nothing for me to stay here for now. Sorry, I didn't mean that in a bad way. I just mean that I want to be on the road again."
"Where are you going? London?"
"No, why did you say London? Ah, the lawyer thing."
"Sorry again, I assumed that you would need to sort that out before you headed off traveling the world again."
"We'll see. I don't know yet. Maybe I will throw a dart at the map and see where it leads to."
"I knew someone like you once," said Ben
"You mean the girl in the mask?'
"Yes."
"It's ok, I asked Mary about her, and she told me what she knew, which was not very much."
"Mmm. Ok."
"Tell you what, I'll make a deal with you, as I will be leaving soon."
"Sounds interesting what do you have in mind?"
"After dinner tonight, you tell me all about the girl in the mask and I will tell you all about the lawyers in London."
"Not sure about that being such a good deal."

"Well, as it's unlikely that we will see each other in the future, what's to lose?
Look I don't want to pressurize you into talking about her. Let's forget it. It was a bad idea."

They were coming up to the house when Anna called out. 'Mr Ben, Christina. Come through the kitchen door; your shoes are all covered in grass.'
"I swear she is my mother sometimes," Ben whispered to Christina.

"You're very lucky to have her; she is lovely."
"Leave your shoes at the door, and I will attend to them later for you."
Ben and Christina went into the kitchen.
"Anna, it seems like Christina will be leaving us soon so maybe we will have a special dinner before she leaves."
"No, nothing special, I hate that sort of thing."
"Ah, Miss Christina, we will miss you so much. Won't we Mr Ben? It's lovely to have a lady in the house. Mr Ben, why can't Miss Christina stay longer?"
"Don't look at me. I have offered, It's not up to me." Ben lifted his arms up.
"There, you can stay longer Miss Christina."
"Yes thank you very much, but I have places to go and things I want to see."

Ben put his arms up again towards Anna. "It's a hopeless case; we have to let her go."
"Ok, enough of the manipulation by both of you. It's not going to work."
Anna made a tutting sound as she turned towards the stove, where something needed attention.

Ben looked at his watch. "I have a tad more work to do ready for Monday morning, so let's say we eat at about 7:30 tonight. Is that ok with you?"

Christina shrugged her shoulders.

"Yes, what works for you is good for me."

Anna turned back from the stove again.

"Si, 7:30 is good."

"I'm off for a hot bath then," said Christina.

"I will run that for you, Miss Christina."

"No, you have enough to do here. I can manage fine."

Anna looked at Ben who threw his arms up again. "I told you, don't look at me. I'm not getting involved. You can sort it out between yourselves."

Ben turned and left the kitchen. Christina followed a moment later.

Christina closed the door to her room, went to the bathroom and started to run the bath. Back on the bed, she pulled one of the hats from the bag and tried it on, looking in the rapidly steaming mirror through the bathroom door. She reached down to the lower shelf of the bedside cabinet and pulled out two brown journals. One of them had messages written on the front the other didn't.

She replaced the one with the messages and then took the other one to the bathroom. She closed the door, undressed and slipped into the warm water, closing her eyes in a moment of bliss.

A few seconds later, she reached for the journal and thumbed through the last few pages and started to read.

Almedio told me that living my life while observing it would take me on the path to my destiny, my purpose in life.

'What is this all about? What sense is there to be made from it? I feel incomplete, lost. I know there is more.'

She laid there in the bath a moment, pondering on the last sentence. 'I feel incomplete; I feel lost. I know there is more.'

After a few moments, she thumbed over to the next page and continued reading.

'My doubts gnaw at me like a dog gnaws a bone. I know I have something in me that is greater than me but why can't I find that and get on with life? Does life have to be a struggle?

I should get a job, settle down and live the nine to five routine; maybe that is the answer.

Stupid!!
Yes, you are stupid to think this way.

Today I am going to cut off my plaster. When I look back at the events of the last few weeks I have not seen any dots in my life that were purposeful.

A car hits me and breaks my leg. I can no longer travel. I am stuck here in this house while I watch my life revolve around nothing. I am angry with life, very angry.'

Next page.

'I have to stop this anger. Ben has been good to me over this. He could have left me in the hospital and not even bothered.

We have talked at night after dinner, and somehow I find myself sharing messages with him. Surely to be sharing messages with someone who has achieved all they want in life, with great wealth is not my purpose.

As I write these words, I feel a pull to thinking about the tattoos and how I have not fulfilled my contract by not having them done. I don't know if I can do this.

Almedio told me that my life, all life, is not meant to be a struggle to be played out in mind, but I feel this sometimes, and it frustrates the hell out of me.'

Next page.

'Today I am feeling confident the last few journal entries have been a bit down. I have let my focus slip.

I have decided to stop being so angry towards Ben and make the most of my time here.

When I leave, I don't know where to go. Almedio thought that New York is a good place for me to visit but cities like these are not to my liking.

Maybe I will go back to Peru. See more of South America or London.

There, you said it, London.

You know you have to face this. You know you have to get over the guilt.

I know that Mum loved me as much as I loved her. I could not watch her being eaten away. I would have liked to have known where she traveled to in her last six months before she was forced to live in that bed wasting
Christina closed the journal and let the tears roll down into the bath water. It felt good to cry and not worry about wiping any tears away.

She opened the journal again.

'London, yes. I must go, I have to deal with this. What could Mum have left in that box that she felt was important?

I can't deny that I am curious, but at the same time, I don't want to remember mum like she ended up. I only want the good memories. Why can't that be so?

Almedio said that memories are neither good nor bad in their existence, it is only the right or wrong life that we breathe into them that gives them power over us.

I should try harder with this and not give life to bad memories or maybe even try to learn a method to swap a bad memory for a good one.

Oh- journal, I even wonder about you sometimes. I wonder why I need write all this about myself?

What if someone read this? They would think it was a mad person writing it. On the other hand, maybe they could relate to my writings.'

Next page.

'Today I have been thinking about the roots that I brought with me. I have since found out that I should not have brought them into the USA. Almedio must have known this when he told me to take them. I can't believe that I brought them in.

If I had known that it was wrong, then I might have been caught.

Anyway, no harm was done. I will continue to carry them until the right occasion comes up.

Almedio said that the roots would leave me at the right time.

I have been writing down all the messages as they come back to me in a separate journal. I have no idea what I am going to do with it or even if it will be completed. Is there ever a completion of anything?

'You're rambling, stop it!'

Next page.

'The tattoos come into my mind almost daily. I know I made the contract, but it's such a big thing for me to have done. It's for life and not sure if I can cope with that.

You are delusional Christina- or rather, you are trying to deceive yourself. You KNOW why you have to have the tattoos completed. The ONLY reason you are fighting this is that you know that those tattoos will release so many more messages.

There- that told me, didn't it?

'Now get on with it and get them done.'

Next page.

'I have decided to go ahead with the tattoos, but I am going to let them come to me. I will allow the right tattooist to find me. I know this will happen and I will meet the right person at the right time.'

Christina closed the journal and put it down by the side of the bath. She slipped further down into the water, and her head tilted back, so only her mouth and nose were above the water line. Then a quick full submerge and back up again.

A few minutes later, wrapped in a large towel, she rinsed out the bath, air dried and then got dressed.

It will be dinner time soon, but the bath had made her tired, so she lay on the bed and dozed a while.

She was jarred back from her doze with a tapping on the French doors. She had earlier closed the curtains so she could not see who it was. She went over and slightly opened the curtains. There was Marcello.

"Hi, I thought you would have wanted me to prepare the roots for you?"
"What? Have you brewed them? You had no right to do that. Did you use all the roots?"
Marcello stood his ground.
"Yes I did, and I did this correctly, and you didn't have the second part that must go with the root to release the compound."
"That is not the point-" Marcello cut her off mid sentence. "Tt is the point. I had the knowledge from my grandfather of how to do this. Ok, you have taken the ceremony, but you do not know how to create the drink. Without me, you have just roots."
"I don't care what you say, you had no right to do-" Christina stopped dead. Marcello looked behind to see if someone was there and that was why Christina had stopped so abruptly. They were still alone.

"What's the matter?" Asked Marcello.
"The roots would leave me at the right time." Christina murmured.
"What? What are you saying?" Asked Marcello.
Christina reached out and put her hand on his shoulder.
"It's Ok. Everything is OK. Let's meet tomorrow at the garden shed to talk about this."
"Christina!"
Anna was calling for dinner.
"Ok, I'll be there in a moment," Christina called back.
"Is that OK? Can we talk tomorrow?" She turned back to Marcello.
"Er- yes, but it's Sunday tomorrow, it's my day off. I have arranged to meet someone at 5 pm to do some work for them.
Why do you want to talk? Are you going to tell anyone? I will lose my job if you do."

"It's Ok Marcello, don't worry. We will talk tomorrow after lunch; it will not take long, ok?"

Christina closed the door and drapes and picked up her journal and thumbed back a few pages. There was the line.

'The roots would leave me at the right time.'
She picked up a pen and turned to a new page and wrote.
'Is this the way this works? Do I have to stop trying so hard and instead just listen and observe? Do I have to accept that the actions of others as they interact with me might be me being on THEIR radar at the right time?

Maybe none of this is as hard as I think it is. But my leg? How can physical injury like a broken leg play a part in all this?'

She closed the journal and headed for the dining room.

Ben was already seated as Christina walked in.
"Amazing," he said.
"What's amazing? Me, you mean?"
"I was referring to your leg."
"How do you know I have great legs?"
"What? What's got into you?" Ben was flustered, seeing a side of Christina he had not experienced before.
"Sorry, it's just me, yanking your chain. I have a habit of doing that when I get to know someone. Mmm… whatever Anna has cooked tonight, it smells great."

"That will be this, then."
Ben lifted the lid from one large dish that was between them. The smell intensified.
"I may get used to all this vegetable stuff after all," said Ben.

Christina served herself and then turned the handles of the large fork and spoon towards Ben, who then served himself.

"So my leg, you were saying?"

Ben swallowed his first mouthful.

"I was thinking how amazing the human body is and how it repairs itself. Bones knitted together and now you are walking like nothing ever happened. Maybe it was all meant to be?"

"What was? You driving into me had to happen, you mean?"

"Ok, that seems a bit extreme, I know but you know what I mean, right?"

"Yes, I know what you're saying, but I'm not sure about breaking bones."

The rest of the meal was consumed quickly, and once again, they were in the lounge. Christina was the first to talk.

"So what about our deal, then?" Christina pointed to the picture above the fireplace.

Christina observed as Ben shifted on the couch.

"Tell you what. As I suggested the deal, how about I go first?"

Ben relaxed and leaned back.

"Sounds like a good plan."

"But a deal is a deal, right?" She said.

"Absolutely, but there is not much to tell about her, believe me."

Christina placed her hands to her face and looked down at the carpet for a moment.

"Ok, where to start I am thinking."

"Where did you go to school? Where did you grow up?"

"I grew up in London. Well, London is a big place. We lived in Willesden Junction to start with. That was where I was born and went to my first school. It was not that nice of a place to live, but when you're young, you don't know those sorts of things.

From when I could remember, Mum was always saying to me 'It's not important where you physically live, but it's critical where you mentally live.'

She would then get me to imagine living somewhere else, somewhere we both liked. From there, we moved to Edgware Road; this was great as it was walking distance to Oxford Street. I made great friends there."

"What about your father?"

"I don't have a father- Well, of course, I have a father, but I don't know who he was. He could be dead for all I know."

"Didn't you ever ask about him?"

"Yes, but it was never a big deal. Mum and I were happy; she used to say we were a winning team, no matter what happened."

Christina's eyes become defocused.

"What are you thinking about?" Asked Ben.

"How much I miss her."

"I'm sorry, I didn't mean to upset you."

"No- it's ok, a few tears never hurt anyone, eh?"

Anyway, mum had a good job working at a law firm.

When I was twenty she become ill, it was a type of bone cancer. She coped well at first but then became weaker and weaker. Two years later she was bedridden. We were very lucky, as she had insurance to pay for all the care that was involved.

She kept telling me to go and travel and not to stay and watch her waste away. Every day she said for me to go and see the world, to explore and live the life that she hadn't.

She talked of distant lands that I could go and see. It was like she had planned it all. She had even set up what she called a travel fund for me.

One day, it all came to a head. She was very fragile and made me promise that I would not watch her die. She said that she had always wanted to go to Bolivia. She said she had seen pictures of it when she was much younger and always wanted to go but never did.

She pleaded with me to go to Bolivia and tell her all about it when I returned. The trip was booked for three weeks' time."

Christina began to cry; Ben moved to the same sofa and put his arms around her. She responded, and they hugged each other for a few moments until the tears subsided. Ben got up to get some tissues and then sat back on the other sofa after he handed them to her.

"I am sorry now that we agreed to share stories. I didn't want to upset you or cause distress in any way. We can forget the whole thing if you like."

"No, it's ok, I feel better for it. I don't know why I told you all that. I was only going to tell you about the lawyers."

"Maybe it had to come out; it's not good to keep all that emotion inside."

"Maybe— anyway, I better finish now."

"Only if you want."

"So while I was in Bolivia, mum died. The thing was I knew it was why she was sending me away. She knew that she had come to the end of it all.

I had very mixed emotions at the time and didn't go back, not even for the funeral."

Ben handed some more tissues over.

"So how long ago was this?"

"Over 12 months ago."

"And for twelve months you kept traveling, and that was how you ended up in Peru?"

"Yes."

Ben leaned forward towards Christina.

"I think your mother was a very special lady and she showed the depth of her love for you to set you free at the time she knew it had to be. I think she knew that if you had been there, then likely you would not have traveled and lived out the things she wanted to do. Now she gets to see the world through her daughter's eyes."

Ben handed over more tissues.

"Are you sure you can afford all these?"

They both had a smile.

"It was a short while after that, that the lawyers tried to get me to go back to London to deal with the estate.
"Maybe that is what you need to do now?"
"I'm not sure the time is right yet."
"May I say something that might not go down too well?"

Christina sat up straight, lips together.
"In my office, there are twenty guys under my supervision. I pass information to them that they are then to act on. Most of them will either stay in those chairs until they retire, leave voluntarily or they get fired. Every one of them wants my job. They all want promotions, and many of them are capable, but they are unable to deal with issues that come about without some form of hand holding.

They are capable, they know what to do, but they do not instigate the action based on their observations. They do not take control of the situation. If they took control and made their own decisions, even if those decisions did not work out at first, they would be well on the way to success.

Now that's a long sort of explanation but— as I see it— and I am sorry if this upsets you, you need to take control of this, and then you will be able to move on."
Christina looked down into her lap and toyed with some tissues.
"I know you're right. I have to face it."
"One more thing that may help you. I think that as long as you leave this all open, you'll likely feel you are not finally on your own".
Christina looked up from her lap, took a deep breath in and exhaled at the end of which she said "I know you're right, I have known it for a long time. I know I have to deal with it."
"If I can help you in any way with flights etc. then let me know; I am sure we can get something sorted."
"Thank you, but I still have some money saved, and I am traveling on that. I will get a job when that runs out."

"Ok, but the offer is there."

"Thank you— well, now it's your turn. Hopefully, you will not need any tissues."

Ben shifted his position and looked up at the picture.

"That was a long time ago, and there has been a lot of water under the bridge since then."

"What is her name?"

"Louise — Lou Lou, I called her.

We met in school. She lived with a distant relative of hers after her parents both died in a car crash. The relative died, and she was all alone in the world."

"Like me," said Christina.

"I was going to ask about that— don't you have any family?"

"No, there was just mum and me."

Ben looked away from the picture and turned back to Christina.

"It's strange, isn't it, when you think about that?"

"What?"

"Being alone; I was alone with my father, you were alone with your mother, and Lou Lou was alone as well."

"The lonely hearts club," said Christina.

"Yes, pretty sad when you think about it."

"So you paint— I mean, it was you who painted the picture? It's rather good."

Ben reached into his pocket and pulled out his wallet. Inside was a faded photograph about the size of a passport photo. He handed it to Christina.

"I painted it from this."

Christina glanced back and forwards from the photograph to the picture. "I take that back; it's not good, it's amazing. You even got the water stain in the corner of the mask. That's cool."

She handed the photograph back.

"So, what's the story with your painting, you went to art school or something?"

Ben rubbed his hands together and then rubbed them down his cheeks, stretching his face down.

"No, I wanted to, and she wanted me to." Ben looked again at the picture.

"Why not then?"

"Dad got me a job in the firm where I am now and insisted that there was no future in painting. He was right, I suppose. I would not have acquired what I have painting pictures."

"Almedio told me once that wealth, true wealth would be better measured by personal happiness, as opposed to dollars hoarded."

"He may well have a point there."

"So where is Lou Lou now?"

"Of that, I have no idea."

"And you tried to find her or just gave up."

"I tried to find her. I did everything I could and even hired detectives. It was like she dropped off the planet."

"Why did she leave?"

"She left the morning after the photograph was taken. Things had been tense for a while; my father insisted that I become independent before I started 'gallivanting' off with anyone, as he put it.

We had a row after the fair ground, nothing too serious but it had been building up for a while. She had also changed a little, in so much that there was a seriousness about her plans for the future.

When I got up that morning, she had gone. There was a note saying that if we were to be together, then now was the time for it to happen. She had it in her mind that we could travel the world on nothing more than my painting skills and our love for each other.

Fuck."

Ben reached over for a tissue.

"It's been a long time since she has caused a tear to flow."

"So she left you on the morning, and that was it?"

"Not quite, in the note, she gave me a deadline for us to both start our adventure, as she put it. That deadline was to meet at the fairground where the picture had been taken at noon that day."

"You didn't go?"
"I couldn't; I had a meeting with the firm that I work for now. Anyway, she had done that before but in a more joking way. For example, she would say meet me tomorrow at whatever time she thought of, and we will elope and be married. Obviously, this time was different, very different. She never called. I knew she was angry from the argument we had the night before, but I had underestimated that."

Ben looked back at the picture and then back to Christina.
"From that day, I never saw her again. Well, that's it, now you know about the girl in the mask. I told you there wasn't much to it."

"Sad though eh! I mean what might have been?" said Christina.
"Sad or happy ever after, we will never know for sure what might have been. As I said, that was a very long time ago-
Look, I'm a bit tired, and tomorrow I want to make an early visit up to see Dad. I need to sit on the grass and have a talk with him. I know that might sound nuts sitting in a cemetery talking like that, but-" — Christina cut in.

"There is nothing nuts about that. It's rather sweet in a way. Why not talk as long as we want to ones we have lost?"
"I was thinking of going on my own if that's ok with you?"
"Yes, perfect. I have some writing I want to do anyway."

Ben got up and left the room. She looked up at the picture and started to think if there was any way he could find Lou Lou.

Chapter Thirty-One

The noise on the gravel from the camper leaving woke Christina. It had been a night full of dreams, but not one of them could she remember.

There was the familiar tap on the door.

"Christina, Christina."

"Yes, Ok. I'm awake."

"Everyone has overslept this morning. I have left some breakfast out for you. I am leaving now to visit my brother. I will see you later, Miss Christina. Is that ok?"

"Yes, fine Anna. Have a lovely day."

A few minutes later she heard more gravel crunching as another vehicle left. She stretched and turned over to look at the clock. It was late - 10 am. She grabbed her daily journal and began to write.

'It's coming to an end. It's time for me to leave and yet there is a part of me that wants to hold on a few more days. I don't usually feel this way when traveling. I get the urge to move, and I go.

Why does this place have this effect on me?

I look back now at all the events since the accident, and it's hard to make any rhyme or reason to it all.

I have to meet Marcello in a couple of hours, but I don't know what to say to him. He has used the roots I brought with me. My concern is what if they should not have been for him.

Almedio said I would find the person they were for. How could that be Marcello? I would never have met Marcello without the accident.

Is universal intelligence willing injury to guide a person's life?'
Enough questions for today Journal. Breakfast!

She showered and went into the kitchen. Anna had left out some cereal and fruit. The house seemed deadly quiet with only her there. She ate breakfast and decided to explore the house, starting upstairs.

At the top of the sweeping staircase, there was a long hallway with tall windows that ran floor to ceiling, with views of the grounds in both directions. Along the corridor, several doors led off into other rooms.

She walked to one of the windows at the end of the hallway and looked out to the grounds. She noticed how everything from plants, bushes, and trees seemed to enhance one another. It was like someone had stood at this window and instructed an army of workers below to plant everything in its perfect place.

'Not quite the jungle,' she murmured to herself.

She started to walk along the hallway, just cracking each door, not going into any of them but seeing bedroom after bedroom.

About halfway along she cracked a door open, but this was not a bedroom; it was another hallway albeit much shorter. There was a set of double doors at the end.

She tapped on one of the double doors and then questioned why she did that, as she was the only one in the house. She pulled on one of the doors which caused both of them to open. The room was bursting with light. She opened the doors up further, and her eyes were immediately drawn upwards to the height of the huge glass domed ceiling. Then down to the entire solid glass wall in front. It was only then that she noticed the easels and the painting. There were paintings on the walls and easels holding paintings at different stages of completion.

They ranged from landscapes to portraits, each one hypnotically carrying the mind into the scene.

She felt the need to sit down and try to take all this in. There was a single chair placed in the front and center of the room, and there it was again. The girl in the mask, only this one was huge. The chair and easel perfectly placed to allow viewing it in the best light possible. The intricacies of this painting were breathtaking, Christina sat there captivated.

Some drifting smoke outside drew her attention from the painting. She got up to investigate; it was coming from the wooded area of the gardens. She knew this was where the garden sheds were and where she had arranged to meet Marcello. She took a last look around the room and closed the double doors behind her.

Back in her room she grabbed a light jacket from her backpack and went out through the French doors, heading towards the smoke.

Marcello was sitting by the stove, stoking it with some larger pieces of wood. There was an old kettle on top that was not far from boiling.

As Christina pushed open the door, she noticed his right leg started bouncing up and down the moment he saw her.

"Tea?" he said, rubbing his hands up and down the top of his legs.

"I'm sorry Christina. I was wrong to make the mixture without you. I wanted to-"

"Stop-" Christina put her one of her palms out towards Marcello.

"Yes, let's have some tea." She said.

Marcello's leg stopped bouncing up and down.

"I brought us some cake as well." He said.

Christina's smile returned as he got up and came back with two mugs containing a tea bag in each. He pulled up another chair. Christina slipped off her jacket and hung it over the back.

He poured boiling water over the tea bags and then placed the kettle on a concrete block beside the stove.

"How strong do you like it?" He was swirling the tea bag with a spoon.

"That's it now; I only like it weak, the color of whiskey."

Marcello scooped both bags out of the mugs, opened up the door on the front of the stove and flicked them into the fire.

"So, I am sorry about-" Christina cut in again.

"I don't know what all of this means. I don't know if you did right or wrong. I was angry at first, as you had not asked me. But then if you had asked me I might have said no.

We are where we are, and that's it. How much is left?"

"Nothing, I used it all. Sorry."

"How much did you make?"

Marcello pointed to the two clear glass beer bottles marked poison.

'Is that all, it doesn't seem like much."

"You can't make much without the proper leaves that only grow where the root grows. My grandfather taught me of other leaves that could be added but nowhere near as powerful, so the root liquid has to be distilled more. This is why there is not so much. But still, enough for two or three people."

A truck engine grew louder until it was right outside the building, where it stopped.

"Oh crap, it's Jerry. I forgot I ordered some bark chippings. Hold on while I tell him where to tip them, so I can get rid of him before he tries to come in for tea."

Marcello closed the door to the shed behind him. Christina could hear Marcello talking to the truck driver.

"Follow me down this way, and I will show you where to tip them."

The sound of the engine faded as the truck moved away.

As Christina was sipping the tea, her eyes caught the bottles marked poison. She got up to inspect them closer. The contents looked the same. The tops were sealed with a piece of plastic and an elastic band.

She took a bottle down and pulled the edge of the plastic up, with caused the elastic band to fly off. She put the bottle to her nose. It caused her stomach to roll and an instant flashback to the ceremony.

She put the plastic back on top and looked down on the bench to see where the band had gone. There was a spiral bound ring pad with a hard cover there, and the band had landed in the spiral. She picked up the book to pull the band free and then put the band back on the bottle and replaced it back on the shelf. She then replaced the book where it had been, and that was when she noticed a faded line illustration on the cover.

She flicked over the top hardcover to see a most intricate pencil sketch. Another page and more sketches, another page and there were five smaller sketches with names written on them. She turned another page over; her stomach rolled, and a sick feeling worked its way right up into her throat. She held onto the side of the bench and took a few deep breaths.

She murmured 'How-'
    The door opened.
    "I got rid of him, told him I was busy."
    Christina continued to hold onto the bench.
    Marcello walked over. "What's up?"
    "Oh, you found my outlines. You like them?" He Said
    "Beautiful, what's this?"
    Christina turned the pad horizontal.
    "Merging rivers, it's a doodle. I sometimes go to the river and take the sketch pad; that probably influenced it.
    It would not look too good like that though, it would need some shading on the final image.

It's difficult sometimes. Customers tell me what they want, but they can't draw so I have to try and interpret their idea before we lay them down."

"Can I add a line to the left of the rivers?"

"Yes sure, go for it. But let me get a proper sketch pencil. He walked over to the door and picked up an aluminum briefcase and brought it back to the bench. He pushed some tools back to clear a space for it and flipping open the catches; he lifted the lid.

Christina's' stomach rolled for the second time, this time it was much stronger. She held onto the bench and took some deep breaths.

"You ok? What's up? You have gone as white as a ghost. Are you sick?"

Marcello looked up at the beer bottles.

"You didn't drink any of it, did you?"

"No- it's ok. How long have you been a tattooist?"

Christina was looking at the contents of the case.

"Oh, for five years now but I have been drawing since I was a kid. My grandfather was a tattooist, but he did not have anything like this."

Marcello stroked the chrome tattoo gun that was embedded in the foam of the case.

"I want to do this full time one day when I have saved enough money to be independent."

Marcello handed Christina a pencil.

"Sure it's ok for me to draw on it?" She asked.

"Yes, go for it."

Christina drew a vertical line which then sloped back down to the left of the rivers. The image was now complete

"That's it? That's all you wanted to add?"

"Yes; it's now complete."

Marcello scratched his head and then shrugged his shoulders.

"Could you tattoo this on my arms?"

"Of course, it's an easy one but show me where."

Christina rolled up her left sleeve.

"It has to go from here-" she pointed from high up on the inside of her upper arm "down to here," pointing to about 2 inches above the inside of her wrist. Marcello tilted his head to one side. "They are big tattoos. Are you sure?"

"Yes sure."

"They are for life, you know?"

"Look— can you do them?"

"Them?"

"Yes, it has to be on both arms, a mirror image of each other."

"Well, it may take a few attempts to line them up when we transfer the outline from the paper to your arms. But yes I can do that, no problem."

"Ok, so when can we make a start? How long will it take?"

"About three to four hours each arm. It will be too much to do in one day."

"Ok, so when? How about tomorrow?"

"Tomorrow is Monday; I have to work. Why the hurry?"

"I'm leaving soon."

"Leaving-where are you going?"

"How can we make this happen?"

"I could come in early and finish gardening by lunch time."

"Then, we can do it here?"

"It's not the best place, it's not very clean, and you will have to lie down."

"How about that?" she said, pointing to an old door leaning against the wall.

"We could put that across two chairs."

"Are you sure? That is not normally how this is done."

"Can you do this or not? I have to know if this is the way it's meant to be."

"Meant to be?"

"I'll tell you tomorrow. So we have a date then, after lunch tomorrow?"

"Ok, if that's the way you want to do it, then yes."

Christina grabbed her jacket and went to leave.

"One more thing- shave your arms."

"What?"

"Shave your arms in the complete area where the tattoos will be."

"Why?"

"Any hairs, even tiny ones, can interfere when I lay down the ink."

Christina nodded and closed the door behind her.

Chapter Thirty-Two

Ben pulled the camper over, beside the overgrown hedge at the cemetery. He pushed through the gate and emerged into the well-manicured cemetery. He walked over and tapped his father's headstone before returning to the bench.

'Hope you're awake, dad. I have fucked up, and right now, I am pretty pissed with life.

I know you only wanted the best for us both and I know that you worked your butt off to make a success of your life that you then passed on to me.

But I have to question this.

I met this girl, and she has - well, really messed with my head. She is very young which makes it even worse in a way as I am very attracted to her.

I don't know what the fuck to do. Where does it end? What is the point in accumulating more and more money? A billion dollars and not a soul I love to share it with.

Sometimes I feel like quitting everything and walking away. You remember Lou Lou Dad?'.

Ben dropped his head and stared at the grass.

When he looked back up, there was a bird perched on the top of the headstone.

'A bird dad?' Is that the best you can offer?' He laughed.

A gust of wind blew some leaves across the grass and over Ben's feet. I have to go and find her Dad; I know she is out there somewhere. No matter what it takes, no matter where she is, even if she has a whole family around her, I have to do it. I just have to say- Well, I don't know what I would want to say- just something.'

Ben got up and walked towards the headstone. The bird flew off, and Ben tapped the top of the stone.

'Thanks for the chat, Dad. See you soon.'

Christina reached for her journal.

She wrote:

'Lost and confused' or 'found and clear' might be a good entry today. Almedio told me that the roots I carried with me would find the right person. How do I know that person is Marcello?

What if I am wrong? What are the consequences of not detecting the right dots, the right twists and turns?

And then, the contract I made during the ceremony to have the tattoos. How do I know that Marcello is right for this?

Tears started to stream down her face and onto the journal. They were tears of enlightenment.

'I have remembered one of the messages from the ceremony.
    As I wrote about the consequences of not detecting the right dots at the right time, tears flooded, as the knowledge came to me. The answer is simple, as it always seems to turn out to be.

If we are living our life like the ship's radar and we are noticing the dots, how can we ever know that we are taking the right course of action?
    If you interpret something and take action on that something, but it turns out that it was not the right choice, it doesn't matter, because the fluidity of the dots will realign, to prompt and reposition you for the right path which you are seeking.

Marcello has the roots, and there are some factors about why that might be right.

He knew about them.

He had the skills to process them.

Then, what about my tattoo contract? Marcello has a drawing of almost exactly the image I saw during the ceremony, on the other side of the world.

I was hesitant and resistant to having the tattoos completed. Was I being directed to a person that I would feel comfortable letting them tattoo my arms?

There appear to be more questions than answers, but the truth is that the answer is not to try and rationalize it; rather, go with the flow of life as it unfolds.

The things that Almedio told me I would find seem further away than ever. Part of me thinks my life has been put on hold by accident and another part of me thinks this had to happen.

Maybe the tattoos will open the floodgates, and I will once again have access to the messages that came to me during the ceremony.'

Ben arrived at the lake and parked in the same spot as when Christina had been with him. He put the kettle on for tea and then grabbed a folding chair.

"How are you?"

It was the original owner of the lake.

"Saw you pull up on your own this time and thought I would come and say hello."

"Hi, Jeff- I've just put the kettle on, sit and have a cuppa?"

"Don't mind if I do, don't mind at all."

Ben pulled out another folding chair and the kettle starting to sing.

"No milk, is that right?"

"Yep, you got it, son."

Ben went into the camper and returned with two mugs of tea.

"There you go." He handed Jeff the tea.

"You know, there is something I have never asked you but always wanted to."

"Well shoot, young fella, but I can't promise anything."

"Why did you sell the place to me?"

Jeff blew across the top of the cup of tea a few times.

"Well, it seems to me that there are right and wrong things in life. That morning with the wire, I remember it like it was yesterday.

You see, my wife, my sweetheart, used to say that we never owned this place. She said that ownership was a great lie of life. She said that we are only ever guardians of what we have around us.

She used to remind me to guard everything around me, not for ourselves living up here but for the next person who would inherit the guardian status. I used to pull her leg about the only thing that mattered were the dollars it took to buy it.

She would give me that look that meant I was wrong and she was right. As they always do, eh? You know that look right, Ben?'"

Ben laughed. "Yes, I do."

"So, anyway before we met that day, I was talking to my dear sweet departed about what was happening and that the bank was going to foreclose the place. I joked with her, saying that the bank would not make an excellent guardian of the place. The morning I met you, I was heading into town. As I drove up the track, I looked out across the lake and imagined I saw my sweetheart down by the waterside. This was one of her favorite spots, right here.

Anyway, as I was driving, the thought of a guardian came to mind and then I saw some careless person with wire around their tire."

He winked at Ben, who returned the same with a smile.

"So that was it?" Said Ben

"No, not at all; you remember we spent some time together that day?"

"Yes."

"Well, it was during that time that I kept thinking about my sweetheart and then all of a sudden, I remembered something that happened to her many years ago.

We were out fencing, and I had stretched up the wire, real tight. It broke and whipped back and started to coil up. It flew down the line to where she was standing and whipped all around her, wrapping her in a wire cage.

I ran down to her thinking, she must be injured, but she was laughing. When she stopped, and I got the wire from her, she turned and said 'There you go, Jeffery, that is because we are guardians of the place and this work is making it ready for the next guardians.'

I said she was a lucky lunatic.

That wire Ben, on your wheel that day, that was the spot where it happened. I didn't give it much thought when it first happened but later in the day, we were talking, and for some reason, I was telling you our life story and all about the place it then started to come back to me. When you later made the offer to buy the place and let me stay here, it seemed to me that my sweetheart had found a guardian for the place."

Jeff reached out, took Ben's hand and shook it, saying

"That sir is why I sold the place to you. Can't say it was not a worry, as you could have been one of those tricksters who kept coming up here to buy the place to build houses. But it all turned out good in the end.

That was another saying of my sweetheart- 'It'll all come good in the end.' "So anyway, what's troubling you?"

"Nothing, all's good."

"Ben, it's me you're talking to. An old fella like me knows a thing or two about people, so what's the story?"

"Oh, I don't know. I have a lot going on. I think of this place and your life, and sometimes it gets me thinking what the hell is this all for. Sorry, not your life Jeff. I mean my life and what I do with it, which sometimes doesn't seem very much."

"My sweetheart used to say that sometimes rich people had little of value in their lives. She used to say that money might overtake a person and they might delude themselves that more money means more freedom."

"I would have liked to have met your dear lady."

"Probably not the first time you wouldn't; she was very straight and to the point. She never said anything with three words when two would do the same job. Ah- she was a darling that one, I tell you. So- you got a lot of money Ben?"

"Seems to me like some of the 'direct to the point' rubbed off onto you," said Ben.

"Maybe so, but we can chew the fat all day here or get down to the bones of things. So-"

"Well, when you say a lot of money what do you mean? Ok, sorry- yes, a lot is a good description."

"Did your daddy leave it to you?"

"Some yes but not most. Most I made on my own."

"Ok and what do you do with that money other than buying up old people's homes and lakes and let them stay living there?"

Ben rubbed his chin without saying anything.

"Like I suspected, not a lot. Tell me, do you have anyone special in your life, anyone that you love enough to give everything away for?"

Ben got up and walked a few steps towards the water side.

"Can you still skim a pebble across the water?" asked Jeff. Ben looked back at him.

"Well, can you?"

Ben looked around on the ground and selected a stone. He threw it out, and it skimmed, making three hops across the water. "Nice, you can still do it. Tell me what you did?"

"What do you mean? I threw a stone, and it skimmed."

"No, that was not what happened at all; back up and tell me again."

"I picked up a stone and then skimmed it across the water."

"Let me make it easier on you, son. You see, most people don't pay attention to their lives. When you bent down to pick up the stone, you had already spent some time looking for the right stone. But that part, you forgot about. You paid no attention to that part. But that part was the most important part. Without selecting the right stone, the rest would likely be a disaster.

This is like life, son. Most people do not pay any real notice to the foundation of their life and what that life is for. You see, we all have a purpose while we are here. I think we are here to make the most of who we are, not most of what we can accumulate and take from others.

You see what I'm saying?"

"Sort of."

"Sort of is good enough for now. But then, there is the second part to consider. When the stone hit the water, it had the momentum wrapped up in the energy that you gave it. That energy was dissipated each time the stone dipped in the water. Eventually, all the energy was absorbed by striking the water, and the stone sank.

The stone is still there; the stone could continue and keep skimming if it had one thing, what is that thing?"

"Energy."

"Right; where that stone is now is like a lot of people's lives. They start off doing the things they love, and there is all the energy that is required to keep the forward momentum. Gradually, they are educated away from their passion into conformity. When this happens, they still exist, like all the other stones on the bottom of the lake. All that potential is there, just waiting for the energy it needs to activate it. But here is the thing, that energy is not a hand reaching down picking up the stone and throwing it. No, no, no.

All that is required is that the person has to start living their life's purpose. Let me tell you about your life and see if I am anywhere close. Is that OK?"

Ben came back to his seat. "Ok, shoot."

"Your life has been skipping across the lake with lots of energy, but you have never stopped to consider if there is a bank on the other side where the stone - your life, might reach. You have been occupied with creating money because you can see on the surface that money provides the energy to keep the stone bouncing along.

Something has happened in your life and brought to your attention, consciously or unconsciously, that this energy is false. Now the forward momentum of the stone is being questioned. If you don't do something about this, then the stone will sink like all the others.

You are now faced with a decision in life. Do you carry on like you have been doing all these years or do you swap out this false energy for the energy of your core driven purpose? That something that you're here to do with your life?

Most people will not do this, and the reason is that they believe they will drown. They believe that if they stop the false energy, then they will sink into the abyss, never to return. The truly successful are those that are fulfilling their purpose. These are the ones providing nourishment for their soul and so providing something of value to others. The person who lives their life like this is like a stone skipping across the surface of the water. Each time the stone dips into the water, instead of dissipating energy it collects energy from the value it provides to others and launches again into the air to carry on forward.

This stone or person can continue on and circumnavigate the world if they so wish. It's all a matter of choice.

So- all that remains is to ask yourself a question.
Do you have the courage to start living out your purpose?"
"Jeff, I have to say that you are a man of many talents. I have never heard you speak like this before and yet every word has resonated with me. I know what I have to do, but I am not afraid to admit that I lack the courage."

"Courage, my friend, is not such a big thing unless we give it power that does not belong to it."
"What do you mean giving power to it?"
"Quite simple; let's say you want a change in your life, you know what this change is but you don't know how it will turn out. That's quite a feasible situation, right?"

"Yes, I'd say so."

"Ok, so you have this change in your mind, and it takes a little courage, bravery or whatever you want to call it, to make that change.

Let's say that courage to proceed with something new will proceed with a thirty percent value rating.

Let's say that anything above thirty percent starts to bring in fear and doubts and will threaten that change.

I had to go through this very same process when I sold you this place. You see, courage is not just about facing down a lion in life. It also takes courage to do all manner of things, if these things threaten the status quo of your life and where you are now."

"I think I'm starting to get this, Jeff."

"Good, now remember that I did not want to sell this place. Deep down the reason for that was because I wanted to spend the rest of my days here. I am connected to this place like the roots of the largest trees that grow here. I want to be buried on this place, alongside me sweetheart which as you know, was one of the conditions."

"Yes, I do, and it will be done as you have asked, right down to the last detail."

"I know it will, and that is why we are sitting here today talking like this. So what threatened me ever selling this place to you was not over the money or what the bank might or might not do but more on acceptance of you and your word. If you remember, it took some days before I finally agreed."

"Yes, I thought at first you were holding out for more money, which I would have gladly paid."

"I knew you would but what would I have done with all the money? I have no family, nobody to leave it to. Money was not the issue. When I went to bed that night after you mentioned it, I thought this was a good idea; this would solve the problem, but by morning, my courage to proceed had wavered. I started to play out different outcomes in my mind. I started to project on what might or might not happen if I went ahead. I was probably running between the fifty to seventy percent mark with all this. It was not going to happen. I was going to dig in my heels. The level of courage I now needed to accept this change in my life had become a huge obstacle."

"That is so true Jeff, I remember coming back up to see you when it all started to go wrong with the lawyers, and I could not understand why. Do you remember that day?"

"Yes I do, that was the turning point. That was the day that I got to know you. I got to trust you, and as that happened, the percentage dropped way back to say only ten percent. The reason for that was simple and yet very powerful.

If more people understood this process, they would be more able to use courage to make a change."

"Tell me more."

"Well, it has to do with the future, that thing that most people think you can't predict.

I say you can predict your future; you can predict where your life is heading if you first turn off the negative conversation that goes on in your head. Secondly, you construct the ideal outcome that you want in your mind."

"You mean like forward pacing into the future?"

"Yes."

"Jeff- you know what is surprising about what you are saying right now? It's that I do this all the time at work. Forward pacing is exactly what has given me all the success I have, and yet I have never thought about this in my personal life choices."

"Most people segment their life like that, but you can't do that. Life is whole, all aspects of it.

Work, play, rest, love- every aspect of what we call living is life, and the moment you segment any part of the whole, you are breaking apart your life into competing parts."

"Fuck Jeff, I am sorry but I feel a little emotional right now."

"It's ok son, that's a good sign. It's you, the real you starting to communicate with itself. You have to pick up this change and run with it or bash it down again. It's your call. It's always our call in how we deal with this. So, getting back to courage; If you listen to the internal dialogue that does not want change, you're building a wall, brick by brick, to keep you exactly where you are in life right now. If you use your imagination and move beyond where you are now, and you maintain a positive internal dialogue about that change, you will be removing bricks from the wall. You will be lowering the percentage of courage that is required to make the changes that you are seeking. Does this make sense, Ben?"

"More than you will ever know, my friend."

Chapter Thirty-Three

Ben drove into the underground car park and handed the keys to Bill.

"It's a great morning Bill."

"That it is, sir."

"How are those plans for sailing around the world coming along?"

Bill laughed. "Well, we are sailing into the wind at the moment, so not that fast a progress but there is no stopping her, that's for sure. Women eh, sir- can't live with them; can't live without them."

"Oh, I don't know about that one." Ben laughed. "Catch you later Bill, have a great day."

"You too sir."

The elevator doors opened, and Ben stepped out. The pile of papers that Ben had asked Mary to type up were still there.

"Morning guys," Ben called out in a raised voice.

There was the same muted response that he had experienced the last time he did this. He decided not to try to increase the reply and instead, signaled Jake to come to the office.

"Good weekend, Jake?"

"Bloody great; went to Scaggys. You should have been there, mate. Wall to wall skin I am telling you, wall to wall, Friday and Saturday night. It took me all day Sunday to get over it.

What about you?"

"Just a quiet weekend at home."

"You're getting too old, mate. We have mountains to climb and crocodiles to wrestle. Talking of which, what's on the cards for today? You run the numbers yet?"

"No, I'm waiting for you to do that, but I will look over them for you."

"Awww- come on mate, don't make me do that again. What's the story here? Why can't we do what we have always done?"

"You want a cage Jake, yes? Then go and run the numbers and bring them back for me to check."

Jake blew a slow but audible breath out as he left Ben's office. The elevator doors opened and out stepped Mary. Ben glanced at the clock. She was half an hour early.

She came straight to Ben's office.

"Got a minute?" She said as she closed the door behind her and pulled up a chair.

"Life should not be full of regrets, Ben. We should not wake up in the morning thinking what we should have done, should have said. Do you get that, Ben?"

"You had a good day out with Christina, I see."

"I like you, Ben, I do, but I don't think I can stay here much longer. I don't think my future is sitting in a cubicle. What's freaking me out is that Michael's plans, those things I used to call fantasies about the future, all of a sudden somehow seem attractive to me. They seem real-"

Ben cut in.

"I went up to the lake yesterday and spent all day with Jeff, just talking."

Mary looked up at the ceiling and let out a sigh.

"No, listen, I hear what you are saying. The reason I mentioned Jeff was because of a conversation I had with him about the courage to change our lives."

Mary sat forward, resting her hands on her knees.

"Tell me more."

Ben looked at his watch.

"Not now. How about lunch today, same place at the park?"

"Yes, ok."

Mary left, and a few minutes later, Jake came in.

"Pull up a chair around this side and talk me through what you have done with the numbers."

Jake came round to Ben's side of the desk and started to talk about what markets he thought they should focus on today. Ben let him continue for some time to explain his reasoning. Then opened a drawer and pulled out his numbers.Six were in direct contradiction to Jake's. Jake dropped his head.

"Fuck, I thought I had this."

Ben slid the two sheets of paper side by side.

There were ten recommendations on each sheet. Ben picked up a pen.

"Ok, so we have the same ten."

"Yes but that's the easy part."

"Maybe so but at least you have them. The contradiction is on six of them which as you know, anything more than four has the potential to be a disaster. So today, you will merge these two lists, and you will instruct the boys to work from your four and my six, ok?"

"Ok but I noticed that even on my four I am buying and selling at different levels. Why not just go with your ten?"

"Have some courage, Jake. Your action levels might be off from mine, but you have nailed the anticipated direction, so the actual levels aren't that important.

Now, a question before you give these to Mary to type up."

"Shoot."

"What was the difference in how you decided on the four, as opposed to the six?"

"I-" Ben cut him off. "Your answer is going to be wrong so stop there, go away and think about it. You can tell me after you have run all the numbers for tomorrow morning. That will give you all night to think about it."

Jakes' eyebrows squeezed in tight, as he raked his teeth over his bottom lip.

"Like I said, don't think about it now. We will pick up tomorrow."

Jake headed to Mary's cubicle.

Chapter Thirty-Four

A beautiful day; the midday sun was streaming through the kitchen window.

"What are you doing today, Miss Christina?"

"Oh- nothing much. I thought I would spend some time in the garden."

"Marcello is a lovely boy, isn't he?"

"Anna, are you trying to say something?" Christina laughed.

"No, no, nothing at all, just thinking out loud; he is a lovely boy."

Christina looked up at the clock as she rubbed the inside of her left arm. This was the arm she had decided to have done first. Her stomach rolled with the expectation of what it might be like. She had heard that some tattoos did not hurt at all and others could be painful.

She pushed away her lunch plate.

"Not hungry today?"

"No Anna, sorry; I was thinking about a lot of things today, and I am not so hungry."

Anna took the plate.

"I will wrap this and pop it in the fridge, and then if you want something in a while, you can come and get it, ok?"

Christina got up. "Ok, thank you."

Anna started washing dishes as Christina returned to her room. She picked up her messages journal and went out through the French doors.

Instead of walking straight down to the garden, she went wide out and into the trees; she then turned toward the buildings so that Anna would not see her.

The sunlight was streaming down like spotlights through the canopy which reminded her of the jungle, minus the damp and humidity. Within a few minutes, she was at the building and could see Marcello out front scrubbing his hands.

He looked up as he heard Christina. "Are you ready?"

"Yes."

"It's ok, ask all you want. For the first tattoo, it's often very strange for the person, as they have many questions and the first question is usually, does it hurt?"

Christina went inside, and Marcello followed.

He had laid the wooden door across two old saw horse benches and had placed a box at the same height as the door, to the left side of the door.

"Ok, so you will lay down there," he said, pointing to the table. Your arm will lay to the side and upwards. This way I can get to this part of your arm." He pointed to the inside of her upper arm. He then took off his jacket and rolled it up as a pillow. "There, you can rest your head on that."

Christina sat gently down on the door testing her weight on it. It felt secure.

"Yes, it's all strong; I tested it already." Marcello smiled.

Christina laid down on the table and got as comfortable as she could.

"Ok, let's get to it," she said.

Marcello laughed.

"There's a little more to it than that". Marcello ran his fingers up the inside of Christina's arm, checking for hair. As he got higher to the inside of her upper arm, Christina let out a giggle. "That tickles, there."

"Sorry, I was making sure you had shaved all the hair off your arm."

He then opened up his case and pulled out some tracing paper that he had drawn the tattoo on.

He then applied rubbing alcohol too much of Christina's arm. Next was to roll on the deodorant stick, used to hold the paper in place and transfer the ink from the paper to the arm.

Marcello placed the paper on her arm, rubbed along it and then peeled away the paper, leaving a transfer of the tattoo.

"There you go, you can take a look."

"It's large, isn't it?"

"Too large?"

Christina looked at the image for a moment, saying nothing.

"Now is the time to say no, or to change anything."

"What do you think?"

"I don't want to say anything about why or why not someone should or should not have a tattoo. People have them for all sorts of reasons. For some, they are symbolic and have personal meaning. For others, they are just there as a fashion item." Christina put her head back down.

"Let's go for it."

"Ok, one more warning. This will take 3-4 hours with the shading, so only one arm today. Also, high up on the inside of your arm it will likely be very painful. I will start in this area first so that things get easier as we move down your arm, ok?" Christina nodded and closed her eyes.

Marcello dipped the gun into the ink, and the buzz of the motor started. "Ok, here we go."

Christina remained motionless as a bee landed on her arm and started to continuously sting her. Well, that was the only thing she could liken the pain too. She wanted him to stop but knew that that was not an option.

'Three hours' she said to herself as she tried to distance herself from the pain.

"Are you ok? Tell me if you need a break."

Christina let out a long slow breath as Marcello dipped into the ink again.

"No all good. I am going to close my eyes to deal with it."

The bee landed again and released its stinging pain like it would for the next 4 hours.

Chapter Thirty-Five

Ben and Mary sat on the same bench they sat on the last time they met in the park.

"So what did you want to talk about?" said Ben.

"As I said, I don't think I can work with you any longer, and I wanted you to be the first one to know that."

"Well, firstly, is there anything that could be fixed? I mean promotion or change of job? You know, I have said many times that you would make a great trader; hell, I reason in a year you could be in your own cage calling the shots."

"Well, that's what I mean, only literally. Caged, that is what I feel now. I have been like this for a while now, what with Dad in the home and now-" Ben cut her off

"Now with Christina on the scene?"

"Has she had the same effect on you?"

"Look, I'm a bit like you. I don't know what is going on in my life right now. Sometimes I think that she has this rose tinted spectacle view of the world and at other times she is some sort of messiah with an insight into my life."

"Well, I'm glad it's not just me."

"Well, if you have made your mind up then, I am not going to hold you back. Are you one hundred percent sure you want to leave?"

"Yes."

"How long have you been with the firm?"

"Just short of sixteen years."

"Don't say anything to anyone about this. I will see what I can pull for you as a severance package, ok?"

"Err- great yes, but-"

"Leave it to me and say nothing."

"So tell me, what are your plans? Where are you going to go? What are you going to do?"

She laughed.

"What's so funny?"

"Well, that you know I am all about organization."

"Absolutely, it's one of your redeeming qualities."

"Well, I have no idea. I have even been paying attention to Michael's ideas." She tipped her head to one side lifting one shoulder.

"I'm starting to like the idea of not being tied to any place in particular. I am thinking of moving around and just see what happens. Michael has some money saved, and so do I. It's not a lot but enough for a couple of years."

"I admire your courage, that's for sure, and actually, it sounds pretty exciting."

"So you'll be alright without me around to organize your work life?"

She laughed as Ben raised his eyebrows, then reached out and touched his knee.

"Well, that's enough about me, what about you? I suspect that Christina is going to be heading off soon, eh?"

Ben looked down at the grass for a second.

"You know what- I don't know whether to be happy or sad to see her go."

Mary's face squeezed up.

"What do you mean, happy? Is there something that I don't know about her?"

"Oh no, not like that. I don't mean she has been any trouble; it's just that- well, she has left a bit of a mark on me, something that I don't know if it's a good or a bad thing for me."

"Oh ok, I see what you mean."

"All in all, I feel like something has changed in me and yet I can't put my finger on anything. It seems like little things. For example, I have been driving to work, parking in the same garage, passing the keys to the same guy for years and suddenly, I realized that I didn't' even know his name.

His name is Bill; his wife has a dream to sail around the world. She enters every competition to do with boating. She has researched vessels, routes, taken a sailing course, learned how to read radar and weather patterns. I learned all this from Bill because I asked his name and paid attention to him.

It's the weirdest thing. I am now rooting for all this to happen to Bill; I want to hear that he and his wife are sailing around the world. I want them to experience the freedom of living their lives as they want."

"Well Ben, here is what I have come to realize, and I might add that I am as guilty of this as you are and probably millions of others."

"Guilty of what?"

"We are all guilty to some degree of trying to live our lives through others. Look at the status that so many so called celebrities hold today. That status can be centered around a large perceived attractive rear end or just speaking out in ways that shock and creates controversy.

The world has gone mad to the degree of what we give our attention to. But the real danger, if we can call it danger, is the way in which we externalize and associate with the so called celebrities.

We see people all the time trying to emulate others, to seek to live the life of the celebrity. They are buying the same clothes, using the same brands and so on.

None of this is real; we only get to see the celebrity side of the celebrity, which is only a tiny proportion of that person's life.

The wannabe believes that the five percent that they see is the complete and whole life of the individual. But the real danger here or the real sadness is the surrender of the wannabe's personal life."

"What do you mean surrender of life?"

"I know that sounds a bit over the top but hear me out. I believe that we all have a purpose and I also believe that following that purpose will provide the most happiness in our lives.

Most people shy away from whom they are as individuals; they shy away from their core purpose. They end up trying to live their life according to the promoted concept of success and happiness.

In short, many try to emulate the celebrities' lives by association. That association costs money, a continuous stream of money that one has to sell their very life time to obtain. By the time I mean the work, consuming a person's living time on the planet."

Chapter Thirty-Six

"Ok, all done. That was a long stretch."

Christina rolled her head to look at her arm. It felt like a dead weight.

"I have to say I have never worked on someone for that long and they have been so relaxed."

Christina blinked her eyes a few times and then took a deep breath.

"How did you do that?"

"Do what?"

"Stay so relaxed all through it."

"Oh, I learned a technique of something like self-hypnosis, when you can train yourself to turn down any pain, sort of like turning down the volume on a music system."

"Pretty impressive. Well, what do you think? You have to imagine it without all the redness of the skin. Has it turned out as you thought it would?"

"Exactly."

"So do you want a couple of days' break before the next arm?"

"No. Can you do the other one tomorrow?"

"Yes sure, but now a couple of things. I have a tube of this for you." Marcello handed over a tube of cream.

"It's actually for nappy rash, but it works great on a fresh tattoo. It's going to itch like hell later on. Do not scratch it. If it bothers you in bed, then put some cream on it and then wrap some cling film around your arm until the morning.

Are you going to tell me why you wanted the tattoos? I mean, I am just interested because I had drawn them as you wanted them without even knowing that. My Grandfather would know about these things, but he has gone now."

"How about tomorrow when you're doing the other arm?"

"Yes- and you will tell me about the ceremony?"

"Let's see how much time we have first, ok?"

Christina got up from the makeshift table and carefully put on her jacket.

"Don't forget the cream," said Marcello.

"Ok, see you later."

Christina left the shed and walked back up to the house, following the same path through the trees to avoid being spotted by Anna.

She went back through the French doors and then into the kitchen. Anna was not there. She started looking in some cupboards and draws. She heard Anna coming.

"What are you looking for?"

"Sorry Anna, I did not mean to go through all the draws. I wanted some cling film if you have any."

"Cling film — you mean glad wrap? What do you want that for?"

"Err- my backpack. If you— wrap it in cling film then when you go through the airport, the straps don't get caught in the luggage belts."

"Miss Christina, you are not leaving us, are you?"

"No, not yet but I like to be organized."

Anna went to the draw that Christina had open and pulled the contents to the side.

"There you go, you were about to find it anyway."

"Thank you. Can I take the roll and replace it later?"

"Of course, take what you need. I only use it sometimes to pack a sandwich for Mr Ben."

Christina returned to her room, went into the bathroom and locked the door. She slid off her jacket. There were a few streaks of blood on her arm. She pulled off some toilet tissue, dampened it and then dabbed off the blood without rubbing. She then applied some cream which had a cooling effect.

She looked at her arm in the mirror and was transported back to the ceremony and her conversations with Almedio about living a deliberate life.

The deliberate life is a life avoiding conformity. He explained that the difficulty with this avoidance was learning to recognize what conformity is and its effect on you.

He went on to explain-

'We function in the world in an upside-down and back-to-front manner, and we are trained to be obedient in this from a very early age.

Take something as innocuous as a school uniform and break down the purpose and long-term effect of this. First is the branding of the organization (the school) and the second is the suppression of individuality. Clothes are often an expression of ourselves, and long after we have left school and hung up our uniform, we take on another. The name of this uniform is called fashion. We are right back into conformity.

Conforming is like sailing into the wind, like peddling uphill while observing a much easier route, but not being mentally equipped to take it.

The organized world is not designed for the individual to rise and reveal their talents; it's designed to turn you into a consumer, a person who lives a mediocre life, a life that will most certainly be one full of regrets.

There is only one escape from conformity and mediocrity, and that path will be found by living a deliberate life.

Living a deliberate life will not be easy at first, not because of any physical effort but because of the mental programming that has taken hold of your life.

This programming, right from your early schooling, will have set up pathways in your brain. These pathways have become well worn; they are the pathways of least resistance. Unless you create new pathways, then the existing ones will continue taking your life along the same path that it's on now. Creating a new mental pathway involves two actions. Firstly, the daily awareness of conformity and secondly, the daily and deliberate resistance against it.

These two actions will confuse and challenge the existing mental pathways; the mind will hate this and will resist.

You will notice devious resistance methods as all manner of 'easy' outs and distractions will appear in your life. The purpose of which is to get you off the concept of a new pathway and back onto your existing one.

Those who become non-conformists are often admired. They stand out by their radical clothes, speech or even their whole life. In some cases, we even give them celebrity status. We see that this person has broken away from conformity and we want to do the same. The celebrity now has a following, has a clothing and perfume brand which we rush to buy, so that we may be like this person, so that we may be the non-conformist that they are.

What have we done? We have identified with something outside of ourselves, and we now conform to this new identity that is not of self. We have not changed, we have not stopped conformity; we have simply changed horses while we are continuing on the same path. We have created a different mental pathway, but the route and destination have remained the same.

The only way out is to return to the two-stage process that will provide the escape route: The awareness of conformity and the deliberate resistance against it.

There is another type of conformity that is a powerful and destructive force that is deliberately used against you.'

Alemdio told me that he had recently been shown a video of a sports person of international fame, who turned up at a random small street cafe.

He sat at a normal table in amongst people living a normal life. He was instantly recognized and was asked if photos could be taken.

There was an outside camera, recording all the people

approaching for these photographs. He said the outside camera gives us the perspective of outside observers.

There was a constant stream of people, all pulling out their phones and then forwarding pictures to friends on social media. The cafe started to fill up; photographs were shared across the world; the simple cup of tea stop for the celebrity had turned into a viral video, reaching millions of people and would circle the globe.

The celebrity returned to his car, where filming continued. When asked why he agreed to so many photos, he stated that he loved the people and it kept him in contact with them.

For this particular celebrity, there was an element of truth in this statement, but this is only the surface of what happened in this event. The real depth, the real value of this cafe stop can be found in what the celebrity had placed around his neck.

In every photograph and video that circled the globe was a special pair of headphones that the celebrity had endorsed.

This is advertising that cannot be purchased over the counter. This is viral marketing that will result in millions of dollars of products sold.

We are unconsciously led to conforming to the headphone brand that is good enough for this international sports star.

Living a deliberate life can be enjoyed as a very stimulating mind game, by asking the question many times throughout the day.

'What am I consciously and unconsciously reading into my now experience?' and 'What am I consciously and unconsciously ignoring from my now experience?'

By starting this mental observation, you will discover things in your now experiences that will have a dramatic impact on your day to day life.

However, all this is only of an academic experience and value, unless it's aligned with what you want your deliberate life to be. This deliberate life can only be lived after you have searched for and discovered that which is your core driven purpose. Now, of course, you may be already living a deliberate life, but that life may not be aligned with your core driven purpose.

Imagine how much more life could be if you were living a deliberate life that was in alignment with your purpose. Happiness and contentment in your life would know no bounds

Chapter Thirty-Seven

B en and Mary exited the elevator together, a little after 2.30 pm. Jake almost sprinted across the floor towards them. Before he reached them, Ben turned to Mary "Nothing about leaving. I will get back to you later."

Mary continued walking as Ben came to a halt and Jake blurted out- "Fuck mate, we have a bit of a sinking ship. Four of your six are not responding to the buying. Price has hit the ceiling, and it will not go higher. If things turn down from here, we will get hammered."

"And what about your four?"

"Steaming on, but your six will wipe that out if they don't break through the ceiling."

"You'd have to be pleased with that, then?"

"What?- No, and one of the head honchos has been down here asking where you were and what I was doing with the situation. He seemed pissed, Ben."

"What are the top two on the list doing, pretty flat?"

"Yes, pancakes."

"Ok, so cover ninety percent of your exposure on those two and leave the others."

Ben walked towards his office and Jake went straight to pass instructions to the foot soldiers. He closed his office door and spun his chair around. He put his hands behind his head and looked out across the city. A few minutes later the door opened.

"It's a hell of a view, eh?"

Ben swung his chair around to see the man who had sat at the head of the table during the boardroom meeting.

"May I take a seat, Ben?"

"Of course, it's your seat after all."

They both smiled as he sat down.

"I'll get right to it, Ben. Upstairs are concerned about you leaving Jake in charge of things."

"I thought you were the upstairs?"

"Well, we all have bosses; one can never tell where the food chain ends, eh! Anyway, all I am saying is that there is a concern." Ben leaned forward and rested his left elbow on the desk while rubbing his chin. With his other hand, he picked up a pen and drew a straight line on his yellow pad.

"I think you might have been right the other day in the meeting."

"Right? What about?"

"Mary has been here a lot of years working with me."

"Ah- upstairs is going to be pleased. I will organize that for you. When do you want it to happen?"

"Severance pay. I want her to get the package that one of us would get. Can that be arranged?"

"It's that bad, is it? Look, I'll see what I can do."

He got up and left the office, closing the door behind him.

As the office door clicked shut, Almedio popped into Ben's mind. He started thinking about what sort of person would choose to live in a jungle village over a city with all the conveniences that it offered.

Mary tapped on the door, entered and closed it behind her.

"All good in here? I saw one of the directors come to see you."

"No worries, all perfect. Remember to say nothing to anyone about your leaving. I suspect there will be an office reshuffle shortly and it will have an effect on your position."

"Er- ok. I don't know whether to say thanks or to shed a tear at the prospect of leaving."

"As I said, say and do nothing. You don't know anything is coming."

"Don't worry, I understand. Changing the subject, Christina?"

Ben put the pen down that he had been doodling with and leaned back in his chair. "I mean, is she leaving or- well, what are her plans, do you know?"

Ben leaned forward and picked up the pen again, assuming the same chin holding position he had earlier with the director.

"I don't know what her plans are. Why do you ask, you have something in mind?"

"How about a send-off get together?"

Ben dropped the pen and sat up straight. "Now that," he said "is an excellent idea. I will have a word with her tonight.

How about we make it on the weekend, depending on her plans, of course."

"Yes, I can do that. I am sure Michael will be keen on meeting her again, as well. I swear that if I had not been there, with all the times he mentions her, I would think there was another woman in our relationship."

Mary turned to leave.

"One thing before you go."

"Yes?"

"You know that junk mail that is always saying you can win this or that?" Mary's eyebrows squeezed together. "Yes."

"How would you find out about organizing a competition like that?"

"I have no idea. Do you want me to find out?"

"Yes if you could, please."

Mary turned again to leave.

"On second thoughts- you would not need to create a competition, would you?"

Mary's arms dropped to her sides.

"You're not making any sense," she said.

"Sorry, I was thinking out loud. Ignore me."

"You still want me to find out about the competition?"

"No, no need to do anything. Ignore me; I'm having a brain fuzz day."

Mary turned to leave for the third time.

"There is just one thing."

She turned back again. "Christ Ben, I am going to get dizzy here."

"Sorry, I was wondering who deals with employee records here. Do you know?"

"Yes Susan two cubicles up from me."

"Could you ask her to look someone up for me?"

"I can try, but she was telling me the other day that you can't just look up someone's personal information unless there is a particular reason for doing so. What did you want to know?"

"An address for Bill."

"Bill?"

"Bill, the garage guy."

"Oh- ok, I'll see what I can do. Are we done now? I don't know if I can cope with spinning around again." Ben laughed.

"Yes we're done- apart from- just kidding."

Mary left, and Ben turned on the trading screens to catch up with the day's trading activity so far. It was not going to be a big day, but currently, open positions were showing a figure fluctuating around $1.800.000 in profit.

He stood up and looked out across the floor at the foot soldiers. Jake was moving from desk to desk, talking with them. He stopped and looked back towards Ben's office to see Ben looking at him. He gave a thumbs up sign and then turned back to talk to one of the traders.

Chapter Thirty-Eight

There was a tap on Ben's door and in walked the director.

"That little issue we talked about a while ago, sorted and with this severance package I think she will go quietly and not make a fuss."

He handed Ben a sheet of paper, laying out the package.

"We will handle this for you; you need not get involved."

"No, better I deal with it. I will talk with her tomorrow

Jake has instructions, and I am leaving it to him, as I have a few things to attend to outside of work."

"A replacement for Mary?" asked the director. "We have someone in mind, best if we take care of that for you."

Ben shrugged his shoulders. "Whatever works."

Ben grabbed his briefcase and popped in Mary's severance package and his yellow legal pad from the desk. They both left the office together; Ben headed for the elevator. Half way there, Mary caught up with him.

"Here you go." She handed him a slip of paper.

"What's this?"

"That address you wanted for Bill, the garage man."

"Oh great, you're a star, thanks."

Mary turned to go back to her cubicle as a young man stepped away from his screen and intercepted Ben.

"Sir- I err- read your note."

He pointed to the pile of papers that Mary had left by the side of the elevator.

"Great. What did you make of it?"

"Still fully working on that, but wanted to ask you one thing."

The elevator doors opened, and Ben stepped in, holding the door open button.

"Well, shoot. You haven't got long."

"The two top currencies on the list this morning. I don't get it; they were never going to amount to much."

The elevator doors started to close. Ben pressed the open door button again, and they opened again.

"So why did you act on that information?"

"Because I was told to."

"Then that was your problem, think about it."

Ben removed his finger and the doors closed.

Chapter Thirty-Nine

The elevator doors opened. Bill was as always, right there.

"Afternoon Bill. How's it going?"

"All good sir, all good. You driving, sir or you want the limo?"

"No, I'll take a car thanks, Bill."

"Very good sir, have a nice day, well, what's left of it anyway."

"Will do- ah, just one thing Bill?'

"Sir?"

"Is there a place nearby where I can buy a phone?"

Bills' eyes lifted up as he touched his chin.

"Turn left out of the garage then four or five blocks up. Look for the AT&T sign. Pretty sure they sell phones in there."

Ben inched the bonnet out of the garage like every day since the accident and turned left. The traffic was heavy, and he realized he had made a mistake by driving, as parking was going to be difficult.

It took 15 minutes to travel the five blocks to where he saw the AT&T sign. There was a parking spot right outside the store.

The shop was busy, and it looked like all the assistants were tied up with other people, so Ben just browsed the store. He couldn't remember the last time he had bought a phone for himself, as they were always company supplied. There was a bewildering array of them in all shapes and sizes.

He was looking for a particular phone that he had once owned several years ago, but there was nothing even closely resembling it.

"Can I help you, Sir?"

An older man approached Ben.

"Sorry, to have kept you waiting, we are a bit busy this time of day."

"Yes, I'd like a phone please but you don't seem to have the model here. I had one like it a few years ago. Best phone I ever had, as it was so simple."

"Ha. I know exactly what you mean. Everything has to be a smart phone these days. What was wrong with the old flip phone, eh?"

"Yes that's it, that's what I had, a flip phone. Like a clamshell. They were great, and the screen was always protected from coins or keys in your pocket."

"Yep- I agree. That was the best. The problem is those phones are all out of date now. Nobody wants that type of phone anymore. Let me have a look on the computer and see if we even have any. I'm pretty sure we don't."

Then the man went off to a computer terminal, and Ben followed. He started to search, but nothing came up. Another assistant looked over to what he was doing and noticed what he was searching for.

"The old flip phone. There are two of those out back brand new, still boxed."

"Nothing is showing up on the computer for them."

"Well, there are a couple there. I was looking to help a customer out with a second-hand cable, and while I was looking, I came across them. I remember them as I thought no one was ever going to buy them. Hold on; I will go and look."

The young man returned a couple of minutes later with two boxed flip phones.

"Yes, that is the exact model I used to have. Perfect."

"Problem is I don't know how much they are, as they are not on the system."

The other assistant was now serving someone else but turned back and said. "You could book them out as second-hand ancillary equipment."

"Good idea but how much to book them out at?"

The assistant looked up from the screen at Ben.

"How does $200.00 sound Sir?"

"Yes, that's fine. Tell you what; I will take both of them. You never know when you might want a second phone."

"Ok, how about $300.00 for both of them, as they are not on the system?"

"Even better." Said Ben.

"Ok, so are you going to use a phone number you already have?"

"No, I will need a new number but only for one phone."

"Ok, what sort of contract were you thinking of?"

"The most basic you have as I don't plan on using this phone much."

"Ok well, the most basic is the pay as you go. You just top up credit on the card when you want more call time."

"Perfect, I'll take it."

"Ok, I'll set that up for you now, Sir. It will take me about 10 minutes, is that ok?"

"Fine — you don't happen to know of a print shop nearby, do you?" Ben asked the assistant.

"Yes, right next door."

"Oh, I didn't notice it on the way in. Tell you what, I will pop next door and be back to pick up the phone in ten minutes or so."

"Perfect, I'll have it ready for you."

Ben entered the shop next door; there was no-one else in there. There was a bell on the counter which was made from a large sheet of glass with an example of print underneath.

A man appeared and looked at Ben over half-rimmed spectacles.

"Afternoon Sir. How can I help?"

"Mmm… help might be the right word, as I'm not exactly sure what I want. Do you print anything like competitions, I mean like competition forms."

The assistant took off his glasses.

"You mean a competition entry form?"

"Yes perfect, that's what I mean."

"Hold on; I have some samples out back."

The man returned and spread out about ten different competition forms. He picked up his glasses from the counter and put them back on, as he pointed to individual forms ranging from black and white to full color.

"Obviously they vary in cost; this basic black and white are, of course, a lot cheaper than this full-color one.

May I ask what the prize is going to be?"

"Yes, it's a Yacht."

"Wow, don't do too many of those. Normally something like that would be run in a magazine. The type of forms we do is pretty much what you see in the junk mail. You're likely going to have to spread a million or more pieces around before you would see a return."

"I only want three."

"Three million is a big run, sir, too much for me, way too much."

"No, I only want three forms."

"Sir, are you serious? Three forms to win a yacht?"

"It's a project that I want to run."

"Well, sorry but it's not something I would get involved in. The setup costs for artwork and copy are $500.00 which we make no money on, and then a print run of less than say twenty thousand is just not worth it. Sorry, I don't think I can help you."

He started to collect up the forms he had laid on the counter. Ben put his hand out and stopped him.

"Hold on, if this is about money then forget that. Just tell me what it would cost?"

He took off his glasses again and rubbed his chin.

"Well, to be honest, you could probably get away with printing something on a good laser printer."

"Could you arrange that for me?"

The man continued rubbing his chin.

"Look, $2,000 take care of it?" Said Ben.

"2,000- Absolutely."

"Ok then, let's agree on $2,000."

Ben stretched out his hand, and they shook on the deal.

"Ok, so when can you have them ready?"

"Mmm I will set something up tonight, and you will have proof by tomorrow lunch time. How's that sound?"

"Fine. Can you email it to me?"

"Yes, I will scan it into a file for you."

Ben wrote down his email address and then pulled out his wallet. "Here, I have $500.00 in cash now, and I will pay the rest on collection. I'll give you a contact number when you email the file to me. No need to bother with a receipt for that right now, as I have to shoot next door."

"Ok, I'll get onto it right away. I'll use some stock images for the boat and lay something up for you to take a look at."

"Perfect."

Ben reached into his pocket and handed over a slip of paper.

"These are the rules of the competition. The winner must agree to these to be able to win."

Ben went next door to the phone shop. The assistant who had served him before was with someone else but acknowledged him and looked towards a bag on the counter.

"Just finishing up here, Sir and I will be right with you."

The assistant rang up the sale and handed over a bag to the customer he was serving, who then left the store.

He then turned to Ben.

"Right sir, all done. I just need to know what credit you want on the phone. Top ups start from $30.00 up to $100.00."

"Fifty bucks will do for now."

Ben handed over his credit card.

"Ok so with the $50.00 phone credit, that's $350.00 all up."

He swiped the card and Ben entered his security pin.

"I have written your new telephone number on the back of my card inside the box. If you need anything else in the future, give me a call direct."

"Thanks."

Ben picked up the bag and left the store.

Chapter Forty

Christina had on a long sleeve cardigan at the dinner table. Her arm felt as it if was on fire. She rested it on her lap and concentrated on eating with just a fork in her right hand.

"You ok?" Said Ben.

"Yes fine, why?"

"Oh nothing, you seem a little different, that's all. Did you have a good day?"

"Yes, been in the gardens and doing some writing. I am thinking about leaving pretty soon, and I want to say thank you for all you have done for me."

"It's been a pleasure — well, apart from the first few days."

They looked at each other and laughed.

"I was speaking with Mary today at the office, and she said that we should have a leaving party for you."

"No!"

"Whoa! Nothing fancy — well not even a party, I didn't mean to say that. Just a get together before you leave."

"I hate goodbyes; I don't like all the fuss and stuff."

"Well, how about I invite Mary and Michael over again one evening before you leave? We can have dinner, and that's it?"

Christina pushed some food around her plate. Ben sensed a no was coming so jumped in.

"Ok, if it bothers you that much, I'll say nothing and not tell them you're leaving just yet. How's that?"

"No, it's ok. Let me think about a date to leave and then we can sort something."

"Well, ok but if you don't want to, then that's fine. It's your call."

They finished up dinner and went to the lounge.

"So you were writing today. Did you get much done?"

"Not a lot but sometimes - what's it they say? Quality over quantity; well, that's my excuse for today."

"So, are you going to tell me any more tonight?" Ben asked.

"Actually, I was just thinking about how I explained some messages I understood and others I didn't. And there were still more messages that I had no idea of the real content of them. Do you remember us talking about that?"

"Yes, I was pretty caught up in it."

"Well' it was just that today something came up, that seemed to be connected to a conversation we had about discovering your purpose.

You remember? Your purpose was about discovering what you were here for?"

"It made me think way more than you realize."

"Well, I may have interpreted the message incorrectly."

"I do hope not, as it messed with my head and I'm only just coming to some understanding of it."

"Well, when I say wrongly, I am only referring to how you find out what that passion or core purpose is.

You see, I had thought that it was all about getting out there and finding yourself; about discovering something that you could turn into your passion.

But that message became clearer to me today. It seems like to look externally is leading you further away from discovering what your passion and purpose really is."

"So what you're saying is that the more you look, the less you're going to find?"

Christina put her hands flat together and started tapping her closed lips with both index fingers.

"What's up?

"Nothing. I'm thinking about how powerful and yet how difficult this might be for some people. Well, myself in a way, because I know that I have been searching externally and I have to stop this. I have to take some of this medicine myself, so to speak."

"So, do you now have the message in full?"

"Yes, I'm pretty sure I do."

"Well?"

"I may have mentioned some of this before, so forgive me if I cover some old ground but it's important.

In a way, I now think this is one of the most important messages I received.

Remember when I talked about celebrities' lives and how people consciously or unconsciously try to emulate them?"

"Yes, to be honest though, I don't think I do that. What I mean is, I don't have a craving for anything that a celebrity has."

"Yes I get that, but this is where it's so, almost dangerous for someone in your position."

"What do you mean dangerous?"

"Well not dangerous in the physical sense of harm but on the mental side of things.

"Sorry, I am not following this at all."

Christina put her index fingers to her lips again.

"Look it's ok; just say what you think you have to say. I will not be offended in any way. Promise."

Christina looked into Ben's eyes.

"You see that's it; that is why it is so hard to explain."

"What is?"

"When you told me to say what I have to say, what led up to that statement? Why did you say that?"

"Well, I could see from your actions that something was bothering you and you were reluctant to say whatever it was. I know the reason for that reluctance is because you don't want to offend me or the like."

"Ok, so you got it exactly but how did you get that understanding?"

"Like I said, from your actions?"

"Well, here is the message.

You didn't get that understanding from my actions; you only think you did.

My actions were, let us say, the lower level of understanding. Then when you knew that I wanted to say something that might offend you, that was a higher level of understanding. The single most important part of that process goes by unnoticed. The most important part is the bit in the middle, the bit before the higher level of understanding."

"So how does this relate to a message?" Ben asked.

"Ok before I get to that, how are you feeling now, right now?"

"Actually, a little frustrated."

"Well, hold on to that feeling for a moment because that feeling can tell us way more than we think it can. You see, if we focus in on the actual feeling, we completely bypass what has triggered that feeling.

So in your case, you have the feeling of frustration, but when you dig deep into that, there is something that is vital to understand about it."

"Go on."

"The feeling was not a result of what I may or may not have said; it was a result of something that triggered within you.

It was something almost hiding, in the middle of the whole experience.

It's that hidden part we need to examine. Understanding that reaction and under what circumstances it can be triggered offers us real insight."

"But what does that insight do for us?"

"It allows us to become alerted to the things that are most important to us."

"Can you do one thing for me?" Said Ben "Tell me what it was that you were going to say that you thought might offend me."

"You mean the celebrity thing and how that would not affect you so much? Well, think about that. You are in a way a celebrity."

"No, I'm not; no way."

"Really? You have created all this wealth. Do people not look up to you where you work, do you not feel a sense of pride, living here in this vast completely impractical house?"

Ben stiffened in his seat.

"STOP. You see, it's happening again; you are getting ready to defend yourself to justify all this with hard work and dedication. This reaction is exactly what we have been talking about."

Ben leaned back into the sofa. Neither of them said anything for a few moments.

Christina was first to break the silence.

"So, that right there was everything I was trying to explain; that leaning back and thinking about what was going on inside. Thinking what was triggering the reaction was the significant part.

By examining and understanding that part, you become deeply in tune with yourself, the real you.

Now don't get me wrong, I am no Guru in this. I may have these messages, but that does not mean I can live my life by them all. Yes, I try, and I am getting better, but nobody is perfect in this- well, maybe Almedio might be right up there.

I am starting to remember something he said about this, but at the time it did not make sense. Now it does. He said.

'You don't have to discover who you are, or what you want to be or do. You only have to remember.'

That was what he said, and at the time it made no sense to me. I mean how can you remember something that you cannot be aware of? But that's it, that's the whole deal here. We have to remember NOT things that we have forgotten. We have to remember our AWARENESS and how that works. When we are at a state of full personal awareness, we are at that moment aware of whom we are and what it is that we are here to do."

"The truth is then, we all know, don't we?" said Ben.

It just dawned on me that all the bullshit, all the hype, and tripe, all the false facades that we put up. In fact, almost every part of what we put out into the world to represent who we are is a wall that we build, brick by brick, that separates us from our real self.

The more bricks we lay, the higher and thicker the wall becomes until it's so thick, so impenetrable, that we are completely removed from who we really are. All our hopes, dreams and ambitions end up behind the wall, where they remain for the rest of our lives."

Christina was the first to speak after what seemed like a long silence.

"I can't believe you explained it like that Ben. It was like I was listening to Almedio. He used the same analogy of building a brick wall.

He finished that conversation by saying.

'Do not try to find out who you are because you already know who that person is. Instead, start dismantling the wall that you have built around that person.'

Some people, he said will smash that wall down in a moment if they should be faced with a life threatening illness or some other catastrophic event.

These people will be seen by those outside to have made dramatic changes in their lives, and they have. But, those changes will be related to what they discover about themselves when the wall comes down.

For those not faced with a catastrophic event, but with an awareness of the wall, it takes the systematic brick by brick removal to reach who they are and to start living that life, that is their true self."

Chapter Forty-One

Christina woke with the sun streaming through a gap in the curtains covering the French doors. It had been a late night talking with Ben, and she had overslept. As she moved and became aware of her arm and how sticky it felt. She had not meant to sleep with the glad wrap on. She went to the bathroom and peeled it away; it felt so good to let the air to it. She set the shower temperature to the coolest she could and stepped in. She stayed a while, letting the cool water flow over the tattoo.

She was careful to pat dry her arm and not rub anywhere. She dressed in jeans, tee shirt, and a long sleeved red, white and black checked shirt. She thought this would be a good choice in case of any blood spots.

She made her way to the kitchen where Anna was busy baking scones. Everything had become very easy with Anna now; all formality had long since passed, but she still called her Miss Christina.

"I let you sleep in late this morning. I was here when Mr Ben left, and he said you had been talking until late at night, so that is why I did not wake you. Marcello missed you at breakfast this morning. I think he likes you a lot. He is a nice boy, no?"

"Yes, very nice. Can I help myself to some breakfast?"

"Si, Si, of course. How about a nice warm scone with butter?"

"Mmm… sounds lovely."

Anna passed over two warm scones which Christina ate before the butter had enough time to melt.

"I have to go to town later. Would you like to come with me?" Asked Anna.

"Not today, thank you. I want to spend a lazy day, thinking about where I am going to go when I leave here."

"Oh, Miss Christina, it's been lovely having you here. We will all miss you very much. Mr Ben said that we would have a party for you and I will be there. I will see if Mr Ben will let Marcello come as well if you like?"

"A party?"

"Well, not a party but I will make special food for everyone, and it will be lovely. Have you decided when you are leaving?"

"No, not yet but I will know later on today or tomorrow."

Christina got up from the table and took the plate to where Anne was still working. She put her arm around Anna's shoulder and squeezed her.

"I just want to say thank you, Anna, for all you have done for me and making me feel so welcome here. You are a lovely person, and I will miss you very much when I leave."

Anna stopped what she was doing and hugged Christina. Christina held on.

"Thank you again, Anna."

"You're very welcome, very welcome."

Five minutes later she was heading across the lawns at an angle that prevented Anna from seeing her. She was nervous of the second tattoo. She pushed open the door to the shed. The door was still there just as she had left it yesterday. Today it looked more like an operating table in her mind.

She could hear Marcello approaching from the side of the shed.

"You're the early bird," he said as he pushed open the door.

"Yes…"

"You wanted to get it over with, eh?"

"Yes, I suppose so."

"It's not good to look at it like this. I mean these tattoos mean something to you. These are to be part of you forever. It's not like it's just ink on your arm, and that's it. Many tattoos I do for people, they are a little fun thing - a picture, a mouse or bird. Most of them mean nothing to the person outside of the idea of just having a tattoo.

My grandfather would say that this, what you have here on your arms, is almost like a sacred thing. The tattoos chose you; you did not choose them."

Christina sat on the side of the makeshift table.

"I had never thought of it like that. I see what you mean. I like the thought that the tattoos chose me."

"Ok, let me have a look at your arm."

Christina took off her shirt, sliding it gently over her left arm. Marcello looked up and down the arm.

"Nice, it looks all good, but you kept the glad wrap on too long. Now is the time to let the air at it. Use a little of the cream to help with the itching if you need to and don't forget, do not scratch - Ok, I will wash up, and we will make a start."

Christina rolled up her shirt to use as a headrest and laid on the table. Marcello put on his latex gloves and applied the alcohol rub and deodorant.

"This one is going to be a bit tricky to position because you want this mirror image. I've never had this request before… for a mirror image I mean."

Marcello had to apply the stencil three times, each time renewing the deodorant and cleaning off old ink before everything lined up.

"Ok, we have it.

Sit up a moment so you can check both arms and see if you're happy with the positioning."

Christina stretched both arms out and compared them.

"Yes, they look good."

"Great, let's make a start then."

Christina laid back down as Marcello dipped the gun into the ink. The stinging bees had arrived again, this time it seemed like they were angry as well.

Chapter Forty-Two

Mary stepped out of the elevator after lunch and went to her cubicle. There was an envelope with a note attached, saying bring it to Ben's office.

She knocked on Ben's door and walked in.

"What's this about?" She said, holding out the envelope.

"Sit down and open it."

Mary sat down, and Ben slid over a letter opening knife. Mary ignored the knife and lifted the sticky flap.

'Dear Mary,

It is with deep regret that we have to advise you that your position with this Company is no longer required. We would like to add that this bears no reflection on your performance. This decision has not been reached lightly but is a requirement, due to the restructuring of the firm.

On the following pages, we have laid out what we believe to be a generous severance package.'

She looked up at Ben. Ben's eyes widened as he saw tear filled eyes. He passed a box of tissues over.

"I thought you wanted this?" He said.

"Oh, Ben you can be so insensitive sometimes."

"What, what I have I done? I thought this was what you wanted; we talked about this."

"Yes, but it's been a long time; we have been together for a long time. I am going to miss that."

"Ben reached out and took her hand across the desk."

"Hey, come on, adventures new and bold and you haven't even read your severance package yet."

Mary flipped over the top sheet and started to read.

"Not bad, eh?" Said Ben.

"I never expected this Ben; it's huge. Five years salary and retain all health care for that period, plus a $20,000 relocation sum."

They looked at each other for a moment, before a huge smile appeared on Mary's face. Mary looked back down and continued reading. Her face dropped, and the smile vanished.

"There is a clause. I have to leave on receipt of this offer to make it valid."

"Yes I know; they want it to be clean and swift with no office politics. You have to grab your stuff from your desk and hand in your pass and leave, without talking to anyone."

Mary started to breathe heavily. "Ok, how long do I have?"

"Ten minutes."

"I feel like I should hug you and cry at the same time."

"Well, a hug is not on the cards. Upstairs concluded that we were having an affair and it was interfering with my work. I let them believe what they wanted to believe.

This is supposed to be our break up, and you are leaving. That is why they have given you the package they have; they don't want any hassles."

"So, I should start screaming and give you a good slap so that everyone thinks the same as upstairs?"

Ben gave a half chuckle. "I hope you're not serious?"

"Well, I don't mind if you want to me too."

"No.. no, I don't like the idea of a beating."

Tears started to build again.

"Right then, I better go and clear my desk."

Back in her cubicle, Mary cleared her desk into a filing box. Pulled down some photographs and was ready to leave. She sat a moment to compose herself; she did not know if she could make it to the elevator without losing it.

She took a deep breath, put her handbag over her shoulder and picked up the box. She decided to look at no one.

Eyes straight-ahead and focused, she turned left out of the cubicle. She had to get past Ben's office and then it was a straight run to the elevator. She decided not to look towards Ben's office as she passed but was helpless to stop her head turning.

Their eyes met for a moment before she turned back to keep on track. What had always seemed like a few paces to reach the elevator now seemed like a long distance marathon with blurred vision through flooded eyes. Please let the door open quickly. She pressed the button without putting the box down and stood to face the closed doors. She was screaming inside for them to open.

"Mary, what are you packing in the box, you're not leaving us, are you?" Jake called out laughing.

The doors opened, and she stepped in. She had made it off the floor, now it was just past reception, hand in her pass and then out onto the street. The reception was busy. Great, she could slip her pass on the counter and leave unnoticed.

She hung back to make sure reception was speaking with someone;

then approached, just resting the box on the counter off to the side for a moment. She unclipped the pass from her waist and placed it on the counter, and she picked up the box. One of the receptionists turned to her. Mary didn't recognize her; she was new.

"Can I help?"

"No, all good. I just want to leave this old pass with you."

"Ok, hold on. I'll check for your new one."

As the receptionist turned away, Mary picked up the box. Just a short way now, just through the revolving door and out onto the street.

She stepped into the revolving door and felt the cool air on the street on her skin. She let out a deep breath as she walked away from the building for the last time. The outside air was drying her watery eyes.

Chapter Forty-Three

Marcello was three hours into the second tattoo. "I need to stretch a minute," he said, getting up from the upturned box that he was using as a stool.

"Me too."

Christina sat up and swung her legs over the edge of the door. She linked her fingers together and put both hands behind her head.

"That's an interesting picture," said Marcello.

"What is?"

"Sorry, I was thinking out loud. When your arms are up like that, the tattoos sweep into each side of your head in quite an unusual way."

"It looks weird?" Asked Christina.

"No, not at all, it's a nice effect; it looks like a circular pattern, with the rivers flowing back into your mind.

Reminds me of something my Grandfather said about circular rivers.

He used to say that people look for the source of rivers, higher

341

and higher until they find a small trickle of water. They then declare this to be the source.

He would say that they are wrong and this is wrong thinking because the river is like the human mind. The mind does indeed have a central source but constantly feeding back into that source is every act of living and thinking, of being who we are.

We play a great part in the source; just as the rain falling into the river adds to the river and so makes it greater than the single source."

"Your grandfather sounds like he was pretty amazing. You must miss him."

"Yes, he was a big influence on me, but I wish I had realized it at the time and paid more attention to him."

"Maybe you retained more than you think you did."

"Maybe. Ok, let's get this arm finished."

An hour later, Christina sat up and looked at both arms.

"How long before I can have a good rub and scratch?"

Marcello smiled. "About a fortnight."

"God, don't know if I can stand it that long."

"You will."

Marcello started to pack away his gun and ink.

"Well, what do I owe you for this work?"

"Nothing."

"No, no way is that going to happen. I have to give you something."

"I have been thinking about this moment. I knew you would want to pay me. I was thinking about it last night when I fell asleep.

I had a dream that I was on a river in a small boat. I was rowing up the river when I saw my grandfather on the bank of the river. I tried to row towards him, but all I could do was row in a straight line. I could not reach him.

I called out to him, and he shouted back to throw away one of the oars. I was reluctant to do so as I knew I would end up going around in circles. Eventually, I threw one of the oars away, and sure enough, I started going around in circles.

I shouted to my grandfather that I was now stuck in the river, going around in circles.

He laughed at me and told me to put the single oar over the back of the boat and to twist it from side to side.

I started to move, and I could steer. I headed over to the shore, and my grandfather stepped into the boat; As we drifted on the river, He said-

Take notice of what you take in life so that you know when to complete the circle of returning because, from these circles, you move forward.

I then woke up."

"So, what do you make of the dream?"

"I don't know, but I am pretty sure it has to do with giving and receiving, don't you think?

I don't know why you brought the root or why my grandfather told me about the ceremony. And I knew nothing about your tattoos, despite the fact that I had drawn them.

When you add all this up, don't you think there is something going on here that we need to pay attention to?" Christina said nothing as she concentrated putting her outer shirt on without dragging the material over her arms. As she did the last button up, she sat back on the makeshift table.

"Well, when you put it like that, I suppose you have a point. I've had no idea of whom I was to give the root to. It may have been you; it might be someone else. Hey, maybe you end up giving it away. Maybe you're right, and maybe your dream had something to do with it. If you're happy to let things be as they are, then let's settle on it."

"Yes, let's say you have helped me and I have helped you."

"Done deal, then?" said Christina. "See you at breakfast tomorrow."

Marcello nodded. "For sure."

Christina traced her steps back through the trees, but instead of turning left up to the house, she walked down the drive towards the main road. The driveway was a good half mile, and little of it could be seen from the house. As she approached the gates, they swung open. She had triggered the sensor that opened the gates when anyone approached from the inside. On either side of the gates were two large trees. She walked around the base of one of them and then walked back past the sensor the other way, causing the gates to close.

She collected up a few small branches and leaves, placed them at the base of the tree and then made her way back up to the house.

She went straight to the bathroom and slipped off her shirt, to take in the full view of both arms. She shook her head as words that she had repeated many times, whenever a discussion arose about tattoos, came to her.

How many times she wondered, had she stood her ground over the futility of tattoos, and now here she stood with ink from the top of her inner arms all the way to her wrists.

Chapter Forty-Four

"So, who's the non-chatty one tonight then? Yesterday it was me, and tonight it's you. What's up?"

"Sorry, I was drifting off with the fairies."

"Where were the fairies?" Christina laughed.

"Who knows? No, seriously, I was thinking about Mary. She left the company today?"

"Was that unexpected? She never mentioned anything to me about being unhappy at work."

"It was all a bit sudden. I think you had an effect on her and got her thinking about a few things."

"Oh crap, you see what I mean. That is why I hate talking about all this stuff. It affects people."

"But isn't that the whole idea?"

"But not to get people to quit their jobs."

"Can't you get her to come back to the firm? She told me she liked her job and enjoyed working with you."

Ben laughed.

"Oh, I don't think she would want to come back. She got a severance package that was more like a golden parachute. She is going to do some of the things that Michael has been trying to persuade her that they should be doing together. I suspect they are going to have a good next few years, with some exciting times ahead."

"So, what about you?"

"Me? Oh, I will carry on as normal. I will miss her though, that's for sure."

"So, you're not going to quit your job tomorrow and head off into the sunset?"

Ben rubbed his hands together, laughing.

"Now there's a thought. Anyway, changing the topic, this get together we planned before you leave."

"You planned, don't you mean?"

"It's no big deal. It's Wednesday today so how about we make it Friday evening?"

"I hate goodbyes. I told you that. I hate them."

"Think of it as something else, like a get together over a meal. Come on; I'm sure you can make an exception this one time. I promise it will be-" Christina cut in. "I can see you're not going to give in, are you?"

Ben smiled. "Right then, I'll gear it all up. You forget about it; any favorite meal that we can get Anna to prepare?"

"See, you're making something bigger out of this than it need be."

"Ok, ok. No special meal."

Christina's shirt pulled on her arm; she looked down to see a small patch of blood that had dried and then pulled away, so it started to create a fresh blood spot. Ben noticed it. "You're bleeding… what's up?"

"Oh, nothing, I was in the garden today and some brambles caught on my shirt. It's just a scratch.

Ben leaned over.

"Here, let me take a look."

"No!"

"Ok sorry, I was just going to have a look and get something to put on it, that was all."

"It's fine; it's just a scratch."

"Where were the brambles?"

"Why are you making such a big deal about this? It's a scratch."

"Hey, what's got into you tonight..I wanted to know so Marcello can tidy them up, that was all."

"Sorry, I'm not feeling too good. Down near the garden sheds, that's where it happened."

"What were you doing down there?"

"What is this? Twenty questions? I think I will call it a night if you don't mind."

"Sorry, I didn't mean to upset you."

"No, look it's not you, it's me. I am having one of those days. It's probably the jitters from thinking about heading off."

"Well, you know you're welcome to stay longer if you want."

"Yes, thank you for the offer, it's appreciated."

"As I said, it's no problem at all. By the way, do you have a phone?"

"No, I lost it in the jungle and never bothered to get another one. It was old, and they don't make them like that anymore. I hate the new phones with the touch screens."

Ben reached into his pocket.

"You don't mean one of these, do you by any chance?"

Christina's face lit up.

"Wow, exactly like my old phone. I didn't think they made them anymore."

"They don't, but I was in a shop today to sort out some stuff and got talking to an older guy who found two out the back of the store."

"Where is the store? I will go and get one."

"You can't; I bought them both. I have no need for the second one. Don't even know why I bought it. Tell you what, how about you have it as a gift from me?"

"Really?"

"Yes, really" Ben laughed.

"Great, thanks so much. I can't believe I have my old flip phone back."

"Well, there you go, it's upstairs in my bedroom. I will leave it on my office desk in the morning before I leave for the office."

"Oh, thanks so much."

Anna came into the lounge.

"Is there anything else I can get you?"

"No, we're all good thank you, Anna." Said Ben.

"Miss Christina, did you finish with the glad wrap?"

"Oh yes sorry, I forgot, it's in my room, I will get it for you now."

"No, in the morning will be fine."

"It's no trouble to get it now. I am going to my room right now."

Christina got up, but Anna started to walk away.

"No, no. In the morning will be fine."

As soon as Anna was out of earshot, Ben said

"I swear she gets more motherly every day."

"I have good ears, Mr Ben."

"Sorry Anna, no offense. I was just saying-"

"He was saying how much he needs a mother to take care of him, Anna," Christina called after her.

They could hear Anna laughing as she walked away.

"Ok, I'm off to my room if that's ok?"

"Yes, ok. One thing before you go, glad wrap? What's that all about?"

"For packing of some gear; see you tomorrow, ok?"

"Ok, I'll say good night now then, as I have something I want to work on upstairs."

Christina locked the door of her room and took off her shirt, which had stuck to her arm again. She ran some water from the shower head over her arms and then patted them dry. She then applied the cooling cream which reduced the urge to scratch.

She picked up her Journal and started to write.

'What I have to do now I am not happy about, but I can't go through with it. I know where the fear comes from but I am not ready to deal with that right now. I feel as guilty as hell, considering what Ben has done for me but I can't override what is going on inside me now.

I have decided to let Marcello keep the Ayahuasca. There is something in what he said about the series of events, and then there was the image of the tattoos without any possible knowledge of that.

It's almost like an unconscious communication circling the planet which surfaces when the time and place is right. I wish I knew more about that, maybe one day I will.

I have been experiencing some strange sort of want since the tattoos were completed which cause me some degree of fear.

Thinking about the fear as I make this journal entry, I sense that it is from what is coming.

I know that does not make much sense but to put it another way-

There were many messages (actually way more) that were only received as flashed light. When I pressed them into the root section that hung around my neck, I sensed they were somehow stored in there.

I know this is illogical in the physical sense, but I can only write that which I believe or sense to be true.'

As I was writing this, I knew where my fear was coming from-

Now the tattoos are completed I have fulfilled my promise, my contract. I sense that now the messages that I stored will start to come out of the root section and into my mind in an understanding way.

This is exciting in a way, but I have to admit to being quite fearful of this happening. The fear is that I will not be able to control or deal with what comes forth.

Ben opened the double doors to his studio at the top of the house and turned on the lights. He dimmed them down until one stronger light shone on the large painting of the girl in the mask.

He sat down in the chair, facing the picture.

'Where are you?' He murmured.

'What a fucking idiot I was!

I don't know where you are in the world, Lou Lou. Probably married with hoards of kids and long since forgotten me. Well, I tell you what my sweetheart, I am going to find you. I know this is selfish like I was that day you left but this time at least. I can tell you this to your face and admit to being such an arsehole.' He leaned back in the chair and closed his eyes, but it was too late, his eyelids were no match for the pressure that had built up behind them.

Chapter Forty-Five

C hristina woke a little after 10:00 am, dressed and went straight to the kitchen. Anna was not there, but she could hear vacuuming in the distance. She helped herself to some breakfast and then went to Ben's office. Next to the keyboard was an AT&T bag, containing the flip phone.

She turned on the computer screen and logged in as a guest.

There were three email messages. One was from a company offering to complete SEO work for business. The other about buying meds online and the third had the familiar heading - Crowe and Horwath Solicitors.

'Jeez, they are bloody persistent.' She mouthed.

The email read pretty much the same, apart from a PS -

'My Name is Vivian. I work here at Crowe & Horwath. I wanted to reach out to you and let you know that I recently lost my mother and I can understand your reluctance to deal with her estate. Like me, you probably feel like once you do that, then everything has finally gone.

Anyway, I just wanted to let you know that if you want to talk anytime, call and ask for me.'

Christina clicked close on the email.

'Best places to travel to,' she typed into the Google search. The moment the results came back' she knew it was a dumb search string to use.

'Warm places in the world right now -' was the second search, which delivered the hottest places on earth.

She then remembered a conversation that she'd had with Almedio about direction. And how she had thought there was a contradiction between following the dots on a radar screen and having a plan.

She recalled him saying that plans if rooted in a person's core driven purpose, would ultimately deliver dots that were in general alignment to that purpose and would be assisting in keeping that person on a meaningful and satisfying life path.

However, he said that if they made a move away from that path, then often there would be an event, sometimes a radical event which would check that deviation to bring about a course correction.

If that course correction were unsuccessful, then a feeling of being lost and confused would exist, until a correction was made.

He had also said that without knowledge of one's core driven purpose, there would still be a connection but it would be unrecognizable.

During these thoughts, Christina had picked up a pen and was doodle writing.

'The radical event-' she wrote, but even before she had completed the last letter, she experienced again in her mind the accident with Ben. Now her mind was racing, looking for connectors.

If that accident was a course-changing event, then what had she missed earlier, that warranted such an event to happen?

Her mind went into radar mode, searching back to just before Ben drove into her.

What had she been thinking? What had she been doing? More and more scanning at greater and greater speed was going on until it all faded into a blur of confusion.

She turned back to the computer screen and typed.

'Flights leaving soon.' A list came up.

Jordan
Wisconsin
London
Greece
Florida

She clicked on Greece. Flight time was good; it was leaving tomorrow at 7.30 pm which meant an overnight flight, with sleep assured for a good part of the trip.

It was also a bargain price, but there were only a few seats left. As she clicked the book now button, her stomach rolled, and a wave of guilt swept over her, as she thought of what Ben was planning on Friday evening.

A pop-up window appeared saying flight could not be booked online at this time; please call last minute bookings.

She hovered there for a moment and then wrote last minute Greece 7.30 pm under the doodle and logged off.

Back in her room, she opened up her journal and slipped the doodle paper inside as a marker on the last entry.

She then picked up the other journal that contained the messages that she had written since the ceremony. She thought that now with the tattoos completed, she might have more understanding about them.

She picked up a pen and wrote.

'Radical Events.' across the top of the page.

'Radical events, what are they? Are they connected to our core purpose? Do they happen in an almost orchestrated manner? If they do, then who is orchestrating them?

In a way, it can only rest with us.

We must be responsible for them because we have, either consciously or unconsciously, deviated from the path that was in alignment with our core driven purpose.

Sometimes I feel lost and bewildered in all this and have to question my reasons for wanting to even live like this. But then the moment I think such thoughts, I know that conformity is not my or anyone's correct path in life.'

I have bags to pack, yes I really do.

Christina separated her backpack into primary and day pack. It took about an hour to have everything sorted.

Right now, her whole life sat there in front of her. All she had to do was pick it up and move but now was not the time, there were a few things that had to be done, and the first was a letter to Ben.

Chapter Forty-Six

J ust before lunch, Jake came into Ben's office.

"Ben, I heard a rumor that Mary has left?"

"Yes."

"Is it true that you were poking her?"

Ben's face turned red.

"Show some fucking respect, will you? She was here for as long as you and fucking good at what she did."

"Sorry, you know what office talk is like."

"Yeah, well. Fuck the office talk."

Jake shuffled his feet.

"From now on, we have a new system. You come in here in the morning with your recommendations. I check them over against mine. When I'm happy with the outcome, you take them and get them prepped for the troops. Ok?"

"Ok, er- sorry about what I said about Mary, it was out of order."

"Yes well, a lot of people around here don't engage their brain before their mouths start to deliver."

The flip phone rang.

"I have to take this Jake, can you close the door on your way out?"

"Sure."

Ben flipped open the phone.

"Hello, Mr. Williamson?"

"Speaking."

"It's the printer here, regarding the competition forms you wanted. I have a proof ready for you to take a look at. I will email it over to you now"

"It's ok; I will call in as I have to call into AT&T next door."

"Ok, see you in a while then."

Ben flipped the lid closed and then stroked the phone with a smile, before putting it in his pocket.

He collected up a few loose pages from his yellow legal pad, put them into a briefcase and headed towards the garage.

"So, Bill. Tell me, this wife of yours-"

"Sir?"

"How committed is she to this sailing thing? I have a boat you know, down at the Beeches Marina and I estimate that ninety percent of boats never actually leave the marina."

"Yes, I heard that one and I told her that. You know what she said, sir?"

"Tell me."

"She said that there are dreamers in this world that dream of fanciful things with no more desire for those things other than to impress others. But then there are the dreamers of passion and purpose. That, by the way, is the name of the boat that she tells me we are going to sail around the world in. 'Passion and Purpose.'

I have to give it to her, that is a cute name, eh?"

"That it is, Bill. Passion and Purpose."

Ben called first into the AT&T store. The assistant who served him yesterday recognized him immediately.

"Afternoon sir, what's it like to be back with the flip phone?"

"Nice."

"Had someone else looking for one right after you came in; he must have been an enthusiast. He told me the phones first came out in 1989, but the patent on the design was filed some nineteen years earlier. It took nineteen years to get it on the shelves." "Well, good things come to those that wait, eh?" Said Ben.

"Indeed, now what can I do for you this afternoon?"

"I would like a prepaid card for the second phone."

"Sure, how much credit on it? Standard one of the shelf is thirty bucks."

"Yes, that'll do."

Ben handed over $30.00 in cash.

"Just tear open the packet when you're ready and inside, you'll find the sim card and the telephone number assigned to it. Pop the sim in, activate it, and you're ready to go."

Ben pocketed the credit card-sized packet and went next door. The same man came from the back of the store to greet him. On seeing Ben, he said

"Hold on a minute; I will get the proof."

He came back and laid it on the counter.

There was a picture of a yacht taken from behind, as it sailed off into the sunset.

"One thing sir, you did not say how this was to be won. I mean what does the person filling out the form, have to do to win the prize. Oh, and where do they have to send their entries?"

"I want them to write something about why they think they should win the yacht and what type of yacht they would like to win, and then send it in. The person with the best reason will be chosen to be the winner. Put a closing date on the competition - two weeks from today."

"Ok, my daughter can enter that now for you. The other thing we need is an address for them to send in the entry to. What address do you want to use? Normally it's a PO BOX Number."

"This is all getting a bit complicated, where do I get one of those?"

"Not complicated at all sir, real easy to get. We use one for most of our post."

"Could I use your address? I mean, have the entries sent here?"

The man rubbed his chin… "Well… I don't see why not. I mean you only have three pieces, it's hardly going to block our mailbox, is it?"

"Perfect." Said Ben.

"Right sir, if you want to take a seat, I will have my daughter complete this and print you off your three copies, ready to go." The man returned to the back of the store and Ben took a seat to wait. He had about reached the back of one magazine when the man came back.

"There you go sir, all completed."

The now full color finished form looked high quality.

"That's perfect," said Ben, as he slid them into his briefcase.

He pulled out his credit card.

"Charge the fifteen hundred balance to that."

"Are you sure sir?" I mean it was not that much work in the end. How about we make it a thousand?"

"A deal is a deal, and I am using your PO Box. Charge it up."

"Thank you, sir. Pleasure doing business with you."

He swiped the card and Ben entered his pin number.

"Ok we're done," said Ben.

"But I'll need to contact you, sir if you get any entries."

"Ah, I forgot about that. Can you give me a call?"

"Sure. Hope to speak to you soon then?"

"Let's hope so," Said Ben, as he left the store.

That evening after dinner, Ben and Christina talked almost into the small hours before they realized the time. They covered everything from the first abrupt meeting, up until now.

Ben checked the alarm clock and turned off the lights. It had been a pleasant evening. How empty his life had been before meeting Christina and how empty it was likely to return to being after she left.

Chapter Forty-Seven

Christina fought off sleep for another hour. She then turned off the lights in her room, apart from a bedside lamp and pulled the curtains apart so she could open one of the French doors.

Out on the patio, she looked up at the house. There were only dimly glowing hallway lights. She went back to her room and slipped on the heavy backpack and one of the hats she had bought a few days ago.

There was a short stretch of crunching gravel she had to cross before reaching the silent grass. It was a moonlit night, and she would easily have been seen if anyone was paying attention. Once on the grass, she quickened her pace and moved to the cover of the trees as soon as she could so that she could not be seen from the house. Every leaf and twig seemed to be shouting out to call attention to her.

She reached the gates and was careful to avoid the sensor that would have opened them. At the foot of the large tree, she took off the backpack and hat and set them against the trunk. She camouflaged them as best she could with the branches she had left there earlier. The adrenaline was interfering with her mind, and she triggered the sensor. The gates started to open, only this time, lights were also triggered. She quickly moved deeper into the trees and then ran flat out towards the house. Luckily, there was enough light to avoid the branches and brush. In minutes she was at the edge of the trees. Now she had to get across the open lawn and over the gravel. She stayed there a while looking back at the house. The same hallway lights were on, but there was also a shadowy figure looking out down the driveway. She could see this was Anna.

It seemed like forever until Anna moved away from the window. As soon as she turned away, Christina sprinted across the lawn, over the gravel and back into her room. She locked the doors and took a quick shower before climbing into bed.

Chapter Forty-Eight

The smell of bacon reached Christina's room as she was cleaning grass clippings from her shoes that she had not noticed last night. By the time she reached the kitchen, Marcello was already halfway through his breakfast.

"Morning, Miss Christina," Said Anna. "Would you like some eggs?"

"Yes please, that'd be great."

"I'll have her bacon," laughed Marcello.

"You've had quite enough. If you eat too much, you will be lazy working today. Did you have a look around the grounds this morning as I asked you to?" Marcello held a constant gaze at Christina while he said.

"Yes, there was nothing down by the gates, so I don't know why they triggered last night. Maybe it was a branch in the wind. We have had that happen before.

I'll drive around all the grounds later in the caddy cart to check everything more carefully. Would you like to come around for the ride?" He motioned his head at Christina

Anna spun around to look at them both.

"Yes, that is a wonderful idea, Marcelo. I don't know why you have not thought of that before."

As Anna turned back away from them, they looked at each other and shook their heads smiling.

Marcello got up to leave.

"I'll pick you up in the caddy truck in about ten minutes outside your room, ok?"

Christina nodded "Ok."

She finished up breakfast, thanked Anna and went back to her room.

A few moments later, she heard the crunch of gravel under tires and went out through the French doors to meet Marcello.

"You can drive," he said.

He slid over to the passenger side.

"How?"

"Easy, two pedals - go and stop. To reverse, press the forward pedal the other way."

Christina pressed the pedal, and they shot forward, spinning up some gravel from the drive.

"Whoa! Gently does it."

"Sorry, I was expecting to push hard."

"So where shall we go first? How about down to the gates, where you tried to cover your backpack over?"

"You didn't move it, did you?"

"Calm down. I found it early this morning when Anna told me to check the grounds.

Don't worry; I didn't say anything to her. I figured you had a reason which you might like to let me in on?"

"I'm leaving?"

"Yes, I figured that but why the backpack down by the gates?"

"I don't do goodbyes."

"Anna told me they are making a party for you, so you're going to blow that all off?"

"Don't tell anyone, promise me you won't tell anyone; promise me."

"Ok, I was not going to tell anyone anyway. It's your business if you want to run away like that."

"I'm not running away. I just can't handle goodbyes."

"When are you leaving? No, don't tell me. But you can tell me where you're heading."

"Athens."

"Why Athen?"

"It's warm, and I want to see the Parthenon."

They arrived at the gates. Marcello went to the back of the sensor and beckoned for Christina to look at what he was doing. He pushed a small button and said "This disables the sensor and locks the gates after ten seconds. The only way to open them after that is by pressing the button again or by opening from within the house. You might need to know that.

Tell me why are you going to leave without saying goodbye?"

"Look, I have my reasons, ok?"

"Ok, but it doesn't seem right. Anna will be pretty upset, I'm sure. Hey, she thought we were going to get married."

They looked at each other and laughed.

"Well, it's your life, and you have to do what you have to do. I will not say anything to anyone."

"Thanks."

"We better drive around a bit before we go back up to the house to convince Anna that I have checked everywhere."

They drove around the grounds for another half hour before Christina was back to the house and Marcello returned to work.

In Ben's office, she found a yellow legal pad and took it back to her room.

'Dear Anna

Even though I have not been able to say goodbye to you, I want you to know that you are and always will be a special person to me. You always made me feel so welcome, and for that, I will always be grateful.

Love
Charlie :-) XX'

She tore off the sheet, folded it in half and wrote Anna on the front. On a second sheet, she wrote

'Dear Ben

I am so sorry that I could not be a part of the get together for my leaving. I tried to explain to you that I can't cope with any more goodbyes right now. I will always remain grateful for the time spent with you and your generosity in taking care of me (but it was your fault after all) But seriously, I have enjoyed our talks, and I am sure that I will soon be missing them. I am leaving you two items.

You will find them both in my room on the top shelf of the main wardrobe. One item is my journal of messages as now I am ready to start a new one. The second item I imagine you taking to the lake one day on an adventure.

Much of what you will read came to me in the early days after the ceremony. There are many things in the book that I could not talk about with you or anyone else. I was, I suppose, fearful of ridicule, although I now know that this would never have been in your character.

I hope you spend many a day at your lakeside thinking of me and the time we spent together while reading some of the messages.

I suppose I should say that I am sure we will meet again but I am not sure of that and if we are honest with each other, we will likely forget each other soon enough. Please give my apologies to Mary and Michael. I enjoyed my time with Mary. She is one very lovely lady, and maybe you missed your opportunity before she met Michael.

You really must be more proactive Ben and watch the radar for the dots.

Finally, I would like to say sorry again that my departure has had to be in this way, but I hope you understand.

We all have things to find in life, and I am not sure yet what mine is. I do know that I will keep traveling for now and keep looking.

I hope everything happens in your life that you wish for and may all your dreams come true.

Love Christina
  XX'

She folded the sheet in half and wrote Ben on the outside. She then put both notes in one of the small bedside draws.

"Mr. Ben, you are early again," she heard Anna call out as she opened the front door.

"Yes, another early day. Is Christina about?"

Christina stepped out of her room.

"Oh, there you are. I have something for you."

"Not a present, I hope?"

Ben turned to Anna. "What do you make of that Anna, a girl who doesn't like presents?"

Christina cut in-

"Well, it depends on what type of present, I suppose."

"Of course it does," said Anna with a chuckle.

Ben reached into his pocket and pulled out the package containing the sim card for the phone he had given to Christina.

"There you go; sorry you'll have to work out how to put it in, it's all a bit techie for me."

Christina took the card.

"Thanks very much, I'll sort it later."

"Everything all set for tonight, Anna?"

"Yes, Mr. Ben everything is ready."

"Great. Mary & Michael will be here about 7:30, and we'll eat by 8:00… if that is ok with you as well Christina?"

"I want to shoot into town and pick up a few things, but I'll be back by say 7:00."

"Ok I will run you in now," said Ben.

"No, I have ordered a taxi already."

"Well cancel it, and I will take you in."

"No- I- I want some time alone to get a few things."

"Oh… ok, if that's what you want."

"I'm going to take a quick shower, Anna and then spend a while upstairs. Can you call me at about 6:30?"

Ben turned to Christina "Don't be late back from shopping, eh?"

"No, I'll be- Oh, I just have to check something on the Internet. Ok if I do that now?"

"Yes sure."

Christina logged on and typed 'local taxis.' There was an online booking service, and one could be here in fifteen minutes. She booked it and logged off.

She went back to her room and grabbed her smaller pack, took out the two notes from the bedside drawer and went back to the office. She lifted the top clean sheet from the yellow pad and slid under the two notes.

As she opened the front door to leave, Anna came out of the kitchen and came over to her. "Come here," she said.

She walked over to Christina and put her arms around her. Christina responded and hugged her back.

"Take care Charlie," she whispered in her ear. "Take care."

Christina broke away. "I better go as I am going to meet the taxi at the gate to save time."

Anna turned away and walked with head down back to the kitchen.

Christina closed the main door behind her and walked briskly down the driveway. When she reached the gates, she pressed the button and disabled the auto close. She could now manually just open and close the gates.

Her stomach was knotted tense. A few moments later she saw the taxi coming. As the driver indicated to turn, she put her hand up to signal him. He pulled up right beside her. "You booked online Miss?'

"Yes, for the airport."

"Bags Miss?"

"Just one, hold on."

Christina pushed open the gate and grabbed the backpack and hat from the base of the tree. She had not seen the driver follow her in.

"I'll take that Miss."

He reached forward and picked it up.

"Strange place for a bag Miss. Don't worry, seen and heard it all in this business. I learned pretty quick not to interfere. Come on, let's get this in the cab."

The driver dropped the bag in the trunk and closed the door after Christina.

"Ok. Straight to the Airport Miss?"

"Please."

"Where are you going? So as I know which terminal."

"International – Europe."

"Talk if you want Miss if not, I can drive just as well."

"Thank you."

Christina watched the countryside flash by and then change to concrete and freeway. The cab pulled outside international departures. "Says here on my ticket that you paid online, right?"

Christina pulled a $10.00 bill from the pouch that hung around her neck that also contained her passport.

The driver grabbed her backpack from the trunk and set it on the curb. She handed him the $10.00 bill.

"Thanks, Miss. You take care over there in Europe, eh?"

Christina put on the main backpack first and then her hat. She then slipped the smaller one over her front, which balanced the load a little. The airport doors opened, and her stomach fluttered; there was an ocean of people all going to different places. She looked around and then made her way to the last minute counter.

It was in the order of time departing.

London, 90 Minutes

Greenland, two hours

Athens, two hours

Michigan, three and a half hours

"I'd like a ticket to Athens, please."

"Lovely over there, went there myself two years ago. Stay off

370

that ouzo drink they have over there. Dynamite that stuff is and makes your head feel like it was dynamite when you wake up the next morning."

"I'll remember that, thanks."

The clerk took payment and then a printer started up. A ticket popped up from a machine which the clerk tore off and handed it to Christina.

"Thank you, where is check in?"

"You can check in over there." The clerk pointed to a long queue at a desk about twenty-five meters away.

"Oh great and I can drop my bag there as well?"

"Yes, you can."

"Don't worry about that queue; it will be gone in about 30 minutes. The bad news is that the departure gate for this flight is at least a fifteen minutes walk. Or you could take one of those for $20.00." She pointed to a row of chauffeured electric airport carts.

As Christina looked at her watch, the clerk said.

"You have plenty of time before you have to be at the gate, even after checking, so you can easily make it."

"Ok thanks."

Christina slid the ticket into the pouch alongside her passport, picked up her backpack and made her way to some empty seats about fifty meters away.

From here, she could monitor the queue, and people watch.

Chapter Forty-Nine

A nna made herself busy tidying up Christina's room. She opened the wardrobe and reached up to take down a hat and journal. She went over to the bed, sat down and put a hand either side of the book cover.

"Oh, Mi Christina," she said softly.

There was a yellow slip of paper used as a page marker. She opened it up, it was a blank page, but on the marker, it read

'If you find this before the leaving notes, you will find them in the office tucked in the yellow pad.'

She closed the journal and then wiped away a tear, repeating 'Oh mi Christina.' She replaced the hat and journal on the shelf, closed the wardrobe and removed all the bedclothes. She loaded the washing machine and then went to the kitchen. She could see Marcello out front, tending a flower bed. She tapped on the window and signaled for a drink and beckoned for him to come.

She poured the boiling water into the teapot as Marcello removed his boots.

"Nice cup of tea for you Marcello. While it is brewing, you can tell me what you know about Miss Christina leaving. Was she unhappy here with us?"

Marcello looked around the kitchen as if someone else might be there.

"When did you know?" he said.

"It's ok; nobody else knows she has gone."

"When did you know?" he repeated.

"The moment she left I knew she would not be back. Women know these sorts of things."

"I didn't know when exactly she was going to leave, but I thought it was going to be soon, because of the party. She does not like such things. That is all I know."

Anna slid a cup of tea over to Marcello. "You don't know where she has gone?"

Marcello picked up the cup of tea and blew on it, looking at Anna.

"It's ok if you don't want to tell me. I don't suppose it's that important."

"Athens that is where she is going to."

Anna looked at the kitchen clock and figured that long enough had passed since she replaced the hat and journal back on the shelf.

"Finish your tea; I have to go and tell Mr. Ben."

Marcelo's eyes widened.

"Don't worry; I am not going to say anything that involves you."

Anna went back to Christina's room, took down the hat and journal and laid them on top of the mattress cover. She pulled out the page marker note and headed upstairs. She went through the first set of double doors and tapped on the doors at the far end of the short hallway.

"Mr. Ben?"

"I'm painting, Anna."

"Yes, I know Mr. Ben, but this is important."

The door opened. Ben noticed her watery eyes.

"What's the matter, Anna?" He touched her on the shoulder.

"I found this."

She handed him the page marker note.

"Did you find the notes in the office?"

"No, Mr. Ben."

"When did you find this?"

"A few moments ago when I was cleaning." Anna dropped her head, which did not go unnoticed by Ben.

He headed downstairs, calling back to Anna to close the studio doors.

In the office, he picked up the yellow pad and the two notes dropped onto the desk.

Anna was now at the office door. Ben took the note marked 'Anna' and held it out to her.

"Here, this is for you."

He sat down and read his note. He then looked up at Anna, who was wiping a tear as she said again 'Oh, mi Christina.'

Ben laid the note on his desk and spun his chair around, facing out into the garden.

"Do you want anything, Mr. Ben?"

He swung back around to face the desk again.

"I wonder where she went to? Do you have any idea?"

"No, I have no thought on that at all, she did not say anything to me."

"When she said she was going shopping, was that it, was that the goodbye?"

"Si, Mr. Ben I think so."

"That will be all Anna, thank you. Can you close the door please?"

The door clicked shut, and Ben picked up the note and read it again. Heat flushed through his body as he tapped his fingers on the desk. He laid down the note and then noticed the imprint of the doodles on the pad and the faint words last minute Greece

"Anna!"

Ben shouted — and again louder

"Anna!"

Anna came rushing through the office door.

"Mr. Ben?"

"Tell Marcello to get my car out of the garage. Then call Mary, you'll find her number in the Rolodex here." He pointed to it on his desk. "Tell her that tonight might have to be canceled- No, forget that, call Marcello to get my car ready."

"Now, Mr. Ben?"

"Yes now Anna, right now."

Ben turned on the computer screen and logged in under the guest account. He opened a browser and clicked search history.

'Last minute flights' was at the top of the list.

He clicked on that and then the link it provided. He scanned the flights and then checked his watch. He went out the front door, but the car was not there, so he went around to the side of the house to the garage. Marcelo started the engine and looked down to where to put the car into drive. At that point, Ben tapped on the bonnet. Marcello startled to see Ben and hit the brake pedal hard. It was the accelerator. The car lunged forward towards Ben. Marcello turned the wheel hard right and impacted the camper van so hard, that it spun it around sideways.

Marcello jumped out "Sorry Sir!" Ben put both his hands on top of his head.

"Sorry, sir I- you made me jump and I-" — Ben cut him off mid sentence.

"I need a car now. The Bentley, get the Bentley."

"It's not here, sir; it was taken for service today."

"Fuck, is there no car here?"

"You can take my car, sir, it's old but" "I'll take it."

Marcello sprinted out of the garage and around the back. The keys were already in the ignition. He drove around the front of the garage, jumped out and held the door for Ben, who jumped in. Ben closed the door; the car made a horrific grinding noise and then stalled. Ben opened the door.

"It's a bloody stick shift."

"I can drive you, sir."

"Get in."

Ben slid over to the passenger seat.

"Airport Marcello, get us to the airport."

Marcello drove slowly so as not to make the gravel fly up from the driveway.

"Gas, give it gas."

Marcello accelerated, and gravel flew up from the rear wheels. The gates swung open.

"Do you know your way to the airport?"

"Yes sir, I dropped my friend off there last week — luggage sir, you have no luggage."

"I'm not going anywhere; we are going to find someone before they leave."

"Christina?"

Ben twisted half round in the passenger seat, so almost facing Marcello.

"Did you know she was going to leave today?"

"No, well, I-"

"No yes? What do you mean no yes? Tell me what you know. Have you been speaking to her? Did you know she was leaving?"

Marcello changed to a lower gear and then back up when there was no need to.

"We met at breakfast with Anna sometimes, that was all."

"Ok, forget it, let's get to the airport."

They traveled for the next 20 minutes in silence, with Ben looking out of the side window.

Marcello pulled up in the drop off zone. There were people every-where. "Drop me here and wait— No, park up and come inside in case I need you."

Ben got out and went through the automatic glass doors. He looked left and right. There were people everywhere. He then saw the last minute flights booth and went over. The assistant was printing some tickets for a customer at the counter.

"Can you help me?"

The assistant and the customer looked up at Ben.

"I can in a minute sir; I just have to finish with this customer."

"I only want to know if-" The assistant cut him off mid-sentence. "Sir, I will help you, but I have to finish up here with this lady first if you don't mind."

Ben turned around, so his back was now towards the counter and looked up at the screens, scanning all the destinations. Athens. There it was. Gate 26. It flashed up. Make way to the departure lounge.

Christina was about thirty meters away jumping her backpack higher on her shoulders. She picked up her smaller pack and started to walk back through the seats towards check in. She stopped and tipped her head forward so that the brim of her hat obscured her face. She then slowly lifted her head, and her eyes went up, controlling what she saw under the brim line of the hat.

"Sir, I can help you now."

Ben turned back around to the counter.

Christina squatted on the corner of the seat, looking back to the last minute flights booth.

"Where do you want to go, sir?" Asked the assistant.

"Nowhere actually, I am looking for someone and wondered if you could help. Did a young girl, 24 years old, book a ticket with you today?"

"Sir, I could not give out that information even if I could remember. Is she family?"

"No."

"Well, sorry I can't help you, sir."

Ben put both his hands on his head and raked his bottom lip with his teeth.

"Greece, pretty sure she was going to Greece. She has long curly hair, very beautiful."

The assistant held Ben's gaze for a moment. Ben nodded his head slightly and raised his eyebrows. The Assistant shuffled some papers behind the counter without looking at them.

"I hear that Greece is very nice this time of year sir, It's also a long way to the departure lounge, and they will be boarding soon."

"Which way is it?"

Christina observed the assistant point, and then Ben quickly moved off in that direction. She sat for a moment and then looked up at the departure screen.

London was displaying, go to the gate.

She walked quickly back over to the last minute booking counter. The assistant was dealing with another woman who was being very expressive with her arms. The assistant was shrugging her shoulders.

As Christina approached, the assistant remembered who she was and smiled. She then turned to the woman again.

"I'm sorry, but there are no more seats left, this young lady took the last one."

The woman turned to Christina. "You have a ticket to Athens?"

"Yes, do you need one?"

"Yes my father is in the hospital, and I need to get back home as soon as possible. Can I buy your ticket from you? I will give you more than you paid for it."

Christina turned to the assistant.

"Can you get me on a London flight and give this lady my ticket?"

"Bless you, Miss, Bless you."

"Let's see if we can do it first," said Christina, looking again at the assistant who was tapping on her keyboard.

"It's going to be very tight to make London. Hold on."

She picked up a phone and then looked across at a check-in desk. Someone on the desk picked up a phone and then looked back towards the last minute booth and waved.

"I have one ready to go now if you can hold for her. She is right here now."

She waved again at the check-in desk and put the phone down.

"Ok let's change your ticket over," she said as she started rapidly typing.

"No, better still go drop your bags then come back for your ticket."

"Thank you so much," said the other woman at the counter.

Christina smiled back at her and went over to drop her bags. A few minutes later she was back at the booth. The assistant handed over the ticket.

"There was a man here looking for you earlier."

"Yes, I saw him."

"Oh, you did."

"I mean I saw him at the desk. I didn't speak to him."

"I thought he was family or something. I pointed him towards the gate for Athens. I did not tell him anything about you or even confirm that you had a ticket for Athens. I just pointed towards the gate. Do you want me to send a message to the gate for him that you are here?"

"No, I don't want to see him."

"Ok, that is fine. You better go Miss, right now. London is boarding right now."

Christina now free of her backpack looked up at the screen and started to walk towards the gate. She walked right into Marcello.

"You told him I was leaving?"

"No."

"Then why are you here?"

"I had to drive him. I crashed his cars."

"Crashed his cars? What- Oh never mind, I have to go. I have to get to the gate."

They both started to walk towards the gate. There was a short queue as hand luggage was being checked. Marcello noticed London on her ticket.

"I thought you were going to see the Parthenon?"

"I will, but I need to go to London first."

She glanced back to see if anyone was following, then turned back to Marcello.

"Ok, that is it. I am going through now. Promise me if he comes back you will not tell him where I am. I need to get on that plane."

"Ok, don't worry."

Christina leaned forward and kissed him on the cheek and whispered 'thank you.'

They both smiled as Christina passed through the gate and waved back. Marcello stood there for a few moments before turning back towards the last minute booth. Not knowing what to do and where to find Ben, he sat looking at the departure screens.

London came up, gate closed.

Ben had managed to get through to the departure by flashing a platinum air miles card and a lot of bluffing about a family member on the flight. The flight was called, and everyone jumped up to get ahead in the boarding queue. Ben positioned himself on a seat near the desk so he would be able to see Christina in the queue.

Twenty minutes later, Marcello saw Ben walking back through the airport towards him. Marcello looked up at the departure screen. The London flight had departed.

Ben made his way over to the last minute booth. The assistant recognized him.

"She was not on that flight. I got right through to the departure lounge and watched everyone board. She was not there."

"I am sorry sir; the girl I think you are talking about was booked on that flight. After you had left, she came back to the booth and changed her ticket to London." Ben looked up at the departures screen.

"Sorry, sir that flight has already taken off."

Marcello stepped up to the counter. Ben just stood there for a moment with a defocused stare before asking Marcello to get the car and meet him out front.

Part Three

Chapter Fifty

The concrete turned back to the countryside before Marcello plucked up enough courage to speak.

"The car, sir... sorry about that; I have some money for saved for-"

"Don't worry about the car; the insurance will cover that. Tell me; you said you used to have breakfast with Anna and Christina?"

"Not all the time, just if Anna invited me."

"But you did spend time with her?"

"We did not talk too much until the last few days."

"She told you she was leaving?"

Marcelo gave himself time to think, by again changing down a gear and then back up.

"Err- I didn't know for sure."

Ben returned to looking out the side window until they turned back into the gravel driveway.

Marcello pulled up in front of the house. Ben sat there motionless for a moment.

"Sir?"

"Just thinking, Anna was going to ask you to the party tonight. Is that right?"

"Yes, sir."

"Make sure you come." Ben got out the car and walked up to the front of the house. Anna opened the door.

"I missed her."

"I am sure she will be in touch with us." Replied Anna

"That I doubt Anna, that I doubt very much."

Ben started to walk towards the stairs.

"Mr. Ben, I put the book and the hat that she left for you in your office."

Ben changed direction towards the office.

"Are Mary and Michael still coming tonight?" Asked Anna

"Yes, let's keep everything the same and also make sure that Marcello comes as well, please."

Just put a few drinks and some snack food around the kitchen table so that it's all informal. I don't want to turn this into something it was not meant to be."

Ben continued into the office and closed the door behind him. Two hours later, Anna opened the door to Mary and Michael.

"Hello Anna, lovely to see you again," said Mary.

"The same to you and Mr. Michael; come, come into the warm. Mr. Ben is in the lounge; go right through, I will hang up your coats."

Mary and Michael walked through to the lounge where Ben was standing, looking out across the grounds. He turned and greeted Michael with a handshake and Mary with a kiss on the cheek.

"Well, not quite what I had in mind tonight but glad that you are here anyway."

"Why... what's the matter?"

"Christina-" Ben paused

"Christina what?" said Mary, looking towards the entrance to the lounge.

"She is not coming- she left a few hours ago."

"Oh, I would have loved to have said goodbye," said Mary

"So would I."

"Sorry- I'm not with you."

"She just up and left, just like that. No word to anyone. I came home; she said she wanted to get some things in town and would be back. Instead, she went straight to the airport and flew to Athens. Well- London, she changed her ticket at the last moment."

"I'm not following how you found all this out if she only left a few hours ago."

"I followed her to the airport. Don't ask me why I did that; I know it was a stupid thing to do. I felt that- well, I don't know why I felt it was a good idea to try and catch her."

Mary looked at Michael, who shrugged his shoulders. Then back to Ben, who did the same.

"So... one minute here and the next gone? No note or anything?"

"Yes, she left a note and one of her journals. Oh- and a hat."

"The Indiana Jones hat?"

"Yes."

"I wondered why she bought two that day."

"What day?"

"When we went shopping. I took her to the hat store and told her what you said about people trying on hats. She bought two of them. Obviously, one for her and one for you... quite sweet don't you think?"

"I suppose so."

"You know what- maybe she was trying to tell you something."

"Well, I will wear it into the office in the morning-" They all laughed.

Anna came into the lounge.

"Everything is ready Mr. Ben."

"Thank you, Anna, we will be right in."

Ben turned to Mary and Michael.

"I hope you don't mind guys, but instead of dinner, tonight I asked Anna to put together a buffet type thing in the kitchen."

"Sounds like my kind of food," said Michael.

Anna had laid out a selection of finger foods and had arranged six stools around the center island. The rear door opened and

Marcello came in. His head tilted slightly down. He avoided direct eye contact with anyone. Anna went over and put her arm on his shoulder.

"Mary, Michael, this is Marcello." They said their hellos while Ben nodded to Marcello. Anna handed him a plate and said: "Help yourself."

With that, they all started to pick at the food.

"So, any idea why she ran off like that?" said Michael. Ben looked up from his plate.

"I don't think it was a runaway; I think it was a bit deeper than that. Looking back now, I made the mistake of organizing this."

Ben gestured his arm to indicate what they were all doing now.

"I think she just didn't like the idea of a get together before she left."

Marcello looked at Ben as if to say something, then dropped his eyes to back his plate.

"So what was in the journal?"

"Messages."

"Messages?" butted in Michael.

"Yes, full of messages from when she took part in the ceremony in Peru."

"What do they say?" asked Michael.

Marcello put his plate down and coughed slightly, which brought everyone's attention.

"They are her interpretations of knowledge as they were passed to her," Marcelo said.

Everyone looked at Marcello. He went to pick up his plate which Anna interrupted by touching his arm.

"What do you mean messages?" she said

Michael interrupted before he could answer. "How come you know this?"

Marcello sat up straight on the stool and rubbed both hands up and down on his thighs.

"When you take the ceremony, you become connected to what is known as the earth mother. You see and hear things, a sort of communication with higher spirits-"

Michael leaned forward, hanging on his next word but then cut in again. "How do you know this stuff?"

"I am from Peru. My grandfather told me all about the ceremony."

"Have you done this?" Asked Ben.

"No sir."

"There is no need to call me Sir, Marcello... Ok?"

Marcello nodded.

"So have you done this ceremony yourself?" Ben asked again.

"No, my grandfather forbade me to do it while he was alive."

Michael leaned forward.

"Why would he do that? He must have known it was a bad thing to do if he didn't want you to do it."

Mary touched Michaels' arm. "Stop interrupting, let him tell us."

"Sorry." Michael leaned back.

Marcello looked at Michael.

"It was never a bad thing to do, and yes, I wanted to do it, but he told me that it was not my time. He said that my time would come after he had returned to earth mother."

Ben turned to Anna and then Mary. "Ladies, please excuse me when I say that a few short weeks ago if I had been listening to any of this, I would have said what a complete load of bollocks. But now-"

Marcello cut him off mid sentence.

"But now it is not so; now it becomes relevant to your life. This is the way of it all. The messages are all around us all the time, but only a few people get to interpret them in the way they are meant to be understood."

"You can do this interpretation?" asked Ben.

"You can do it; we can all do it."

Mary put her hand up to signal that she wanted to speak.

"So are you saying that Christina was a messenger?"

"Well, look around the table. I didn't know that Christina had touched all the lives here tonight. I only know now that she has had a big effect on us all."

"So, Marcello are you going to do a ceremony?" asked Ben

"I have to consider that meeting Christina was meant to be. Up until then, I had not given it much thought. But after the tattoos-"

Marcello touched his chin and then reached for a sandwich that he didn't want.

"Tattoos," said Anna "I found some blood marks on the sheets of Christina's bed. Was that it? She had some tattoos made?"

Marcello took a bite out of the sandwich and made it last.

"She told me about the tattoos," said Ben.

"Where did she get tattoos made?" asked Anna.

"I didn't know she had had them done."

Everyone looked at Marcello who could no longer hold onto the mouthful of sandwich and had to swallow.

"I did them for her."

"You tattooed those images on her arms?"

"Yes."

"Where… when… did you do them?"

"Here, down in the garden building — it was on my own time, Sir. I was not cheating on work. I started early to do my hours and-" Ben cut him off. "I don't care about that. They were big tattoos. When she told me about them, she showed me how much of her arm they had to cover, and it was a lot."

"Yes very big, from the top of her upper arm to her wrist."

"Hold on here a minute." said Michael.

"Christina came here without tattoos; she told you Ben about the tattoos, then she gets you, Marcello, to do them…

How the hell were you able to tattoo her arms?"

"Yes, I am intrigued with that." said Mary.

"You do tattoo, Marcello?" Anna put her hands on her head. "Madre Mia, it's all too much for me."

She turned away and filled a kettle of water, muttering "Madre Mia," under her breath.

Ben looked at Marcello prompting him to continue.

"I am a tattooist. I have studied for a few years, and I do this in my spare time for people. It was extraordinary with Christina as I think that she was not going to have any tattoos until she saw the drawing."

"Drawing?" asked Mary.

"Yes, I make sketches sometimes, and Christina saw a design that was the same as her tattoos were meant to be. It was then that she decided to have them done and I did them for her."

Anna cleared some of the plates then placed a cake in the center. They all stopped talking and read the pink icing.

"Safe travels and much happiness, come back soon."

Ben stroked his chin and slid his index finger just under his left eye that was in danger of leaking.

Anna cut the cake and served it on the plates while they all watched. As she reached Marcello he put his hand out "Not for me Anna, I can't manage the sweetness of the icing."

"Just a little of the sponge then."

Marcello knew it was futile to resist, so took a small bite of the sponge.

"Well, if you don't mind I have to go now." said Marcello.

"Why? It's not late." Ben looked at his watch. "It's only nine, just after."

"Sorry, but I have arranged to meet someone at home tonight who needs a place to sleep, and I said I would be there to meet him."

Marcelo stood up.

"Thank you for everything." He turned to Anna.

"It was lovely Anna, thank you."

Anna put her hand on his cheeks and then gave him a motherly kiss. Marcello looked back at everyone, shrugged his shoulders and then beamed a smile at Anna.

"Nice meeting you." said Mary.

"Yes, very pleased to meet you," echoed Michael.

"Maybe we can chat again soon." said Ben.

Marcello nodded and left via the back door.

"Lovely Boy." said Anna.

"Yes," echoed Mary.

"Shall we take coffee in the lounge?" suggested Ben.

"Yes, a good idea Mr. Ben; I will bring it in shortly, you go to the lounge now, and I will tidy up and bring coffee."

They all got up and went through to the lounge. As Ben was going to sit down, he said. "Hold on; I'll be back in a minute, I'll just grab the journal that she left."

Mary and Michael sat down facing the fireplace.

"Who is that?" said Michael pointing to the masked girl?

"Don't ask, it's a touchy subject."

Ben came back in the room to catch the end of "touchy subject" and saw Michael looking at the picture.

"No, not a touchy subject anymore. She was and still is my childhood sweetheart. She was the girl that I didn't come through for. She was and is the love of my life. She was my greatest happiness and my greatest sadness. I am going to find her and let her know that I made the biggest mistake of my life letting her go."

"Wow- and when is all this going to happen?" said Mary.

"I don't know, but after tonight I think Marcello has a part to play in all this. I feel so bloody stupid that all this while I have seen and ignored so many pointers in my life."

Chapter Fifty-One

Ben sat down opposite Mary and Michael. He opened up the journal that Christina had left him.

"I don't know what to make of most of these messages, but some of them speak out to you. Here is one, for example, it's called 'Living half a life.' I'll read it to you.

'This message troubled me as death seemed to be all around me. I asked Almedio to help me to try and understand; he agreed but showed some reluctance.

I explained that I had a vision where I was standing on railway tracks. I was one of many people. In fact, as far as I could see in front of me and behind, was a single line of people extending to the horizon. On the horizon line in front of me, I could see a whiff of smoke and hear a whistle.

The people on the tracks were not moving; they just stood there talking to each other.

Then someone tapped me on the shoulder. This person was off to the side of the tracks. He was dressed in expensive clothes, and I could see that he had arrived in an expensive car. He kept trying to talk to me, but I kept thinking about the whiff of smoke and the whistle. I could not see the train, and it was so far off that I could not judge its speed and what was happening to the people on the tracks.

I shouted to the people up front to get off the tracks; they just looked around and then went back to chatting. The man tapped me on the shoulder again and said.

'They can't move, they can't even hear you.'

The man then produced a trash can and emptied it on my feet, which made me feel calm. I no longer shouted to anyone on the track. I turned to thank him, but he was walking away. He was now dressed in plain clothes and had a small dog with him, who turned and barked at me before going back to walking beside the man. As he got to his car, he ignored it, and it turned to rust and fell into the ground.

I started to chat with another person on the tracks about the trash around my feet and noticed how everyone had trash around their feet. I heard a whistle and looked up the line. The train was getting closer. I went back to chatting and listening to others.

The whistle went again, and this time I could judge the speed; it was coming fast. I tried to move off the tracks, but my feet were stuck. I started to shout for everyone to get off the track, but they ignored me. I could now see the train was striking bodies and they were being thrown into the air and killed.

The train got closer and closer but it was no good, I could not move. I was hit, and everything went black. I thought I was dead.

Almedio laughed at me which made me feel rather stupid.

'Why are you laughing?' I asked.

'I'm sorry,' he said 'but sometimes I hear a message and it's difficult to understand; other times the full translation is clear. This is one of those cases. The imagery tells you all that you need to know about this message.

Let's work through it together, but before that, I must remind you that you have not completed your part of the contract yet. You agreed to the tattoos and I will only be able to help with those translations that are, let us say, on a lower level. When you have the tattoos, there will be a time of synchronicity in your life. You will learn the importance of all the messages that you received and those contained in that.'

Almedio pointed to my necklace.

As we sat there, on Almedio's favorite log by the river, he picked up a small stick and scratched two lines in the dust.

'These are the train tracks. These tracks represent time. Now time is not a linear thing like most people think it is but that is for another day. For now, we will treat it in the linear form.'

He then paused for a moment as if thinking which carried on too long and prompted me to ask what the matter was. 'Nothing, it was that now is the time for me to mention time and I was about to pass that over. Close your eyes for a moment. Now go back in your mind to when you saw the train crashing into the people and all the bodies were being thrown into the air.'

With my eyes closed, I was able to pull the entire image back up. He told me to signal with my hand when I had the image restored in my mind.

I lifted my hand.

'Ok,' he said, 'now examine the bodies as they are flying through the air. Examine them carefully. What do you see?'

'It's horrible; there are body parts flying everywhere.'

'Now focus on the body parts.'

My face must have screwed up because he said

'There is something wrong, isn't there?'

'Yes, I said, 'there are way too many legs.'

'Now look at the legs and what do you see?'

'Ah, they are not all legs, they are sections of railway tracks. The tracks are being destroyed as the train is coming.'

He then said it was ok to open my eyes.

He continued to say that the train tracks represent your current life path. The train represents a time line. Where you are now standing represents your point of death on this line, if you stay on the tracks. We can't stop the train, but we can fool ourselves that there is plenty of time to stay on the track with the trash and enjoy life before the train reaches us.

We can fool ourselves that is it better to work now at something we don't like, accumulating trash, with the dream that one day we can do something that we do like.

We fool ourselves that one day if we work hard enough, we will be able to stop work and enjoy a full life. We associate a full life with that last part of life where we can see the train.

The reality is of course that we have not been living at all up to this point in our lives and that is a waste of our lifetime.

'But what about the tracks being destroyed?'

'That is very simple; this is telling you that there is no going back. The train cannot be sent away from you, no matter what you do.

Like I have explained before, it's not uncommon to hear stories of how people are given only months to live and on hearing that news, they quit their job and engage in something they have always wanted to do.

Not only that, everyone encourages them to do this. Not one person says 'Oh, you can't do that, what are you going to do for money? How will you manage? I am not sure that is a good idea?'

No-one will say such things; in fact, none will even think of saying such things because what will be going through their minds is what they would do the same if they were in that person's shoes.'

'So what about the man that tapped me on the shoulder?" I asked.

'Well, he emptied a trash can on your feet which tied you to the tracks. The trash was symbolic of all the trash that people have in their lives that ties them to their life tracks. When he walked away from you, he had simplified his life. He was in plain clothes, and the car turned to rust and disappeared into the ground which symbolized the fleeting moment of joy at buying something new.'

'And the dog?'

'Ah the dog, that was very important because a kindly cared for dog will give you unconditional love and loyalty. You must have unconditional love for what you do in life. The value of this unconditional love is how you measure the value of your life timeline.

The loyalty of the dog symbolizes that to live a life of high and satisfying value is to be like the dog that remains loyal to his keeper. You must remain loyal to your true life, the life you know that delivers not only value to yourself but also to others.

There is the life we live and the life we don't live. The life we live we could say is the life of half-awareness. This half-awareness gets us through the day, through work, relationships and all the other myriad of things that make up what we call our lives.

The other side of life is a different side of us. This other life is our essence. Our essence can be thought of as what we are at our core.

The opposing side to our essence, the opposing side of our core driven purpose, is our presentation of ourselves to the outside world. Our essence can be buried and distorted and never acknowledged, but it will always be there in its pure form.

This form many do not get to experience until the train is bearing down on them at full speed.

If you stop for a moment today and look at what you are presenting to the world, you will know whether this is the real you, the real essence of who you are. If it is the real you and you are engaged in living your core purpose, it will be a foregone conclusion that you are a happy and content individual.

Likely, however, things are quite different. Likely you are living a different life, a life that is acceptable, a life that has been molded to conform in one way or another to society 'rules.'

This is living half a life. To live a full life you cannot live by rules that do not emerge from the essence of whom you are. Rules that emerge from within are rules that lead to happiness and contentment. Rules that are provided to us via social acceptance provide us with conformity and oppression of self.

What prevents us from living our core driven purpose is not so much that we are not aware of it but that we cannot see a way where we could achieve that lifestyle, that way of living.

Most of us tread the same path. We go to school, get some good grades, go to university, get some good grades, get a job, obtain debt, work for the next 45 years to pay off the debt while carrying the false dream that this is the way to freedom.

During all this time, we are busy burying who we really are and what we are meant to be doing with our lives. Remember, every day, every moment that passes has a value. We are conditioned to measure that value by the amount of money that we extract from another and then accumulate for ourselves.

We often hear the conversation about the value of time. How much you charge for or get paid for your time. But where is the value in this? At the end of the week or whenever you are paid, draw that money in physical cash. Lay that money out on a table and look at it for a moment. Is it all there or have you already been forced to automatically pay some of it to another organization? Whatever you have left in physical cash is a direct representation of something you have given up, something you can never get back. You have exchanged your time for this.

But now add a word to time, an important word. The word 'life' and now we have 'life time.' What this money represents is the value that you have placed upon your life TIME.

Now as you look back at the table before you, ask the question: 'If I could have obtained this living from anywhere and doing anything of my choosing, what would I have done with my time, my LIFE time?'

This is a big question, the answer to it will sometimes allow you a glimpse towards your essence and your core driven purpose.'

Ben closed the journal and looked up at both Mary and Michael; their eyes were defocused.

"It's an interesting message, don't you think?" said Ben. Mary reached out and took Michael's hand. Ben looked at their interlocked hands and remorse rolled through his stomach.

Chapter Fifty-Two

"Morning Bill how was your weekend."

"Morning Sir. It was amazing, went out to the ocean and got some sand in between our toes."

"Starting to get a bit cold for that, isn't it?"

"You can't keep my Suzy very far from the ocean, no matter what the weather."

Ben started for the elevator, but about half way, he stopped and turned back.

"Bill."

Bill was just getting in the car to park it.

"Sir?"

"I didn't leave any documents in the car, did I?"

"Hold on; I'll take a look."

"No sir, just what looks like some junk mail."

Bill held up the competition form.

"Is that what you meant?"

"No it's all good, I must have them in my case."

"Did you want this sir or shall I get rid of it?"

"No, I don't want it."

Ben turned back to the elevator.

Instead of calling for the elevator, Ben waited and watched Bill park the car. He watched him climb out with the paper in his hand. He glanced down at the paper and then screwed it up. Ben pressed the elevator button, and the doors opened.

It seemed like a time lapse had taken place by the time the door opened again. Ben looked around the office and for the first time, noticed the speed. He became aware of his own pace being much slower. By the time he reached his office, he had become so involved with his slower pace that he didn't notice an older woman was already inside sitting down.

He closed the door behind him as the woman stood up.

"Morning, Sir."

Ben turned back from the door.

"I'm your new PA sir. I have lots of experience in what you do here; I worked for some competition for years."

"Why did you leave them?"

The woman adjusted her clothing and stood up a little straighter than was comfortable.

"Honestly, Sir?"

"Yes please."

"Well, not to be crude sir, a younger model you might say; still wet behind the ears but with other assets."

Ben smiled.

"Well, I'm the lucky one getting the more experienced model, and I don't think there is anything wrong with that."

The woman smiled and came off the uncomfortable stance.

"Sarah, sir. That's my name, Sarah."

"Sorry, I should have asked you that earlier."

"My name is-"

"Ben Sir, they told me at the interview."

"Best you drop the sir from now on. I don't like the sir title ok."

"Yes, s... sorry Ben."

"Have you met anyone else?"

"Jake, you're second in command."

Ben sat down at his desk smiling. He opened up his case and pulled out his yellow pad and envelope. He handed the envelope to Sarah.

"Could you see to it that this goes in the morning post-run please?"

Sarah took the letter and looked at the address.

"It has no name, Sir."

"That's fine, just send it as is."

"Ok and the worksheets for this morning?"

Ben tore off several sheets from the yellow pad.

"My. you're as efficient as Mary."

"Thank you, sir, I heard about Mary from the other girls."

Sarah left with the sheets of paper in hand. Ben spun his chair around and looked out across the city. He thought how this was becoming a ritual for him and how he had never really taken any notice of the view before.

Jake knocked.

"All good Mate?"

Ben spun around and slapped his hands on his desk.

"All bloody great, actually."

"So you're back! Scaggs tonight?"

"No, I have other plans."

"The backpacker....... is she......."

"She left."

"Oh..... I thought that was......."

"You're over thinking things again, which leads to mistakes. Speaking of mistakes, have you checked my numbers yet?"

"Is that necessary Ben...... I mean......"

Ben slapped the desk hard.

"Jake, you want all this." Ben waved his arms around his office, "but you don't want it because you don't want to take responsibility."

"Ben....."

Ben pointed to the door.

"Not now, I have work to do."

"Ben……"

"I said not now; we're done ok? Done."

Jake closed the door as Ben turned his chair back around.

Bill had screwed up one of the three competition forms; one had been posted. There was one remaining in his briefcase.

He pressed a button on his phone, and Sarah answered. "Sir? I mean Ben?"

"Sarah, could you find out if any of the directors are in the building this morning and if they are, could you arrange a five-minute meeting with them?"

"Ok, anything else?"

"No, that's all for now."

Ben hung up and turned again to look at the city. How many, he wondered, were sitting in cages like his.

"Ben."

Ben spun his chair around. A director was standing in the doorway.

"That was quick."

"Yes, the call came straight through to me."

He pulled up a chair.

"What's the issue? Sarah?"

"Sarah…. no, she seems fine. I want a holiday."

"Want or need?"

Ben leaned back in his chair.

"Does it matter?"

"No of course not Look we were at a meeting the other day, and it was mentioned that maybe you were having some issues. To be honest, there were several around the table that were not happy with you passing so much responsibility to Jake."

"What!"

"Don't get me wrong Ben, returns are good, but they are not at your level. Take that over a couple of weeks, and we are talking several million."

Ben leaned forward and pushed both palms down on his desk as he stood up.

"I'm taking a month off, starting right now."

"Ben, don't be-"

"Don't be what?"

"I'll talk to the other directors ok?"

"Talk all you like; I am out of here today."

Ben picked up his case and walked out of his office. The director was still sitting down. Jake saw Ben leaving and started to walk towards him. Ben held his hand out and gave a stop command. Jake turned and went back to his desk. Ben waited at the key booth while Bill fetched his car. He folded the last competition form in half, tore a tiny corner from it and slipped it under some papers. Bill held open the car door for Ben.

"There you go sir; you have a beautiful day."

"You too Bill, you too."

Ben seated himself in the chair, facing the girl in the mask and opened the journal to read.

'Intelligence

As I reached up and touched the sloping form that I thought was a skull, I knew that this was the source of universal conscious-ness, of intelligence. The message relating to this came to me later, during the ceremony. It was given in a rather abstract way. I found myself floating in what I thought was warm water; no light, just blackness but a blackness that provided complete peace of mind.

I didn't have a single care in the world. In fact, I remember that the more I tried to think of something; it seemed to move further away from me. It was like my thoughts were slipping out of my mind and sliding off into the blackness somewhere. I then had a vision of two warring armies. They were equally matched in every way.

Each army was standing on hilltops looking down into a flat valley, where I assumed the battle was going to take place.

I then walked down the valley and at first, no one noticed me. I looked up to the left and right, and all they were doing was shouting at each other from hilltop to hilltop.

The shouting stopped, and I looked up at both sides, to see that they had noticed me walking below. They started shouting again, but this time they were shouting at me. Then both sides ran down each hill into the valley and stopped, leaving a gap of about twenty meters with me right in the middle.

Both sides had now stopped shouting at each other and were now shouting for me to join them. If I took a step to the left, the army on the right showed fear and called louder. If I took a step to the right, the army on the left showed fear and called louder. Both sides were trying to convince me that they were fighting for a just cause and I should join them so that the other side would be outnumbered. The noise became so great that I had to hold my hands over my ears and when they saw me do this, they lowered the volume of the shouting.

Lower and lower it went until there was silence again. Then a soldier from the left side broke ranks and walked towards me. A soldier from the right did the same. We met in the middle where they both tried to reason with me to go to them. Again I put my hands over my ears.

Once again they fell silent.

Slowly at first, the two armies started to merge, and then they fused into a single mass. Tighter and tighter the mass became until a single being emerged and stood before me.

I asked 'What does this mean?'

The being did not speak but instead conveyed thoughts directly into my mind. I knew that these thoughts were not emerging from within myself but rather from an intelligent source. These thoughts were telling me that we are all capable of contacting and receiving intelligence from universal consciousness. The problem is that we erect barriers to this by the constant internal noise or dialogue in our minds.

Intelligence is something we receive when our minds are held in a freefloating state of nothingness. It is then that our mind can merge with universal consciousness. When this happens, we do not have access to universal consciousness; we become universal intelligence.

Today we only know this in fleeting moments; we call this intuition, and only a few are so tuned that they can live an intuitive life. Intuition is like a portal into universal consciousness. As long as we can hold open this portal, we can access the whole of consciousness.

I remember entertaining a thought that this seems like a fanciful idea and was mentally reprimanded. That reprimand was of itself a message about how we close off this portal by that very process. Thoughts and feelings are not intuition. Intuition is pure knowledge. Intuition is always correct but the instant we receive it, we contaminate it with thought.

The idea of living an intuitive life is appealing and at the same time unnerving. We have erected structures in our lives, similar to that of scaffold around a building. This scaffold gives us a safe and secure feeling. The scaffold that we build around our lives becomes a permanent fixture. We believe that this scaffold must be maintained at all cost because to remove it would mean that we are suddenly naked and vulnerable.

The truth is the complete opposite. The scaffold is an illusion that is based on self-imposed rules and self-inflicted obligations to conform. Academic intelligence is not the same as intelligence that resides in universal consciousness. One is a surface intelligence; the other exists as a living, breathing entity that is the conscious universe itself.'

Ben closed the journal and looked up at the centerpiece of the studio - the girl in the mask. He sat there a few minutes as if in a trance and then closed his eyes. His mind started to drift. It was a crazy idea; it was so far off the wall, what would happen, what would be the purpose of going there? He reached down beside the chair and picked up the hat. It caused a smile to run across his face.

He put it on and looked up at the girl in the mask.

'Well, Lou Lou, I said I was going to find you. Maybe the hat will be the thing that makes it happen. Shit,I am going to do it.'

Two days later, the plane was coming into land. He looked out of the windows either side; the jungle seemed to extend to what looked like the curvature of the earth.

He picked up his backpack from the conveyor belt and put it on. He adjusted his hat and walked out of the airport. The air was thick with humidity, which caused sweat to run down his back. There were hundreds of taxi bikes, all vying for business and shouting to all the arrivals.

"You taxi."

Ben looked down at a young man.

"I help you get a taxi. I English speak."

The Boy held out his hand to shake. Ben unconsciously automatically responded.

"My name is Pablo. What is your name?"

"Ben."

"Meet you very good Ben, nice hat."

"Where you go?" said Pablo.

"To the port."

Pablo's face contorted and Ben knew he had not understood.

"Where the boats leave from," Ben said.

"You want a boat?"

"Yes, I want to go to a place called Bora."

Pablo gave an ear-to-ear smile.

"That is my village. You are the man in a hat; this all good. Come, come, we have to go now."

Pablo walked towards a motorbike taxi and waved for Ben to follow. Ben felt like he was being manipulated but decided that he had nothing to lose as his name was Pablo. It couldn't be, could it? I mean what are the odds of meeting the same Pablo that had guided Christina. How many Pablo's were there? Probably a hundred in the airport crowd alone.

The taxi weaved its way through the city of Iquitos. The port was one jetty out into the river, with at least fifty boats all tied up in what seemed like no particular order.

Ben went to pay the taxi. The driver asked for $20.00. Pablo launched into a tirade at the man who then said $10.00. Ben handed over the $10.00 and followed Pablo towards the boats. Several boat owners called out to Pablo, who ignored them. He then waved to an old man sitting in his boat, almost in the middle of all the other boats. It would have been much quicker to take a boat from the outside, but they waited until the old man came alongside so they could climb in. They were soon out on the river with only one or two other boats to be seen.

"You go to see someone in my village?" asked Pablo.

"Yes well, I don't know."

"He told me you come."

"Who?"

"Man in hat, a man in the hat is coming to the village. That is how I see you at the airport."

"You were sent to meet me?"

Pablo spoke rapidly to the old man in the boat. The old man laughed and then kept nodding to Ben and smiling. He then reached out to Ben's hand while keeping the other steering the boat. He shook hands and spoke in Spanish to him.

Pablo interrupted.

"No hablo Espanol." But not before Ben had heard the word Almedio.

Ben wished he had paid more attention to Anna when she spoke in Spanish and vowed to do so when he returned home. Pablo tapped Ben on his shoulder and pointed up ahead.

"Bora."

Ben nodded and then asked. "Almedio lives here?"

The old man butted in.

"Almedio si, si, Almedio," and waved his arm in the direction they were heading. Pablo moved to the front of the boat as they came alongside a platform, where a few tables and chairs had been placed.

He tied up the boat, and they climbed out.

Pablo turned to Ben.

"Fifteen dollars is ok."

Ben nodded and took out $15.00 and handed it to Pablo, who climbed back in the boat and gave it to the old man. He leaned forward and pulled Pablo to him, kissing him on the cheek. Pablo climbed back out the boat and untied it, pushing it clear.

The old man waved to Ben and then turned the boat around, going back in the same direction they had come from. They walked up into the village, where several locals nodded to Ben and then Pablo.

"You stay for time?" asked Pablo.

"I don't know yet."

"We have good places to stay; clean and nice to eat."

Ben noticed a signup front that had a spelling that caught his eye.'BedZ.' This was where Christina had stayed. Ben tapped Pablo on the shoulder and pointed to the sign. "Suzi? This is Suzi's place?"

Pablo glanced around as if looking for answers from somewhere. "You know Suzi?"

"No, I know someone who stayed here."

"You want to stay here?" asked Pablo.

"Yes."

Pablo went over to where the sign was and called out. A woman came to the front of the house and ruffled Pablo's hair. Pablo straightened his hair and then they both spoke rapidly. The woman rubbed her chin and then spoke again to Pablo.

Pablo turned to Ben.

"She says she has room, but I must ask if you want another place."

Ben rubbed the back of his neck.

"She does not want me to stay here?"

"No, it is not because this but she was thinking to help someone else with a guest."

"Can you tell her that I want to stay here because a friend stayed here?"

Pablo spoke again to the woman who threw her arms open and beaconed for Ben to come in. Pablo followed.

"Who was your friend?" asked Pablo.

"Her name is Christina."

Suzi turned around. "Christina- pelo rizado, muy largo?"

Pablo translated.

"She says your friend had long hair very much twisted."

"Curly hair…. Yes," replied Ben.

Pablo scratched his head and then spoke to Suzi. They both became highly animated, then they both agreed on something. Pablo turned to Ben.

"Christina, I remember; she stays here in this room." Pablo pointed to a room.

"You can stay there if you want."

"Yes, that would be great."

Pablo spoke to Suzi again.

"Si, si…" She pointed to the room and gestured for Ben to go that way. Ben went into the room and took off his rucksack. He took out $20.00 and handed it to Pablo.

"Is too much."

Ben got the idea that this was a well-rehearsed routine for Pablo and just smiled at him and pressed the $20.00 into his hand.

"I tell Almedio that you here," said Pablo as he left.

Suzi appeared in the doorway of Ben's room. She made a gesture of putting food into her mouth.

Ben replied "Comida."

Her face lit up.

"Habla Espanol….?" She said.

"Un poco," replied Ben, wishing again that he had paid more attention to Anna.

The chicken and rice were not something Anna would have prepared, but it was tasty and filling. One other person was staying at the place that had come to look at the butterfly farm and had never heard about any ceremony. Ben decided on an early night; it had been a long day.

Chapter Fifty-Three

Ben was already up and had eaten breakfast by the time Pablo showed up. "Buenos Dias," Pablo.

"Good days" replied Pablo. "Your Spanish is good today."

"Did you see Almedio?" asked Ben.

"Yes, but he says you not ready for two days."

"Two days?"

Pablo shrugged his shoulders. The butterfly tourist overheard.

"Come with me to see the butterflies if you have time."

Pablo waved his arms to imitate a butterfly and then put his thumbs up.

"Well?" said the butterfly man.

"Sure, why not? Let's take a look."

It was about a ten-minute walk through the village and butterfly man knew the way, as he had been here before. They handed over their $5.00 entrance fee.

"Keep hold of everything in your pockets. I mean everything. The wee monkeys are very used to humans, and they will come right up to see what you have in your pockets." Butterfly man said to Ben.

The canopy of trees above locked in the humidity. This was the jungle, albeit with signs and walkways. There was a bit of a commotion up front; a monkey had got hold of a mobile phone and then dropped it into a stream when it discovered it was not edible.

"Told you."

Ben checked his pockets and buttoned everything down. Within seconds he felt a hand in his pocket. A monkey had come up behind him and was exploring to see if anything edible was around.

Then another one on the other side. Ben stood there amazed at how confident they were around humans. After a few minutes, they wandered off empty handed.

"How come they are so friendly?"

"They're rescued as orphans; locals still hunt in the jungle, and these are normally the casualties of the mothers being killed. There are a few other animals in here as well. Look out for Pedro Bello. That's the name of a jaguar that was brought here as a wee cub. He's not a cub anymore but don't worry; he will not be checking your pockets."

They walked over a small wooden bridge, passing parrots and even a tapir, and not long after that an anteater. Butterfly man had wandered off ahead a little as Ben stopped from time to time to take in the place. He had never been so preoccupied with just being and experiencing. Suddenly, the hairs on the back of his neck stood up. Pedro Bellow was looking at him. He was only feet away, and for a moment Ben could not see the fence that was camouflaged with foliage.

He breathed a sigh of relief. The Jaguar gave a low growl, which sounded like it had come from deep within the ground before he disappeared back into the foliage. Butterfly man had walked back and saw the Jaguar walk away.

"Pretty impressive, eh?"

"Yes, shame he is locked up though."

"He would be dead in a matter of hours if he was let go. He came here as an orphan and is not scared of people. The locals would kill him for fear of having him around. Come, I want to show you something."

Butterfly man was excited at the thought of showing Ben this next attraction.

"This is Morpho Menelaus. Well, that's its Latin name. It's known as the owl butterfly."

"My god, the size of its eyes."

Butterfly man laughed.

"Look again; they are not its eyes. They are its camouflage to avoid being eaten. The eyes are markings on its wings."

"It does look like the eyes of an owl." Said Ben

"Wait until it opens its wings and we can see inside; you will see the most fantastic colors."

The butterfly was not so accommodating, and after a few minutes, they wandered further into the reserve. They spent the next few hours exploring the reserve together before going their separate ways. Ben walked along the pathways spellbound by the beauty of the butterflies. Occasionally, one would land on him and cause him to stop and take in the moment.

He was getting hungry so decided to go back to where they had come in, as he remembered a small stand there, selling coffee and biscuits. It took a good fifteen minutes to find his way back. He bought coffee and a large biscuit looking thing, which turned out to be more like soft dough. Checking his watch, he realized that he had been in the reserve for nearly six hours.

"You can come back tomorrow to Pilpintuwasi," called out a voice.

Ben turned around to see the woman who had spoken.

"Pilpintuwasi is what they call this place. It means "home of the butterfly.""

She introduced herself as Gudrun Sperrer. She was Austrian and had studied zoology before coming to the village, where she decided with her partner to set up the butterfly farm.

"I was just thinking about how one could spend days in here, wandering around and still see something different every day."

"Yes, it has that effect on people."

"Well, that's good for business," said Ben.

The woman laughed. "Business - no, this is not for money, this is to leave something behind and to show the locals here what they have and the real value of protecting it."

"Is it working?" asked Ben.

"Yes, it is. We are getting more visitors, and each time they see another visitor arriving, they see the value that visitors place on their work."

The woman motioned to a bench to sit down as she was handed a coffee by a staff member.

"So what brings you here, all the way from New York, I would say."

Ben smiled." Is it that obvious?"

"It's a harsh accent, that one."

"Truthfully... I don't know why I am here."

"So you're not here for a ceremony?"

"Well-"

"Ah, so you are here for a ceremony. You heard about it and came to try it but don't know why."

"I am being truthful. I don't even know if I should be here. It's a long story."

Ben gave her a potted history since the accident to the present day.

"So the girl…. Christina you mentioned. I remember her. She spent a bit of time here. It all sounds a bit circular to me."

"Yes, I suppose it does."

"I am pretty sure that you are here for a reason; maybe you will find your purpose like we did when we found the butterflies."

The woman got up to leave.

"Do you know this Almedio fella?" Ben asked.

"Yes, he spends time in the village and out in the jungle. Nice talking to you."

"You too."

The woman walked back towards what looked like a large bird aviary. As she opened the door, she called back.

"If you come tomorrow, come into the breeding room. I am sure you will find it interesting."

She disappeared into the aviary.

Ben decided that he had walked enough for one day and headed back to Suzi's place.

He took a refreshing shower and changed clothes. Suzi showed up to offer to wash them. Five dollars seemed like a good deal, and he handed them over. He lay back on the bed and slept a while. Suzi knocked on his door and placed the clean clothes in a neat pile on the bed.

"It's late, dinner soon, you want?"

"Yes please."

Butterfly man was there again, and they talked about the reserve over a meal of rice and vegetables. It was starting to get dark outside by the time they finished. Ben decided to sit on the porch outside and watch the sun drop below the horizon. A man was sitting there, who moved along the bench to let Ben sit down.

"It's a beautiful thing isn't it?" said the man, without taking his eyes off the setting sun.

"That it is."

Ben was just about to speak when the man put his hand up for silence. He continued to stare at the setting sun, which caused Ben to do the same. Eventually, the sun dipped below the horizon, and the man turned to Ben.

"Sorry," he said, "I like to end the day by letting the sun wash me down for tomorrow."

"Washing you down?"

"Well, I think of it like taking a shower, but that shower passes all through every cell of my body and takes away everything that is not required, to start tomorrow fresh."

They sat in silence for a moment. Ben was thinking about what the man had said and how he started every day by going over the previous day and the day ahead.

"It's interesting isn't it?" said the man, as he got up to leave.

"What is?"

"The things we carry with us as we greet a new day. I often wonder what effect that must have on us and cause us to become so distracted from the things that we should be taking notice of."

The man walked off into the night, leaving Ben alone on the bench.

Ben spent another two days at the butterfly reserve. It was a long time since he had enjoyed time for himself like this. It was having an effect on him. He was walking slower and taking the time to notice life going on around him. On the fourth morning, he slept in and was woken by a tap on the door.

"Almedio says ready," Pablo called out.

"Hold on."

Ben got up and quickly dressed. By the time he opened the door, Pablo was unable to speak due to the amount of toast he had in his mouth. Ben let him finish the rest of it as he grabbed a slice from the center plate and waited until Pablo swallowed before taking a bite himself.

"Almedio say ready now. Go to the butterflies and turn to-" Pablo put his right arm out to signal right."

"Turn right," said Ben.

"Si, si. Then follow the path into the jungle. He sees you on the road in the afternoon."

Chapter Fifty-Four

Christina had seen all the sights of London this past week and was getting restless. Usually she had little trouble knowing where she wanted to go but here in London she felt in limbo as if nothing was happening in her life.

She logged on to check her email and was surprised not to see any mail from the solicitors. She scrolled to the last one she received from them and read Vivian's message again, saying how she had lost her mother.

She flipped open her phone and called the number.

"Howe and Crowath Solicitors. How may I help you?"

"Vivian, I would like to speak to Vivian."

"Speaking."

"Vivian, you don't know me, but you wrote to-"

"Christina?"

"Yes."

"I was thinking of my mother this morning, and at the same time I thought of you, and here you are calling. Let's meet." They arranged to meet for coffee at lunch time.

Chapter Fifty-Five

"You're not going to bother with that, are you?"

"Of course I am, maybe its destiny." She laughed.

"Are you allowed to do more than one?"

"I don't know, why?"

Bill pulled out a crumpled piece of paper.

"I found this one today; they must be everywhere. It's junk mail you know that, don't you?"

She took the paper from Bill and then kissed him on the cheek.

"So you do want to quit your job and sail the world with me. I always knew you were a secret adventurer. Imagine waking up to golden beaches in far-away lands."

Bill gave her the same smile he always did, never wishing for one moment to shatter her dream.

"When has the competition got to be in by?"

"Three days time."

"What do you have to do to win?"

"You have to detail the best boat for sailing the world, write about why you're willing to set sail immediately and also come up with a catchy name for the boat."

"Well, that should take you about twenty minutes knowing you. I'm off to work; I have a garage to run."

Chapter Fifty-Six

I t was about 2;00 pm by the time Ben started down the road, which soon became a track about a meter wide with thick jungle either side. It was a well-worn path and dead straight; unlike the paths through the butterfly reserve. In the distance, he could see someone waiting, so quickened his pace. As he got closer, he waved at a man who waved back. As he approached the man, he could see a fork in the track. A woman was approaching from this other path.

Ben held out a hand, which the man took.

"Pleased to meet you, I've heard a lot about you."

The man spoke back in Spanish and through gestures made it clear that he didn't understand what Ben was saying. The woman called to the man who tapped his watch and then turned his palms outwards before tapping his watch again. The woman paid no attention to his impatience. They started speaking in Spanish and Ben heard the word Almedio.

He butted in. "Almedio- I am looking for him."

The woman turned back to the man, who started waving his arms down the right track. The woman waved her arms in the direction of the track that she had just come from.

She then turned to Ben.

"You go see Almedio?" she asked.

"Almedio, yes, si, Almedio."

She pointed down the path she had come from; the man started waving his arms again.

"No, no, no," he said as he waved his arms again.

The woman started to walk off, and the man ran to catch up with her. He continued to shout at her and wave his hands towards the right track. Ben stood there watching them go back down the single track he had arrived on. He sat down on a large log that had been used by a lot of people to wait on. There were names and markings scratched into the wood that looked years old. An hour passed and the light was starting to fade under the canopy, and it started to rain a little.Ben decided to follow the path the man had indicated. He reasoned that since they were both convinced they were right, both tracks would eventually lead to Almedio.

Chapter Fifty-Seven

Christina was sitting at the cafe when Vivian approached her.

"Christina?"

'Yes."

"Hi, I'm Vivian, pleased to meet you. It's strange we meet like this. I was instructed to keep sending you the same company email, and then I had this thought about how I felt when I lost Mum, and that was why I added the PS to the mail.

My Boss would not approve of such personal contact. They are about as dry as you can get. Anyway, I am talking too much."

The waiter came, and they both ordered coffee.

"Do you know what is in the box?" asked Christina.

"No, sorry I don't."

"Could you find out?"

"No, not even Mr. Howe knows what's in it. Your mother left instructions that you must open it in the company of Mr. Howe.

I can understand how you feel. When my mother died, the house was full of all her stuff, her clothes and all those little things that you didn't even know that she kept.

I kept everything for weeks and then months. I could not bring myself to clear anything out. She left me the house and so I just kept it as it was. One day I went into her room and sat on the bed crying."

"Yes, I did a lot of that," said Christina.

Vivian reached over and stroked Christina's hand.

"I opened up the draw on her bedside cabinet, which I had done many times before. This time I thought about clearing it out and started to take out some things. I came across what I thought was a letter, but it turned out to be some thoughts that mum had written down at some point. A short while after reading it, I got my life back on track. I cleared out all mom's stuff and felt good doing it."

Vivian reached into her bag and pulled out the letter.

"I don't know why but I brought this for you."

She handed it to Christina who started to open it.

Vivian put her hand out.

"No, don't read it now; it's better to read when you're alone somewhere."

"Are you sure, how will I get it back to you?"

"I don't want it back; you keep it and pass it to someone else if you think they could use it."

"Thank you."

"Just one thing," said, Vivian. "My boss doesn't know I'm here or that you have contacted me. He would go up the wall if he knew he could have met you and wrapped up your mom's estate. He's obsessed with loose ends, as he calls them."

"Ok, no worries."

They both finished their coffee and Vivian got up to leave.

"I have to go now; it was lovely to meet you. Have a read of mum's letter sometime when you're ready and if you want to contact me, give the office a call on this number." She passed a card to Christina. "Ask for me."

"Thanks, I really appreciate meeting you."

"You're welcome."

Christina was alone at the table.

"Anything else Miss?" The waiter asked as he cleared away the cups.

"No thanks. All done. Oh, yes, which is the quickest way to the park?"

"Straight down here," said the waiter, pointing down the street out front of the cafe.

"Take the second left and keep walking, you'll come to it."

"Thanks."

Christina turned to the second left, and the first shop was a travel agency.

'Special offers this week only' read the sign.

"How can I help you?" said the assistant, as they both sat down either side of the desk.

"Greece, do you have any deals on Greece?"

"Sure do."

The assistant hit a few keys on the computer.

"Ok, so when do you want to go?"

"I can leave tomorrow if need be. Flexible on what you have. Just don't get me a 2 am flight or something like that."

The assistant's search came back.

"The best deal I can do you is a week today for £ 49.00. Flight leaves at 2 pm."

"I'll take it."

A few moments later, a printer started up under the assistant's desk. Christina paid and tucked the ticket away. She continued down the street and into the park, where she found a spot under a tree and pulled out the letter that Vivian had given her.

It read:

'Regrets of things that could have been.

I wonder what would have been if only if. If - what a word that is. If only I had said or done things differently, then would I still say if? Yes, I think that would be the nature of being humans, of thinking the way we do. If allows us to paint a different future of things that we assume would have been. But this future is not real; it was a future based on if. How do we know that if we had lived the if and created a different future, then we would be creating the imagined if future that we actually lived? It's all a bit of a conundrum.

If is a spurious word, a word that I cannot live my life by. If I live by if, then I live a life without direction because this small word distracts me into a world of regrets about making decisions and actions.

If challenges me to consider that the action I have already taken may have been wrong. How can I know this?

I can't and if I am living at this moment, based on my action that is now creating the 'if I had' thought, then by default I cannot be living in the here and now where I need to be.

I need to be alert to my life now, from where it is and to where it's moving. It seems to me that 'if' has great power and at the same time, can have a debilitating force that can wreck a lifetime.

The power of the word if lies in its ability to open your mind to a created future that you want to live. That word if can take us anywhere we want to go. That wonderful word IF.

But there are words that we can attach to that word that wrecks its power in a moment.

We can attach. 'Only' or 'I had.'

'If only, if I had.' These thoughts cause us to look back and question the actions that we took at the time.

If we do this looking back often enough, we start living a life that questions every action and thought that we take. The word if takes over and robs us of living a life of spontaneity.

A life that allows us to reach decisions quickly and then act on them.

Sure, some of these decisions will not be the best, but the secret is to move forward with the decision and be open and ready to accept the next thing that comes along, which may change that decision. We must never forget that without the perceived wrong decision, we would not be in the position that we would be in right now. If we were not where we are not, what fantastic events in our lives might we have missed.'

Christina put a finger to each eye and wiped away two single tears. She folded the letter, put it back in her bag and pulled out her phone.

Vivian answered.

"Hi, can you fix me an appointment with Mr. Howe?"

"Yes sure, that was quick."

"I read your mom's letter; it got to me, and I need to sort all this out."

"That's great! How does 10 am tomorrow sound?"

"Yes, that's good."

"Ok, come to reception, and I will make sure I am there to meet you."

Chapter Fifty-Eight

The track that Ben was walking on closed in; soon he had to push past vegetation that was trying to reclaim the path back to the jungle. The light was fading which made Ben push on faster. All the damp from the jungle growth coupled with sweat had now soaked his clothing, and his strength started to fade. What had started off as a pleasant and enjoyable stroll had now become an adrenalin and fear filled struggle through the jungle.

He stopped for a moment to catch his breath. Earlier the jungle had been full of sound, now what sound there was seemed to be far off into the distance. The closest noise to him now was his heavy breathing. He leaned against a tree to rest and looked back down the track. It had vanished, as that which he had pushed aside earlier, had now closed in behind him. Suddenly the hairs on the back of his neck stood up. The Jaguar from the reserve, had it escaped? He was sure he heard the same growling sound that he had heard when he visited the butterfly farm. Nonsense, he convinced himself before pushing on harder. The track had now all but disappeared, and the light was now so bad that he could only see about ten feet in front.

He stopped again, and this time the noise of the jungle had come back, but now it was a different noise. Now all the night animals were out in their environment and were everywhere around him. Burning, yes he could smell burning. He lifted his head to get a better taste for the air. It was burning. He pushed forward continuously checking the air. There was a fire burning somewhere, and that would surely offer safety from being eaten in the jungle.

He stopped again to check the smell and now heard a steady rhythmic beating. He pushed forward, and in another twenty meters, the jungle gave way to a circular clearing with a single hut. He dropped to his knees in relief for a moment. The fire and the beating were coming from the other side of the hut. He walked around the side, and there was the man he had watched the sunset with, sitting out front of the backpackers. He was beating a stick on a larger stick.

He looked up at Ben.

"Ah, you found me. I thought you might be lost."

"I was lost."

"Take some water."

The man pointed to a plastic container, hanging from the side of the hut.

Ben guzzled down what felt like liters.

"I was supposed to meet someone on the track, and they never showed up."

"No, you imagined they would turn up. I don't think that Pablo told you that someone would be waiting. Come and sit by the fire, the night air is cooling."

Ben sat down and looked into the flames for a few moments.

"I gave a message to someone to give you, to tell you which path to take. Why didn't you take the path she said?"

"They were arguing — are you Almedio?"

"Yes."

"Why didn't you tell me that when we met at the backpackers?"

"You never asked who I was."

Ben started shaking his head and pulled his legs in tighter to the squat position he was in.

"You are angry." Said Alemdio

"No, just frustrated; this could have been all very easy instead of waiting around for days and then fighting through the jungle."

"That is true, but you are a man that misses many things. Most things in life that we seek are either very close to us or if not, then there is something else close that has a connection to that which we seek. You may have heard of this before?"

"You mean like connecting the dots?"

"So you met her, then?"

Almedio looked up from the fire; the flames danced across his face revealing a huge smile. "Christina."

"Yes, I suppose that is why I am here, but that was an accident."

"Accident?"

"Yes, I ran into her with my car and broke her ankle."

Almedio turned back to the fire and poked it a few times, before watching the sparks take off into the sky before disappearing.

"So you came here to meet me for what?"

"I don't know. Well, that is not true, I think what I mean is that-" Almedio cut him off.

"You don't know what you want or where you want to go or what you are looking for. Is that what you mean?"

Ben stared into the fire for a moment, saying nothing.

"Maybe it was like in the jungle a short while ago, before I lit the fire for you."

Ben looked up from the fire.

"You lit the fire for me?"

"Yes, I could hear you a long way off thrashing about, so I lit the fire and put on these leaves to create smoke."

Almedio dropped a large green leaf on the fire, and they were soon surrounded by smoke.

"Why didn't you call out if you could hear me?"

"So you came here to find something that you lost many years ago, and you would like to take the ceremony that Christina told you about. You are thinking that maybe the ceremony will help you find what you are looking for?"

"You're probably right, but the truth is that I am not sure about anything anymore. When I look back a few days and then forward to where I am now sitting here with you, I can't comprehend how much my life has changed. And all this you are saying, is because I ran into a random person on the street."

"I'm not saying that, you are. You are now connecting events and reading from them. This is good, very good; this is why I made you wait three days. You were not ready, and now you are."

Ben looked away from the flames at Almedio, who had also turned towards him.

"I am not sure about any of this." Said Ben

"Good."

Almedio got up and went to the water bottle. Hanging beside it was an old plastic coke bottle about a third full of a thick brown liquid.

He brought it back to the fire.

"Here, drink this." He handed the bottle to Ben.

Ben unscrewed the cap and smelled it.

"What is it?"

"Don't ask questions that you know the answer to."

"How much do I drink?"

"Drink."

Ben tipped up the bottle and drank. It took three attempts to drain the bottle, before replacing the cap.

"I didn't think you would drink so much.

Mother earth must want to meet you. Whatever happens, know that I am here, never far away from you."

Almedio put more wood on the fire and sparks danced high into the night sky. He looked up to follow them as did Ben, just before he fell back on the ground unable to move.

Chapter Fifty-Nine

The Crowe Horwath building was from an era of quill pens and parchment but inside was crisp and modern. Christina approached reception, but before she reached it, Vivian came from behind a screen and saw her.

They greeted, and Vivian took her to a small waiting room off to the side.

"Nice to meet you again. Mom's letter was convincing eh?"

Christina handed it back to Vivian.

"No, no, you keep it." Said Vivian

"No, I can't. It's a special letter and one that you should keep. It had a great effect on me, and maybe it will help someone else."

Vivian took the letter back.

"I'll go see if Mr. Howe is free; he's expecting you."

Vivian walked to the reception desk and spoke to the girl there, who picked up the phone and pressed a single button.

"Mr. Howe, your 10 am is here."

Seconds later, she replaced the receiver and nodded to Vivian. Vivian took Christina along a short hallway to a large black door that was partially open.

"Give me a call before you leave, ok?"

"Yes ok, I will."

Christina pushed open the door.

Mr. Howe looked up from his desk and motioned for Christina to come in and sit and then returned instantly to reading a document.

Christina sat down and Mr. Howe still looking down, said.

"Well young lady, you have given us the run around for a long time."

"I'm sorry I was not ready to deal with anything like this."

Mr. Howe leaned forward with both hands flat on his desk.

"These things are unfortunate, but they have to be dealt with and wrapped up, do you understand?"

Christina nodded on the outside but inside something else wanted to come out that Mr. Howe caught a glimpse of, which made him uneasy.

"Err - sorry, I know this is a difficult thing, but even so, it has to be done."

He looked back down to the document on his desk.

"I will explain to you what your late mother's will contained."

He sat back in his chair.

"I don't know if you know, but your mother was very astute with money over the years. She had accumulated just over £ 130,000 in a high interest bearing savings account. This money will be transferred to your account at the same bank today.

The family home is mortgage free and has been valued at over £ 600,000 despite its condition, because of its location.

Now, I have taken the liberty as executor of the estate, as we could not find you, to have some maintenance completed.

I also installed some high-quality tenants so that there was income from the property and also security to have someone living there.

These tenants are under a short term contract, so can be vacated at short notice.

Are we clear so far?"

"Yes, all clear."

"Fine. The rental from this property is quite substantial, again given its location to the city. It is, in my opinion, a valuable asset and as executor of your mother's estate, I would advise you to keep and maintain that property. The rental income alone will provide you with a good monthly income with little expense."

Christina nodded.

"Now that is that out of the way. That only leaves this."

He reached down to a low drawer on his desk and lifted up a small tin money box.

Christina recognized it instantly.

"My instructions are that this is to be opened here, in my presence."

He slid the box over to Christina.

"What's in it?"

"I would not know that Miss, Crowe and Horwath follow instructions to the letter; it is not for us to go through things that we are not instructed to."

"Sorry, I didn't mean-"

"Doesn't matter, please open the box and we can proceed."

Christina opened the lid. Inside was a leather bracelet that looked like it had been made by hand. She took it and placed it on the desk. There were several small items of jewelry and two sealed envelopes which she also placed on the desk. One had the word 'letter' written on it, the other 'DOCS.'

"Is that it?" said Mr. Howe.

"Yes." Christina tipped the box toward him so that he could see it was empty.

"Splendid, now the envelopes please."

Christina picked up the small items and then the two envelopes and stood up.

Mr. Howe looked up at her and motioned for her to sit again.

"We have not concluded our business."

He pointed to the envelopes.

"They need to be opened in my presence."

"No, they don't. You told me that your instructions were that the box was to be opened in your presence. There was no mention of the letters."

Mr. Howe looked down at the document for a few moments.

"I am sure that is not what your mother meant. She meant for you to open them here today."

Christina slipped the letters and jewelry into her bag and slipped the leather bracelet over her wrist.

"It does not say that I have to open them here, so I am not going to."

"But your mother intimated to me that you might need some further help with the contents."

"Intimated or told you?"

"Look miss, I am trying to do my best, but if you don't comply, then my hands are tied."

"Is there anything for me to sign?"

He turned around three pages and pushed them towards Christina.

"Please initial the three pages and sign the last one."

Christina did as asked and then slid the papers back.

"What about your fee for this?"

"That has all been taken care of. Do you have an address where we can forward any correspondence to you?"

"No, I don't. I am continually traveling at the moment."

"May I suggest that you use our office to have any email held on your behalf and also so that you have a point of contact for the management of your property? Speaking of which, do you want to maintain the property with the tenants or would you like that terminated?"

"No, please leave them in the house and yes, if I could use your office as a mailing address, that would be appreciated."

Mr. Howe stood up and extended a hand.

"I am very sorry for your loss Miss, something we all have to go through and all these loose ends do have to be wrapped up."

Christina shook his hand.

"Thank you."

Back at reception, Vivian was talking to a man with his back to Christina. Suddenly, she put her arms around him and kissed him on the cheek. On seeing Christina, she broke from the hold and turned to her. The young man turned at the same time.

"Christina's eyes widened, as she stopped and just looked."

"You decided to look me up then?"

Vivian slapped him on his shoulder.

"Don't be cheeky."

"It's her Sis; this is who I was telling you about."

Vivian looked at Christina and back at Mark.

"So you know each other?"

"Yes, we met on the plane." Replied Christina

"Well, you obviously made an impression; he has not stopped talking about you and your adventures." Vivian and Christina smiled together.

Mark jumped back in. "Did you get everything sorted here today? I mean, are you leaving now? How about-"

Vivian slapped him on the shoulder again.

"Give someone time to answer, will you?"

"Yes, I'm heading off to Greece in a few days."

"Meet up before you go?" said Mark.

Christina shrugged her shoulders.

"Ok, let's meet at the same coffee shop where we met," Christina said, looking at Vivian.

"Yes, that's fine, what time?'

"Can we make it tomorrow say around lunch time, as I have a few things that I need to do today."

"Sorry, I can't make it tomorrow. I have to attend court with Mr. Howe."

"I can - it's a date." Said Mark, smiling first at his sister then at Christina.

"Do you want me to give him another slap?" Vivian said, raising her hand again.

They all laughed.

"Ganging up on me you are-"

"Mark."

Mr. Howe appeared at the reception.

"Mark, I'm waiting on you."

Mr. Howe looked at Christina and nodded.

"Sorry, be right with you sir."

"Meet you lunch time tomorrow and don't stand me up."

He touched her shoulder as he walked past towards Mr. Howe's office.

Vivian shook her head and smiled at Christina.

Chapter Sixty

Ben lay there, staring up at the stars. He was still unable to move but at the same time was not concerned. His body felt warm and comfortable. He started thinking about the effects that he now felt and how relaxing and enjoyable it was.

Almedio reached out and touched his arm.

"I will not be far away."

Ben heard something approaching fast through the jungle. Fear raced through every vein in his body. He turned his head back towards Almedio; he had gone and in his place was Marcello. Ben tried to speak, but no words would come out. Whatever was coming through the jungle was almost there.

Ben turned his head back to the jungle, his eyes now white with fear and then back to Marcello who was now Almedio again.

He touched Ben's arm again.

"Fear only has the power that you give it."

A group of warrior-like men burst from the jungle. They had painted faces and carried long spears. They continued to move fast towards Ben. One of them stuck his spear into Bens' thigh, and Ben let out a scream of pain. The leader of the men spoke to the others, and two of the warriors grabbed Ben and dragged him to his feet. They all turned and headed back into the jungle.

Ben called out to Almedio, but there was no response.

Ben was being dragged through the jungle. His legs were not working properly; he continually fell and was dragged on. Sometimes they would stop for a moment as if checking where they were going. Each time they did, Ben called out for Almedio and each time he did, someone would club him from behind, knocking him to the ground. The next time they paused, Ben said nothing.

They were listening, and now Ben could hear it as well - a faint horn blowing sound. They started running again. This time it was faster and faster. Ben's legs were still not working properly. The jungle had dragged both his shoes off, and his shirt was a torn rag.

Suddenly, they burst into a clearing where there were several huts. The leader said something to the two men who had let Ben collapse on the ground. They then dragged him towards one of the huts, tore off the last of his shirt and threw him inside. He collapsed on the floor, and they closed the door behind him.

Ben called out for Almedio; the door opened, and one of the men came in with a large club. He hit Ben at the side of his head, and everything went black.

When Ben opened his eyes, some feeling had come back to his legs; he moved them to make sure. The room was completely black; he could not see a hand in front of his face. Ben was aware of someone else in the room, and as he became aware, the light lifted just enough so that he could make out shapes. There were three more people in the room, laying out in a fan-like shape.

A woman whispered across to Ben.

"Don't hit me again, please."

Ben sat up and looked across at her shape.

"I have not hit you. I have been beaten as well."

The other two bodies sat on either side of the woman.

"They said we were to wait here until you came." Said the woman

"I have been kidnapped I was dragged through the jungle, they even stuck a spear in my leg." Ben put his hand down to feel the wound, but there was nothing there.

"This is not about you and your troubles; this is about us. They told us that someone was coming to us. They said that this person would set us free."

"I am not this person you're waiting for. I need to be saved as well." Said Ben.

"They told us the person coming had no legs and had a wound in their leg. Do your legs work?"

Ben tried to move his legs again.

"No, not properly."

"Do you have a wound in your leg?"

"No, it's gone."

"But you did have a wound?"

"Yes."

"Oh god, it's coming again, help me." The woman whispered.

"What's coming?"

The woman lay back down.

"What's coming?" Ben repeated.

Out of the blackness of the woman's body came another body but this body was a black shadow of a being; not a person at all. More like some entity that was connected to her. Ben replayed Almedio's words about not being afraid over and over in his mind. The being looked at Ben and started to laugh and then retreated into the women's body. Ben reached out and grabbed it and pulled it towards him. It started yelling and screaming. The more he pulled it apart from the woman, the more it fought. The woman's body was convulsing rapidly as this was going on.

Ben pulled harder, and when he could, he punched a blow to the being. With each blow the being weakened and where the blow fell, there was nothing of the being left.

Ben sensed he could win this battle; at the same time, the being sensed it was going to lose. More and more he pulled and beat down with his fists when he could. The being weakened and then finally gave up the last connection to the woman's body. Ben beat the last of the shape until every part of it had gone. The woman let out an enormous sigh and went to sit up when Ben saw a flicker of another entity in her body.

"Lay down; there is another one."

The woman lay down, and Ben reached over to grab hold of it. This was a child of the first shadowy figure and was nowhere near as strong. Ben pulled it out, but as he did, it turned white and became happy. When it was all the way out it stood up, smiled and then vanished.

The woman sat up.

"What did you do?"

"I pulled something out of your body."

"What was it?"

"I don't know. I knew whatever it was it was not meant to be there."

"Thank you. I can't tell you how I feel. Light has returned to the inside of my body. I feel healthy, I can see clearly into my life. I know now where the blackness came from. It's time for me to leave."

The woman got up and pushed open the door. Ben could make out a large group of warriors outside the door, who parted and let the woman walk free. One of them then looked back into the hut at Ben and then kicked the door shut again.

One of the men opposite Ben sat up. Ben could make out that he was blindfolded.

"Hey, you." He called out to Ben.

"How did you do that? How did you pull those things out of her?"

"How did you know what I did? You are blindfolded."

"I heard the terrible noises it made."

"It didn't make a noise." Said Ben

"It was screaming like the devil; the noise was horrific. I thought it was going to kill us all; then when you pulled out the child, the child turned white and became happy. When it was all the way out it stood up, smiled and then vanished."

"How did you know it was a child?"

"I saw it was a child as you pulled it out. My eyes worked at that point. Are you here to fix my eyes?"

At that moment the man's shadow started to light up with small white specks of light contained within it. The specks of light became larger until they were like millions of white dots, contained within the outline of his body.

"That's amazing," said Ben.

"What is?"

"Can't you see your body and the light?"

"I can't see anything. I am wearing a blindfold. Tell me what you see."

"It's amazing and the most beautiful thing I have ever seen. Every part of you is connected to the next part. Each movement of your body, even the twitching of a finger, sends a ripple like an effect through the dots of light and they dance together like a symphony orchestra."

"What does it mean? I can't see anything."

"Wait-"

"What is happening? Tell me, what is going on?"

"They are spreading."

"They are leaving me?"

"No, they are spreading out from your body to the man next to you. Wait, it's not a man."

"Oh god it's not another one of those beings, is it?"

"I don't know; it's not moving at all."

"What are the dots doing?"

"They are spreading through this body; now they are coming into my body."

"Did you move?" said the blindfolded man.

"Yes, I just put my hands up to my face."

"Do it again."

Ben moved his hand to his face.

The man in the blindfold started to laugh.

"We are connected," he said.

Ben looked at the man and saw that the blindfold had gone. He was looking down at his arms and legs and was smiling.

"Look at your arms when I move mine."

Ben looked down and saw the dots in his own body reacting.

"Don't you see?" said the man.

"We are connected, we are all connected. This building is connected, everything is one. We are all the light. We may think that we are alone in this world, but we are not; we are part of a larger whole. Now I understand my life, my meaning. Do you see how beautiful this is? I have to show this to others. I have to rescue my family from the blindness that I have given them."

The man got up and opened the door. Again the warriors parted and let him pass before closing the door again.

Ben turned to the last shadow that was the other man. The dots slowly disappeared, and the man's shadowy outline reappeared. The door opened, and a warrior came in, carrying a flame light. Ben looked across to the other man, and now he could see that he was also a warrior. He spoke to the warrior with the torch in a dialect that Ben could not understand at all.

He then turned to Ben.

"Tomorrow you tell us the meaning of these things; you tell all of us."

"How? I don't understand."

The warrior got up and walked out of the hut, closing the door. Ben had sat a moment in silence before everything went black again.

Chapter Sixty-One

Christina arrived early at the cafe. The waiter remembered her and made small talk for a moment about finding her way to the park using his directions. Mark showed up and interrupted. They ordered coffee and a sandwich.

"You could not have made it up, eh? I mean meeting on the plane like that and then here now."

The waiter brought their order.

"So what were you up to with Mr. Howe? Sorry, I should not have asked that I'm bumbling aren't I."

Christina sipped her coffee and looked across the top of the cup at him and smiled.

"So the plane seating - random or you wanted it to be so?" said Christina.

Mark picked up his coffee.

"Ok, busted. Well, not entirely true. I could have found another seat but yeah ok, I wanted to sit with the most beautiful girl on the aircraft, who wouldn't?"

Christina shook her head, smiling.

"What?" said Mark.

"Nothing, it's ok. Anyway, why was I with Mr. Grumpy?"

"That's his name alright, eh?"

"I had to deal with my mother's estate."

"Oh, I'm sorry. I should not have-"

Mark touched her arm for a little longer than necessary, which Christina noticed and didn't mind.

"It's ok. It was some time ago, and I have used up most of my tears now."

"So what are you doing now? I mean what are your plans?"

"I'm off to Greece soon for a while and then, well then I don't know where."

They both ate their sandwiches and ordered another coffee each.

"Must be great to travel like that, I mean just going somewhere and not knowing where to next. I travel all over, I love traveling, but all I get to do is sit on planes for hours, collect and deliver papers and then do it all over again. It's not what I had planned for my life, that's for sure."

"Hey, I have a couple of weeks holiday owing, how about I come with you to Greece? We can hang out a bit together. I promise I'll be no bother at all."

They both laughed and took a sip of coffee each. Mark held a stare on her long enough to get her to speak first."

"What?"

"What do you mean what - I'm asking you if I can come to Greece with you."

Christina flashed a grin.

"Why not, but I warn you, I can change my mind about where I want to be in the world in a flash, ok?"

Mark shrugged his shoulders.

"Suits me fine. Ok, I'm going to shoot back to the office and clear it with Mr. Howe and then get back to you. So, this time you will give me your number?"

They both laughed again as Christina pulled out her phone and flipped open the lid."

"That's a good start," Mark said, putting his hand in his pocket.

"We're both old flippers."

He flipped open his phone, and they exchanged numbers and checked flight times and details."

"Ok, I will call you later to let you know."

Christina sunk a little in her chair.

"You mean you haven't decided yet?"

"Of course I have, but I have to get the ticket sorted. Hopefully, I can get one."

Christina sat back up; she was looking forward to traveling with someone else.

Mark left, looking back to wave before he turned the corner. Christina was still looking at him.

Christina's phone rang.

"It's me, Mark, just wanted to make sure I had your number correctly."

"What would you have done if it had not been correct?"

"I would have come back, made an excuse about having forgotten to pay the bill and then worked out another way to get your number."

"My, what a forward thinker you are and a real charmer, not paying for lunch."

"That's paid for; I did that when you were not looking when the second coffees arrived."

Christina looked up towards the corner Mark had gone around a few moments ago. He was standing there with the phone to ear. He put his hand up, and Christina waved back.

"See you later."

He closed his phone and disappeared.

Christina picked up her cup but halfway to her mouth; she realized she had already finished and beamed a smile to herself.

Straight ahead, second left and the park would be at the end of that road, where it had been last time. As she passed the travel agent where she had booked her Greece ticket, she noticed some more last minute bargains being advertised. She popped her head in the shop door. The same assistant looked up.

"Oh hi again, you must be getting ready for Greece."

"Yes, I was wondering if there were any tickets left as I have a friend that is thinking of coming with me."

"Last time I looked there were plenty of seats. Do you want me to check?"

"No, all good, catch you later."

Christina continued to the park and sat in the same spot as the last time she was here.

She took a deep breath and tore open one of the envelopes marked 'letter.'

'My dearest sweetest darling,

By the time you read this, I will no longer be with you in body but be assured that I am always by your side, one way or another.

Sending you away as I did at the end was something I had to do. I hope you can forgive me for that, but I wanted to go with the memory of your face looking at mine, knowing you were going on an adventure of some kind. I always wanted to travel and see the world and now I can, through your eyes.

I now have to tell you about your father.

Your father was a good man. He did not deserve what I did to him. I left him, and he never knew of such a beautiful daughter. It was a very complicated situation at the time and looking back; things could have been very different.

I loved your father dearly. I know now as I write this, that all the steps I took to run from him were nothing more than self-punishment for my actions. I was a stupid girl that went on to become an angry woman for many years. Later on, it seemed all too complicated to put right.

I would have been so ashamed to admit to you that I kept your father from you and wanted you all for myself all this time.

In the envelope marked Docs you will find some photos taken just after your birth and some of your early paintings as a child. I want you to have those photos so that you can forever see the real love in my eyes and heart for my precious darling that you will always be.

Your early paintings were so special to me, so I kept them, and maybe they will make you smile today.

Soon after you were born, I changed my name and moved to London. I then passed my new name to you on all documents from then on.

I am so sorry for what I have done. It is only now as I am writing this that I realize I should have sat down with you and explained all this. The truth is I was a coward and feared that you would run away and find your father and leave me alone as I left him. How selfish that thought was and how stupid of me for not knowing that together, you and I could have got through anything.

I say again that I loved your father with all my heart. You were born as a result of that love for him. I am sorry for repeating myself, but I want to be sure that you know this.

When you read this letter in front of Mr. Howe, he does not know the contents. However, he will be waiting for you to ask him for another envelope. I have instructed him that he is not to reveal that he has this third envelope unless you specifically ask for it. Neither does he know the contents of the third envelope. He has been instructed to hold that envelope indefinitely, should you ever wish to open it. The contents of that envelope will provide you with a path to find your father if you wish.

I now have tears streaming from my face as I write this. Tears knowing that I will not see my dearest darling daughter again. I hope you can forgive me and we can go on loving each other until one day we will hold each other again in some way.

Your always and forever loving mother. Take care, my darling

XXX'

Christina looked up from the letter to see a mother playing with her children. She took a tissue from her bag and tried to wipe away her tears.

After a few moments, she opened up the second envelope. There were several photos of her as a baby and also a delicately folded piece of paper with some elastic attached. She unfolded the paper. There were two holes in it and a small water stain at one edge.

Her stomach rolled over, her head started to spin, and she started to cry again, only this time it came in floods. After a few moments, she grabbed her phone. She wanted to call Mr. Howe but didn't have his number. She called Mark.

"Mark?"

"Yes, hi. I didn't think you would be calling so quick, I have only just got back to the office."

"Mr. Howe has a letter for me. I want to come and get that letter."

"Hold on; I am standing now with Mr. Howe. I will pass the phone to him."

"Hello."

"You have another envelope for me."

"Yes I do, but I am leaving the office right now, you will have to come tomorrow."

"No, I need it now."

"If you have opened the letters here as the instructions said, then this would have likely all been sorted. I have to go now. I can see you tomorrow afternoon."

"Please Mr. Howe, I want to know what is inside that envelope."

She heard a drawer open and close.

"Miss, I have the envelope here. I have to leave, but if you instruct me to, I can let Mark have the envelope, and he can open it for you."

"Yes, yes that will do."

She heard Mr. Howe instruct Mark on what to do, and then a door closed shut.

"Hi, are you still there?"

"Yes, can you open the envelope?"

"Sure, hold on."

She heard him tear it open and then pick up the phone again.

"Ok, there is an American birth certificate and some photographs of a young couple."

Mark spread the photos out on the desk.

"Look at the photos."

"Ok, looking."

"Tell me about them."

"They are photos of a young couple."

"Is that all?"

"Yes, the only difference, apart from the scenery, is that in one of them the girl is wearing a mask, you know one of those fairground eye masks."

The phone slid slowly down Christina's cheek and closed.

A few moments later it rang. She flipped the phone open.

"You there? We got cut off," said Mark.

"I can't go to Greece with you, sorry."

"Why not? I was just about to book it. I have cleared time off work. I'm ready to go. What's wrong?"

"I have to go to New York."

"Ok, I'll go with you to New York then."

"There is something I have to do personally."

"Ok you can do your personal stuff, and I'll not get in the way. When are you going?"

"Now."

"Right now?"

"Soon as I can get a flight."

"I can work with that. Come on, let's go together. I can do with a bit of drama in my life right now."

"OK, well it's up to you. Bring the envelope with you, and we will meet at Heathrow."

"Hold on, don't book a ticket or anything yet. I have an obscene amount of air miles stacked up. I can probably pull a quick flight. Call you back in ten minutes?" He hung up and went to the reception.

He handed his airport card to the receptionist, Julie.

"Can you see if you can get me two business class flights to New York, please? Leaving as soon as possible."

The receptionist picked up the phone and Mark went to tell Vivian what he was doing. They both arrived back at the reception in a few minutes. Julie moved the phone away from her mouth to speak to Mark.

"Flight leaving in 4 hours and they can get you on that. There is only first class which they will bump you up to if you use your air points to pay for two business class rates."

"Done deal," said Mark.

"The person you're traveling with. They need a name for the ticket."

"Christina."

Vivian interrupted- "Wilkins, Christina Wilkins." Julie repeated it to the airline and confirmed the flights, then hung up.

"You pick your tickets up at the British Airways desk," Julie said to Mark.

"You're a diamond," he said to Julie and then turned to Vivian and kissed her on her cheek. He then started to walk toward the front door.

"Wish me luck sis, wish me luck."

"Bye, have fun."

Mark waved over his shoulder with his left hand as he was dialing with his right.

Christina answered.

"I got us two tickets; we leave in four hours. I'm going home to pack a few things, and we will meet at the British Airways desk, say in a couple of hours ok?"

"Ok."

"I'm hanging up now and turning my phone off, so you don't change your mind on me," said Mark as he flipped his phone closed.

Chapter Sixty-Two

Ben made out the first shards of daylight from inside the hut, as the door opened. He was beckoned to come out. The tribe was sitting in a circle. Ben was taken to the center and given a stick, to draw in the sand.

One of the warriors said, "Tell us."

"Tell you what?" he replied.

One of the other warriors got up and beat Ben with a club, knocking him to the ground. Then he went and sat back down.

"Show us," said the other warrior.

Ben picked up the stick and drew two short vertical lines and in the middle of them three small circles. Then a couple of inches under that, a short horizontal line; then below that, again two short vertical lines. The warrior who had beaten Ben jumped up and went to stand by Ben. He pointed to the drawing and talked to them in a language that Ben could not understand. The whole tribe nodded in agreement. The warrior knelt down and wiped away the sand to start again and then sat down.

Ben drew a series of circles all interlinked and then stood back.

Again the same warrior jumped up and stood by Ben to explain to the rest of the tribe. They all nodded in agreement. Ben immediately drew another shape but the moment he completed it, it vanished. He looked at the tribe, and they were all nodding in agreement again. He drew again, this time faster and again as soon as he finished, it vanished. Faster and faster, he drew more and more shapes until he was exhausted and sat down.

He looked around the circle of warriors, and they all started to get up and leave. They were smiling and happy.

Ben lay down on his back and looked up at the bright sun. The heat became intense. Suddenly, the sun turned to flames and then a voice called to come back. It was the voice of Almedio, and the sun was a flaming torch that he was holding.

Ben opened his eyes to see Almedio looking over him. He lifted Ben's head and helped him drink some water, then laid his head back down. Ben stared up at the night sky and became in awe at the stars. He rubbed his stomach as nausea overcame him. He rolled over away from the fire and vomited.

When he rolled back, Almedio wiped his face with a wet rag and then covered him with a blanket. Ben closed his eyes and fell asleep.

It was cool when Ben woke. The fire was just smoking embers. He pulled the blanket up tighter around his neck and then realized how hard the ground was that he had slept on. A dog wandered up to the fire embers, sniffed at Ben and then flopped down and stretched. A cockerel crowed a way off; apart from that, everything was still and quiet. He looked towards the jungle and was amazed at how green everything was. He had seen it before of course, but now everything seemed so lush, with a halo of light around it.

"You see it do you?" said Almedio "The light."

Ben turned over to see Almedio coming towards him with two plates.

"Breakfast. You will be pretty hungry about now."

Ben sat up and took the plate. Two fried eggs and some flat heavy bread. Almedio put some wood on the embers, which caught almost immediately.

"What's the twinkling light?" asked Ben, as he took the first mouthful of eggs.

Before Alemdio could answer, Ben, cut in

"My God, these eggs, I have never eaten anything like this."

"Yes you have, but you have never tasted like that before."

Ben spent the next five minutes not wanting to reach the last mouthful.

"The light you see, the way you taste and if you become aware of your body for moment-"

"What is happening? I feel like superman."

"A normal man would be a much better description. What you are experiencing right now is a level of awareness that is about 50% of what we are all capable of. Tell me, what do you feel when you look at the jungle?"

"It's so green, so alive and the light around things is just - well amazing."

"Anything else?"

"Yes, but I felt silly saying it. Love, the jungle is oozing love."

"Love is the word that you have given to connection. You are experiencing a deep connection to your life force and the life force of everything else. Touch the soil."

Ben rubbed his fingers on the ground which caused a smile.

"Yes, even the soil because there is not a thing that is not connected in this universe and you are part of that universe."

"Will it last? I don't want it to go away."

"It will fade in a while, but the important thing is that you remember the experience so that you know this is the truth of the future.

You can, through training, open, closed doors in the mind that will let this into your daily conscious awareness."

"What about the warriors? I was beaten pretty hard."

Almedio looked hard into Ben's eyes for a moment, then pointed to the empty bottle that Ben had drunk from last night.

"The ancestors came for you. You have experienced a connection with mother earth that few experience. They must have had something special for you. Do you want to share anything with me?"

"I was dragged through the forest. They beat me and imagined or not, it was painful."

Almedio laughed and pointed "Imagined- is that why I had to attend to that this morning?"

Ben looked down to where the spear had been jabbed into his leg. There was an orange paste-like substance on it. He went to touch it, but Almedio caught his arm.

"No, don't touch; it will be okay in a couple of hours."

"You didn't imagine anything; you entered a different dimension. We are here and now are in one dimension. There are many dimensions, maybe even limitless."

"You met the ancestors; I am interested in what you learned from them."

"I was taken and thrown into a hut with some other people. There was a woman who had something inside of her. It was a blackness or some shape, but it was like it was living."

"Were you afraid?"

"Yes, very. They told me they were in the hut, waiting for me to help them. When I saw the entity or whatever it was, I felt a tap on my arm and then grabbed it and pulled it out. Then after that another one but smaller, a child. It was pretty full on and frightening. The woman then got up and walked out of the hut through the warriors, and they did not bother her at all."

"What next?"

"There was a man in a blindfold. It was completely black in the hut, but I saw specks of light, like little stars. They grew to be like small dots of light.

The dots spread through his body, then into mine and then the hut and at that point, I thought there was another black entity in the room, but it was another man. We were all connected with each other and everything. A bit like you explained a moment ago, with the way I was seeing and feeling everything around me.

The blindfolded man grew excited and said he had to go and rescue his family and tell others of this experience. He got up and left the hut. Again the warriors parted and let him walk away."

"You said there was another man in the hut."

"Yes it turned out he was a warrior, and he had seen everything that I had seen in the hut. He told me that in the morning I would have to tell all the warriors what this meant."

"You look tired," said Almedio.

"I am exhausted."

"Lay down."

Ben laid down, and Almedio pulled the cover back over him.

"We'll talk later."

Ben didn't hear him, he was already asleep.

Chapter Sixty-Three

Heathrow was busy, but with first class tickets, it was a different world. They were ushered in and sat back in the soft leather seats. The hostess brought some fresh orange juice, which they sipped.

"So tell me, Greece. What happened?"

"It's a long story." "Well, we have got a whole flight ahead of us, and you can't get away from me now so you might as well make a start."

Christina stared straight ahead and began.

Apart from stopping for meals and the odd drink, pretty much the whole flight was taken up with Christina telling Mark the story.

"And here we are now, back in New York." Christina turned to Mark.

"Miss, excuse me."

Mark looked to his left to the woman on the other side of the isle and then nudged Christina, who looked over.

"Miss, I am sorry, but I got hooked on your story the moment you started. I couldn't help myself. Whatever you do, write a book it's a best seller, and you're a lovely couple as well."

The woman reached into her purse and took out a card. "My name is Anna Bearing. I am a director of one of the largest book publishers in the world today. I know a best seller when I hear one."

Mark passed the card to Christina.

"I don't know if I could write a whole book."

"Miss, you just did over the last eight hours of this flight, and I have a confession to make. About ten minutes into your story I was hooked but so tired, I thought I might fall asleep, so I flipped on this."

The woman held up a personal recording device. "All bar the first ten minutes I have your whole story, your whole future book recorded.

I am willing right now to have this transcribed at no cost to you whatsoever and offer you an advance of say $100,000 on the publishing rights. If this sells like I think it will, you will be one very wealthy young lady."

Mark's jaw was way down when he looked back at Christina.

"I- I- think you need to think about that."

The woman reached over to pass the recorder to Mark to pass to Christina.

"No," said Christina, "keep the recorder and let's do this. I am starting to see the synchronicity of the universe. Everything is conspiring to create that which I create. As I picked up my ticket today, the thought of writing a book came to my mind. I dismissed it just as fast, saying to myself that I could not do it. I told myself that I could tell a story but not write it."

Christina leaned forward from her seat and looked at the woman, pausing long enough for the woman's attention to peak.

"We are in this together, and you are part of the story." They shook hands over Mark and across the aisle.

Ben stirred, it was just after midday. His stomach hurt from hunger. There was a wonderful smell of cooking coming from a hut not far off. Almedio was sitting at the door under a sort of ramshackle porch. They caught each other's glance, and Almedio waved for him to come over. A woman appeared from within the hut with the same two plates that the eggs had been on this morning.

"You like fish?" said Almedio

"I could eat anything right now."

The woman passed both plates to Almedio, who then gave one to Ben. The woman then went back inside the hut and Ben sat on the porch opposite Almedio.

"Eat slowly this time; think about the hunger and how the food is satisfying that hunger. Pay attention to what your body does with the food."

Both men ate slowly and methodically. Occasionally looking at each other and smiling as they swallowed and then paused to pay attention to the effects of the food.

Finished, they put the plates down on the porch, and Almedio passed a water jug to Ben.

"With the water, the same, pay attention to it."

Ben drank and became aware of the water flowing into his body.

"Everything is different," said Ben.

"No, everything is as it is; only now you are aware of it. To be aware of something is to be conscious of it. To be conscious of it is to absorb it into your consciousness which is part of the greater consciousness."

"So…. everything that happened to me, what does it mean?"

"Some of that I cannot answer, that you will have to work out for yourself, but I can help you get that started."

Ben adjusted his position on the porch to turn more towards Almedio.

"When anyone has an experience like this, the first reaction is to externalize it, that is to project the experience away from themselves and observe it from a distance. A moment ago you adjusted your seating position like a child getting ready to be told a story."

Ben looked down slightly and smiled.

Almedio continued. "There, right there was a moment that is rather important that you learn how to bring on at will. When you looked down and smiled, where were you?"

"I was here, thinking about my father."

"Stop! You are here in body but were you? The memory of your father took you somewhere else. Where was that?"

"Back to my room when I was younger. I was laying in bed, and my father would read stories to me of a great adventure. I remembered that and that was what made me smile."

"Ok, yes you remembered it, but you immersed yourself for a moment into the experience. Do you understand that?"

"Yes, I think I do."

"Good because that is what you need to carry forward with you. You need to be able to immerse yourself in an experience so that you can draw from it the guidance that is there for you. This is reading the language of universal intelligence."

"I have heard that term universal language before," said Ben, as he dropped his head slightly and again a half smile appeared on his face.

"There, well done, I can tell by your face that you immersed in that experience and travelled to the memory. Ok, so let's try and work out what happened to you and what it means. What do you feel? What the most important part of the experience?"

"That would have to be drawing pictures to the tribe and them understanding. I did not know what they were understanding, but it felt good to be passing knowledge to them. It changed them, they stopped being angry and were appreciative of what I was explaining to them, as I drew on the ground."

"Ok, we will leave that and come back to it later. On the journey to the hut, you were beaten and experienced pain. When you were inside the hut, you were no longer beaten but were forced to experience things, right?"

"Yes, that was what happened."

"Ok, so I want you to think of the journey as being outside of yourself and the inside of the hut as being inside yourself."

Ben felt a tear run down his cheek.

"Pay attention to that tear, Ben. Go into that tear and tell me what it contains."

"I don't know what it contains as such, but I know why it came."

"Knowing why it came is within you. Remember the food and the jungle. Awareness of self and everything around you allows translation of the language of universal consciousness. To genuinely experience something is crucial, as it opens up understanding."

"Ok, well, the tear came as a result of me gaining understanding. It came like a flash. When I replayed the journey and then the hut, I had the feeling that the journey was everything that was happening to my life on the outside. But inside the hut, I was forced to take notice of my inner self."

Almedio nodded "Continue."

"The spear in my leg was the pain I have in my life for a huge mistake I made. This was for one single event. The rest of the journey to the hut was plain hard and exhausting. This I think is symbolic of my current life but I don't understand that, as I don't have any hardships in life. I mean I-"

"You mean you have accumulated wealth in your life and you have associated this wealth with ease of life."

"Yes, that's it, that's what I mean."

"Have you considered that the wealth and ease might take more from you than it has given you?"

"That is exactly how I feel sometimes."

"Ok now, what about the hut experience?"

"Yes, one part of that troubles me."

"Pulling the shadows out from the woman?"

"Yes, one of the shadows was dark and violent. I had to fight and beat this shadow into submission. The other shadow turned out to be a child. Once out, it turned white and vanished."

"Remember that the hut represents you. So everything in the hut is who?"

"Myself?"

"Yes, so if that is the case, then you must look to yourself to help with the translation, but I can help a little with this. Tell me more about the entity that you pulled from the woman."

Ben's head rolled forward, and he began to cry. It was two minutes before either of them spoke.

"That was hard on you," said Almedio. "Do you want to tell me about it?"

Ben nodded and wiped his face.

"The woman was someone I knew. She has remained part of me all my life. This was the pain from the spear in my leg. When I dragged her out of the woman, I was dragging her out of myself. The reason I got upset was how I had to beat the entity to kill it. I felt like I was killing her. Now I understand that I was setting her and myself free. Her kicking and screaming were her not wanting to let go, just as much as I did not want to let go. The child like entry I am not sure of."

"Ok, I can help with that. The darkness of the entity that you pulled out would tell me that the person the entity represents has already passed; they are dead in the physical sense. The child-like entity signifies ongoing life in the physical sense. Now tell me more about the specks of light."

"The man in the blindfold was me, wasn't it?"

"If you say so then you likely know that to be true, so let's go with that."

The light was me beginning to see, to understand that I am not alone, that nobody is alone or separate from anything. We are all connected at the most microscopic of levels. There are some huge implications to this truth; one being that to hurt another, whether verbally or physically, is to hurt yourself. If people truly understood this, then the world would be a very different place. The human need for profit and dominion over others would evaporate, as what would be the need for profit and dominion over self?

It would be like negotiating with yourself to pay a continually higher price for something, in an attempt to get more from something that was already yours. The same with causing pain in another. If you felt that pain on an emotional and physical level, then it would be futile and self-damaging to continue."

Almedio reached over and held Ben by the shoulder for a few moments.

"I could not have explained that better," he said.

"There is part of this that I do not understand, which is the drawings in the sand and how they understood."

Almedio cleared his throat.

"This part you do understand but this, you do not want to face. I am going to hazard a guess here that your profession is as an artist. Am I right?"

"No, I am a currency trader."

"Define that for me?"

"I buy and sell money. That is how I make money."

Almedio rubbed his chin.

"So, you don't buy or sell anything of value? Is that what you're saying?"

Ben paused for a moment before nodding.

"Yes, I suppose you could say that."

"In that case, I do not understand the drawing in the sand for the tribe."

"But I do paint for pleasure, although I don't sell anything or even show anyone what I do. I don't think they are good enough."

Almedio paused for a moment and looked straight into Ben's eyes.

"I am going to let you process that for a moment and then tell me what you think."

Ben sat silent for a moment and then said: "I should have been an artist instead of a currency trader."

"You, my friend, are on the edge of something much larger than yourself. That is what this is all about. Your drawing in the sand for the tribe gave them what?"

"Understanding in some way but I did not know what they were understanding."

Almedio laughed.

"They understood themselves. As they nodded to each other, so they understood themselves. Which means that your drawings were offering what?"

"Understanding?"

"Yes, but self-understanding; by looking at your drawings, they achieved self-understanding. This is the greatest gift that you could give to anyone. Understanding self is to understand others and everything around you."

"The love of my life-" Almedio cut him off.

"The love of your life knew this; she tried to tell you many times. She carried the message for you to do what your purpose is and you ignored this in pursuit of what?"

Ben hung his head.

"For money, power, and dominion over others."

"Do not feel the way you are feeling right now. You now know more about your life than you would ever have and now it will never be the same because of this awareness. This is not a time for sadness or regret; this is a time to look forward to what you are going to do with this understanding."

Chapter Sixty-Four

New York airport was as busy as always. Mark, Christina, and Anna collected their luggage together before exchanging contact details.

"Best flight I ever had. I tell you, it's going to be a big hit," said Anna as she walked away.

Mark looked at Christina.

"Holy crap, does this sort of thing happen to you all the time?"

"What- you mean meeting you and getting a publisher for a book? Oh yes, every day."

She turned and knocked her backpack into Mark deliberately. They both laughed.

"So what's the plan from here?" said Mark

"I don't have one."

"Surely you want to go and see him?"

"Now that I'm here, I want to think about it a bit more. Let's grab a cab and get a place to stay. There is a backpackers place not far from here."

"Not tonight, I have a lot of travel points built up. We can do much better than that."

Outside, Mark hailed a cab.

"Washington Jefferson, please."

"Right on."

"It's a nice hotel. I stay there every trip I have to make, and it's only a short walk to Central Park. By the way, I never said it before; I love your hat. Makes me feel like we're on an adventure."

Mark squeezed Christina's hand.

The receptionist recognized Mark.

"You're back quick this time. Your regular room is free if you'd like it?"

"Er….. no, it has to be a double with twin beds."

Mark turned to Christina.

"Is that ok?"

"Yes, fine."

The receptionist handed over the key card to Mark.

Ben turned to Almedio.

"Do you think I should be painting? Is that my core purpose? I love painting; it sends me into a different world."

"The fact that you asked that question provides you with the answer. I don't know where your painting will lead you, but I do know that it will offer guidance to others."

"It's strange," said Ben. "I have often had urges to paint in a different way and yet I have never understood the feeling."

Ben paused, then grabbed Almedio's arm excitedly.

"I know- I know exactly what I have to do. The drawings in the sand with the tribe; even though I don't remember them all, these are what I have to paint."

"And now it's time for you to leave," said Almedio with a smile.

"Yes, yes, I have to get back home. I have to-"

"Don't plan, just go home and let the consciousness of the universe lead the way."

Almedio looked up and saw Pablo walking towards them. He waved.

"Pablo… right on time, as always. Ben is leaving us now and going home. I want you to take him straight to the airport."

"But I was planning on spending a few days-"

"No- you have things to do at home that need attending to. Go now and come back another time."

"Well, I'm not going to argue with you."

Pablo picked up Ben's pack and swung it on his back.

"We go now?"

"Er….. yes, I think so." Ben went to shake Almedio's hand. Almedio looked down at his extended hand and knocked it away, before stepping in close to embrace him. They hugged.

"Thank you for the experience Almedio, it's been a- well, I don't know what it's been but it has changed my view of the world and what I have to do. I want to pay you for this."

"There is nothing to pay and no thanks to give. I have all I want, so what use is more? I know you want to give, and that is a good thing but wait until you find those that you know you must give to. Giving in that way will be the best giving of all."

Two hours later Ben was at the airport, he managed to get the last ticket out as there had been a cancellation.

He pulled out $50.00 and handed it to Pablo.

"There you go, and thank you for everything."

Pablo took the $50.00 and shook hands with Ben. Ben went through into the departure lounge. The flight home was every bit as tough as the journey there, and by the time JFK was approaching, Ben was exhausted.

Chapter Sixty-Five

Mark and Christina had breakfast at the hotel and then decided to go to the park.

"So, you got a plan yet?"

"Well, to be honest, I'm as afraid as hell."

"Why don't you call first and arrange a meeting?"

"Yes, maybe that's a good idea, but I don't have a number."

Christina rummaged in her back and pulled out an AT&T card and called the number.

"Hi, I don't know if you could help me but a few days ago we bought two flip phones from you and ….."

"Hold, I will ask."

Another voice came on the phone.

"Hi, yes, the two flip phones. I remember we don't sell them anymore and they were the last two."

"I was wondering if you could let me have the numbers for them." "No, I can't sorry. That's confidential information."

"Is your name James?"

"Yes, it is. How do you know?"

"I have your business card here."

"Oh- yes, I remember more now. Is there a number on the back of the card?"

Christina turned the card over

"Yes, there is. Is that the number."

"I don't know Miss, you could always try- I mean, you never know until you try, do you?

Anything else I can help you with today?"

"No, all good thank you."

"You have a good day, miss."

Christina flipped the phone closed.

A few moments later, Ben's phone rang.

"Hello."

"Hello- It's the print shop here. Just letting you know that you have an entry for your competition. I opened it up as we agreed; it came to our PO box number, and I was not sure who it was for."

Ben paused for a moment and smiled.

"Sir, are you still there?"

"Yes, sorry I was thinking-"

The man started to laugh.

"What's funny?" asked Ben.

"The name of the boat sir, at the top of the page It says- Name of the boat: 'Passion and Purpose.' That is the name of the boat. 'Passion and Purpose.'"

Ben smiled and shook his head.

"Thanks, I'll call by soon and collect it."

They hung up the call.

The gravel gave the familiar sound as the cab pulled up in front of the house. Anna came out to investigate who it was.

Ben stepped out of the taxi.

"Mr. Ben, why you here, Mr. Ben. You on holiday, no?"

"I'm home early.

Let's have some coffee and something to eat. I'm starving."

"Si, si. Yes."

Anna turned and went back inside.

Ben paid the cab and went into the house through to the kitchen. Anna put some coffee on the center Island and Ben pulled up a stool. Two slices of toast popped up.

"Scrambled eggs ok for you, Mr. Ben?"

"Perfect Anna, perfect."

Ben cupped the mug of coffee in both hands and sipped slowly. Anna slid the eggs over to Ben and then came round to take his bag.

"I just put the washing on now, then I'll be back."

Ben nodded ok as he had a mouthful of eggs that were unmistakably Anna's."

Ben finished up as Anna came back in the kitchen.

"You had a good time Mr. Ben? Was it a good holiday? Not a long time for you?"

Ben smiled at how Anna had managed to get three questions into one sentence.

"Yes, it was good. I had a nice time, but I am still on holidays for a while yet. I am going to go up to the lake for the rest of the day. I will be back around 6:00 pm."

Ben pushed the plate into the middle of the island.

"Ok, I have dinner ready for about 7.30 pm?"

"Yes, perfect."

It was incredibly beautiful at the lake; the birdsong seemed to merge into Ben's senses. He had never before felt so connected to everything around him.

Chapter Sixty-Six

"So, are you going to call him?" asked Mark.

"Not yet, I have somewhere to go first. It's a good distance, shall we get a hire car?"

Mark called back to the hotel and asked them to arrange a hire car to be picked up out front of the hotel in fifteen minutes.

"Ok all sorted, where are we going?"

"It's way out in the country. I'll tell you on the way."

An hour later, they were driving along a country lane.

"It's not marked very well, and it's all overgrown."

Mark was staring out of the side window, scanning.

"There, pull over here."

Mark pulled the car tight into the side.

"Is this it?"

"Yes, can you give me a minute alone before you come in?"

"Yes sure, of course."

Christina reached over and kissed him on the cheek.

"Thank you."

Mark felt a rush of a sensation.

Christina pushed through the overgrown entrance and the gate, to the immaculately manicured cemetery.

She sat on the bench, staring at the most important headstone for a few minutes and then pulled out her phone.

Ben answered "Hello."

"Hi."

"Who is this? Who am I speaking to?"

"Christina."

"Christina- great, I have so much to tell you. Where are you?"

Christina stood up and walked towards the headstone.

"I found my grandfather."

"That's fantastic, where are you?"

"I'm standing right by him."

"I'm so pleased for you. I would love to talk to you. I could come to London, and we could meet up. I have just got back from-"

"I'm standing next to my grandfather in a small well-manicured cemetery. Where are you?"

"I- I'm up at the lake. Cemetery? I-"

"You could come now and tell me all about my grandfather."

"But I don't understand…"

"Could you come now? I'll wait for you on the bench." She closed her phone.

Ben sat there, processing for a few seconds before jumping to his feet. He went around to the driver's door and drove off, leaving the chair and table by the lake.

Christina heard a cough behind her.

"Ok? Everything ok?"

"He's on his way."

"He's coming here, right now? Do you want me to go?"

"No, wait with me until he arrives."

They both sat on the bench. Christina started to shake. Mark didn't say anything, he just put his arm around her, and she leaned into him. They stayed like that without saying a word, not knowing how much time was passing. A vehicle engine grew louder and then stopped.

Mark stood up. "You probably don't need me here right now. I'll wait outside."

As he pushed out through the overgrowth, he saw a man only a few meters away, coming towards him. Ben's eyebrows had pulled in tight together, and he was tugging at his right ear. He looked up to see Mark, who gestured towards the gate and then stepped to the side.

Christina opened her bag and pulled out the envelope containing the mask. As Ben pushed open the gate, she held it up to her face and turned towards him. Ben stopped in his tracks; tears streamed down his face. Christina took away the mask, and they walked towards each other.

Christina reached out and hugged him like she used to hug her mother. They held each other for a moment without saying anything.

Mark pushed back through the gate as they both turned towards him he said. "So, a family reunion what's next, a party?"

Ben turned back to Christina.

"I have just got back from Peru; I met Almedio. It was a wild experience. You were the child in the hut that I pulled from the woman's body."

Christina tilted her head to one side.

"Sorry - I'm confusing you. We have so much to talk about. Ben motioned for Mark to come closer and then pulled him into a three-way hug.

"I don't know where you fit into all this young man, but I'm glad you're here with - with my daughter."

As they separated apart again, Mark turned to Ben.

"Well, it's been a hell of an adventure so far, that's for sure. What's likely to happen next I have no-" Ben cut him off. "Have you been to Peru?"

Christina and Ben laughed. Ben put his arm around Christina.

"Come on, let's go home. Anna will be so surprised, but just one thing to do first."

Ben pulled out his phone.

"Hi, it's Ben here, the competition that came in this morning."

"Yes, I have it right here."

"Is there a contact phone number?"

"Yes."

"Call the number and tell them they have won the competition and they will be picking up their boat next week, and you will be in touch shortly with all the details."

Christina turned to Ben as he closed his phone.

"Competition… boat…?"

"It's a long story that I think is going to turn into an adventure. Let's go home to Anna."

The end

Afterword

This book came about as a result of traveling to Peru and experiencing an Ayahuasca ceremony. Today I would like to offer you the opportunity to receive some extra free material that will help you get more from the book and the messages contained within.

There is a lot more that I have been unable to weave into the story, some of which hold the potential for great personal life changes.

Go to this page now to find out how you can be part of the next adventure. www.martincole.com

Please leave a review on Amazon for others - I very much appreciate you taking the time to do this, and I am sure other will appreciate it also.

And finally.

If you find any editing errors (There always seems to be some slip through) please do let me know so that I can correct them.

About the Author

Martin believes that everyone has a core purpose to their life and discovering this purpose is of the utmost importance. Out of purpose comes passion and there is little that contains more power than a person living their life with these two forces combined.

Martin hopes that through his books readers may catch glimpses of their own lives and discover that their life can be every bit as empowered as the characters in the story.

Martin uses skilful story telling to invite you into a world of exciting possibilities for personal growth, successful living, and a joyful life.

Please drop by and say hello

www.martincole.com

martincole(AT)martincole.com

~

OTHER BOOKS BY MARTIN COLE

HOW THE MARKET MAKERS EXTRACT MILLIONS OF
DOLLARS A DAY

& HOW YOU CAN GRAB YOUR SHARE

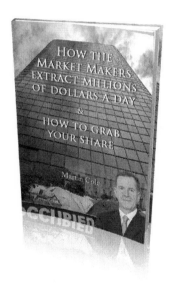

~